D1544813

CARNEGIE INSTITUTE

OF TECHNOLOGY

THE LIBRARY

VINTAGE VERSE

P.G. Tappenden

VINTAGE VERSE

An Anthology of
Poetry in
English

COMPILED WITH COMMENTARY

by

CLIFFORD BAX

HOLLIS & CARTER LTD.
25 ASHLEY PLACE,
LONDON,
S.W.1

First published 1945
Reprinted, 1946

821.08
B 35

TO

COMMANDER C. B. FRY

HERO OF MY YOUTH, FRIEND OF MY MIDDLE AGE

THIS BOOK IS PRODUCED
IN COMPLETE CONFORMITY WITH
THE AUTHORIZED ECONOMY STANDARDS

PRINTED IN GREAT BRITAIN BY WILLIAM CLOWES AND SONS, LIMITED,
LONDON AND BECCLES

ACKNOWLEDGMENTS

I HAVE TO acknowledge the courtesy of the following persons or houses for permission to reprint copyright poems:

Messrs. G. Bell & Sons (poems by Coventry Patmore); Mr. E. C. Bentley (*A Ballade of Souls*); Messrs. Jonathan Cape (poems by W. H. Davies and the Rev. Andrew Young); Mrs. Frances Cornford; Messrs. J. M. Dent & Son (Mr. Arthur Burrell's lines from Langland); Messrs. Faber & Faber and Mr. T. S. Eliot (*The Hollow Men*); Mr. Cecil French; Miss Kathleen Hewitt; Mr. Vyvyan Holland (poems by Oscar Wilde); Messrs. John Lane (poems by Ernest Dowson and poem by John Davidson); Mr. Wilfred Meynell (poems by Francis Thompson); Mr. Walter de la Mare; Messrs. Macmillan & Co., and the trustees of the Hardy Estate (work from the *Collected Poems of Thomas Hardy*), and the author's representative (work from the *Collected Poems of A.E.*), and the author's executors (work from *Poems by W. E. Henley*), and the author's representative (sonnets from *Poetical Works of W. S. Blunt*), moreover the poems taken from *The Collected Poems of W. B. Yeats* are reprinted by permission of Mrs. W. B. Yeats and of Messrs. Macmillan & Co.; the Oxford University Press and Mr. Alban Dobson (poem by Austin Dobson), also—and by permission of the poet's family—(poems by Gerard Manley Hopkins); Mr. A. D. Peters (poem by Mr. Richard Church); Miss Phyllis Reid; Messrs. Secker & Warburg (poems by J. E. Flecker); the Society of Authors and Mr. Lloyd Osbourne (poems by R. L. Stevenson); and Sir John Squire. Also Messrs. Sidgwick & Jackson and the author's representative, for the sonnet from Rupert Brooke's *Collected Poems*; and Messrs. Heinemann for the use of poems by Swinburne and by Mr. Arthur Symons, and Mr. Symons himself for the use of his lyrics.

CARNEGIE INSTITUTE
OF TECHNOLOGY LIBRARY

CONTENTS

PART ONE

Part One

WE HAVE TO admit on the evidence of publishers that poetry is not a popular excitement. I wish that large crowds would surge against the barriers when it is known that the Poet Laureate is due to arrive at King's Cross, or Manchester, or Glasgow, as I have seen them surge in hope of cheering a prizefighter; that policemen had to regulate the impatient queues which gather because somebody has espied in Hatchard's window a copy of a new book by, say, Mr. Andrew Young; that Universities were sundered, and friendships jeopardised, over the importance of Dante Gabriel Rossetti: but the world is not so fashioned, and we do well to make up our minds that poetry is an aristocratic delight or, in a famous phrase, caviare to the general. By aristocratic I mean, of course, that only the best minds put poetry among their front-rank pleasures, though very little experience will assure us that these best minds may be found in any except the darkest stratum of society. There was that 'bus-conductor in 1900 whose favourite reading was Dryden's verse; and the poets themselves come up from almost every social condition: Shelley and Byron, aristocrats; Burns, a ploughman; Keats, the son of a livery-stable keeper.

It is not difficult to see why poetry should appeal only to the few. It has no news-value. To appreciate it a man must relish the power or the grace or the grandeur of words; he must be capable of standing back from life and considering the immense procession of history as a spectator; and he must have a sensibility above the average. Let us first recognise that the opposite to sensibility is not sense but crudeness, and we shall then understand why poetry is kept alive only by a judicious minority in each generation, a small but inextinguishable aristocracy. It is an art revered and loved by most Actors, Actresses, Composers, Painters, Priests and Statesmen; by many Explorers, School Teachers and Army Officers; by some Architects, Doctors, Journalists and Sportsmen; by a few Hospital Nurses, Lawyers, Farmers, Scientists, Naval Officers, Singers and even Stockbrokers; but, so far as can be known, it has never delighted a Politician, a Newspaper Proprietor, a

2

Surgeon or a Financier. After all, a love of poetry is of no help whatever to those who mean to get on in life, and many a sound man must
have sympathised with Mr. Justice Eve when he pilloried himself in
perpetuity by asking, 'What is the use of music?' There were ages when
men cared passionately for the arts. In our own time passion is excited
by ideologies, machinery and sport: but the winds of the world are
continually veering and there may come a day, however distant, when
the arts will again go proudly.

Great poetry remains throughout life in the outlook and very blood
of those who have memorised it: nor is it at all easy for a poetry-lover to
imagine how differently life must look to those who have altogether
ignored poetry. Such persons seem to us like men who are born colour-
blind and for whom Titian's utmost miracle of tint is worthless, or
like the tone-deaf persons who never know that by listening intently to
the Fifth Symphony we may unite ourselves for a little while with a soul
much mightier than our own. Now, poetry and youth are inseparably
associated. If we find nothing in it when we are in our teens, we shall
miss it for good. Moreover nearly all poets do their best work before
they are thirty, or perhaps thirty-five. This book itself is being constructed for young readers, for certain people of (say) seventeen or
eighteen who are predestined poetry-lovers. It is not a book for the
scholar, seeing that I owe much to him and can give him nothing; nor
is it for the experienced reader, who may well have a subtler appreciation of the subject than I have. And, again, any reader to whom poetry
is a passion, as music is to so many people, will obtain very early in life
a copy of The Oxford Book of English Verse, and that is my reason for trying
not to duplicate the contents of that much larger anthology. In consequence, of course, I have had to forego many of our literature's crown
jewels.

As for the subject-matter of poetry, it is not for nothing that until the
world became over-sophisticated, comedy was expected to end with a
wedding, and tragedy with a death. The hope, the ecstasy and the anguish
of sex-love, and the sorrow of impermanence, or the dream of a more
brilliant existence when the body has worn itself away, these—the
sense of life and the knowledge of death—are the substance of most

3

poetry because they are the fundamental perturbations of humanity. This too is in my belief a part-cause of the deep appeal of poetry when we are really young. It records what other men have thought and experienced about life at its most intense. And lastly I suggest that in our teens, and sometimes even in childhood, we mysteriously apprehend emotions which we cannot have experienced; and that our youthful delight in poetry is largely due to the fact that it causes our awakening selves to vibrate with eternal emotions, and is therefore in some measure a prevision of life.

The first three poems in this collection come to us from an exceedingly distant England. We do not know who wrote them, but it seems that they were composed at least no later than the end of the thirteenth century. They are written in what is called Middle English. This Middle English, which is held to have begun about 1120, 'with the death of the generation who saw the Norman Conquest', is so difficult to read without practice that, preferring to infuriate the purist rather than discourage the reader, I have presented the poems in modernised versions. The original texts will be found in the Appendix (pp. 318—324).

For a time the conquerors naturally conducted the affairs of the country in their own language. By degrees, however, English words came back into use, and eventually, according to the historian J. R. Green, 'toward the middle of the fourteenth century' (about the time of Chaucer's birth), 'the perfect fusion of conquered and conquerors into an English people was marked by the disuse, even among the nobler classes, of the French tongue'. An ancient writer declares indeed that after the Plague or Black Death of 1349, 'in all the grammar schools of England children leaveth French, and construeth and learneth in English'; but it was by that time an English that was half-French.

These three Middle-English poems offer us three characteristic pictures of the mediæval mind. The first shows that intensity of religious feeling which inevitably flames into poetry. The second is a startling expression of mediæval high spirits. The third is a delightful example of that refinement of sex-love which reappeared after the Dark Ages with the troubadours of Italy and Provence.

The social reformer, thinking of serfdom, leprosy and local tyranny, cannot imagine the mediæval world without grieving over it; the artist, remembering the arts and crafts of the time, the pageantry, the brilliant and varied costumes, and the religious passion which produced so much magnificent architecture, cannot think that those far off men were any unhappier than we are ourselves. It was precisely to the fourteenth century, for example, that the Pre-Raphaelites in mid-Victorian England were looking back so enviously: and perhaps we shall do well to realise that human beings can often be marvellously happy in most unpromising conditions. Let us then listen to these poets of six hundred years ago, while following the counsel of William Morris who wrote in *The Earthly Paradise*:

> 'Forget six counties overhung with smoke,
> Forget the snorting steam and piston-stroke,
> Forget the spreading of the hideous town;
> Think rather of the packhorse on the down,
> And dream of London, small and white and clean,
> The clear Thames bordered by its gardens green. . . .'

1   At the Cross. (*Anonymous*), c. 1290

This noble and sombre poem is modelled upon the famous *Stabat Mater*, a thirteenth-century Latin hymn. The hymn opens with the two words which have become its title, and they mean 'The Mother was Standing' (that is, at the foot of the Cross). It is read in the Roman Catholic Church during the Mass of the Seven Dolours of the Blessèd Virgin Mary and is sung by Catholics when making 'the Way of the Cross'. Our poem in its original form (see Appendix) opens with the words, 'Stand well, Mother'. There are said to be several versions of the English poem.

> 'O Mother, draw thou near the Rood
>   And, seeing thy son, be blithe of mood;
>   Happy, Mother, shouldst thou be'.
> 'O Son, how may I be blithe-souled?
> Thy feet, thy hands, do I behold
>   There nailed to the pitiless Tree'.

'Mother, put weeping out of mind.
Not for my guilt but for mankind
   Must I endure my death this day'.
'Son, my own death now cometh on.
To my heart's core the sword hath gone,
   As to me Simeon did foresay'.

'Hush! let me die and, dying, win
From hell both Adam and all his kin,
   Who else were utterly accurst'.
'O Son, where shall I turn? This pain
Hath me already well-nigh slain.
   If thou must die, let me die first!'

'Have pity on thine own child, I pray,
Mother, and wash thy sorrow away:
   Death hurts not like the sight of it!'
'How should I stanch my tears, O Son,
Who see the streams of blood that run
   From out thy heart here to my feet?'

'O Mother, better it is that I—
Hearken thou well—alone should die
   Than that mankind to hell should go'.
'I see thy body that was sore lashed,
Thy hands and feet pierced through and gashed;
   It is no wonder if I make woe'.

'Yet must I die. Were it not so,
Even thou, Mother, to hell shouldst go.
   This I endure for thy dear sake'.
'Gentle thou art. Upbraid me not,
O Son! it is a mother's lot
   That I for thee this sorrow make'.

'Mother, thou knowest in full this day
What sorrow comes with children,—yea,
   What sorrow to go with child it is'.
'Sorrow in sooth, I can thee tell,
For if it be not the pains of hell
   There is no greater sorrow than this',

'Wherefore, although pure maid thou art,
Mother who knowest the mother's heart,
   Unto all women lend thine aid'.
'Yea, Son, at every turn do I
Give help to those who on me cry,
   Be it wife or wanton wench or maid'.

'Mother, here may I no more dwell.
The time is come. I must to hell:
   And on the third day shall I rise'.
'Thither, O Son, let me too fare,—
Thy wounds have brought me death so near!
   Never came Death in such dark wise'.

Whenas he rose, down fell her sorrow:
Up sprang her bliss on that third morrow:
   A true blithe mother then wert thou.
Lady, by that same joy, beseech
Thy son that he forgive us each:
   And be thou our shield against the foe.

Blesséd be thou, full of bliss;
And let us not of heaven miss,
   But help us through thy sweet Son's might.
O Lord, by virtue of that blood
Which thou didst shed upon the Rood,
   Bring thou us all to heaven's light.
                        Amen.

2   Hop along, Hubert! (*Anonymous*), c. 1290

The author of 'At the Cross' may well have been a monk or an abbess. It is a safe guess that the author of the wild poem which now follows must at least have started it as he came rolling out of a tavern on a brilliant Spring night.

When we suddenly find the French words 'dame douce', we must wonder whether perhaps they are the original of Jacques' mysterious word 'ducdame'. If the *dame douce* means a decoy-girl, she could certainly be said 'to call fools into a circle'; if it means the 'woman of the house', perhaps she called them around her on pay-day.

With legs at the stride stands the Man in the Moon:
　High on a pitchfork his burden he bears.
Great wonder it is that he never falls down,
　So sore doth he shudder and shake with his fears.
When freezes the frost he is chilled to the bone;
　The thorns rend his clothes all to tatters and tears.
There's not a soul knows if he'll seat him anon,
　And only a witch could say what he wears!

Whither away doth he journey, this man
　Who sets his one foot the other before?
Nobody marked it if ever he ran,
　He's the slowest of men that woman e'er bore.
He is gathering sticks in the field, and his plan
　Is with their thorns to fasten his door.
With his two-edged axe he must hew what he can
　Or his toil in the field will be idle and sore.

This man, just as though he had always been there,
　As though in the moon he was born and fed,
Leans on his fork, like any grey friar,—
　This crookback sluggard who is so much afraid.
Full many a day hath he been with us here,
　And in doing his errand he hath but ill-sped.
A bundle of briars he has hewn him somewhere,
　And the bailiff will sue if the price be not paid.

Get thy sticks home ere he comes for the fee!
　That other foot forward! Step over the stile!
The bailiff a man of high office is he
　And shall home to our house and make merry the while.
We'll pledge him in liquor right warmly; and she,
　Our *dame douce*, beside him shall sit down and smile;
And when he is drunk as a drown'd mouse can be,
　Quite clean from his purpose we will him beguile.

In vain do I cry! If the dolt be so dull
  And deaf, let him go to the Devil, I say!
I yell at him, filling my lungs to the full
  But no whit he hurries, still will he stay.
Hop along, Hubert, thou lily-faced gull,
  Thy bowels, I wot, are all water and whey!
I grind my teeth at the ill-mannered fool
  But he'll never come down till dawning of day.

3   The Clerk and the Lady. (*Anonymous*), c. 1290

The word 'Clerk' is a twin-word to 'Cleric', but here it must mean
not a priest but a scholar or merely a person able to read and write.
Mediæval poets think nothing of referring to Virgil as 'a learnéd
clerk'.

Psychologically the poem is unusual in that the lady yields to the clerk
because he reminds her of a bygone adventure with another man of
letters. We ought to remember that the high-born woman in Plan-
tagenet days—the lady in her bower or tower—was almost certainly,
like the modern American woman, more cultured than most of her
male associates. The barons and their castle-defenders may not all have
been of the 'brutal and licentious soldiery', but we have evidence that
the manners and conversations of the troubadours or country-wandering
minstrels came as a pleasure and a stimulant to some of the women.
This, after all, is the Age of Froissart, of chivalry, of the famous Courts
of Love, of romantic passion which, as a Swiss writer has recently
shown, is fundamentally a longing to die in ecstasy, because life cannot
produce an experience splendid enough.

CLERK   My life I loathe, my death I love, because of a lady's mien
        Who is more bright than the day's light, as may full well be
            seen.
        I wither away as doth the leaf in summer when it is green,
        And if wise thought can cure me not, to whom shall I tell my
            teen?

Sorrow, sighs and woeful moods bind me now so fast
That much I dread lest I go mad if longer they should last;
Yet all my care with one sweet word she could from me out-
  cast;
And if thou destroy my life, fair love, tell me what gain thou
  hast?

LADY   Begone, sir clerk! Thou art but a fool. I'll talk not with thee
  moe.
Thou wilt not live to see that day when thou my love shalt
  know:
And wert thou caught here in my bower, 'twere shame for
  thee and woe.
Better then ride a wicked horse, it were on foot to go!

CLERK   Alack, have pity on me, thy man. Say not that I must pine
Who hold thee ever inside my thoughts where'er my steps
  incline.
If I should die from love of thee, great shame must then be
  thine.
Let me still live and be thy love and, sweetheart, be thou
  mine!

LADY   Be still, thou fool! (I call thee aright.) Must thou again
  begin?
By night, by day they wait for thee, my father and all my kin;
And wert thou taken within my bower they would not deem
  it sin
Me to make fast and thee to slay: so shouldst thou thy death
  win!

CLERK   Sweet lady, do thou change thy mood; teach me not more
  distress;
I know as much of sadness now as erst I knew of bliss.
Standing in a window once, we fifty times did kiss,
And many a man makes light of pain for such fair promises.

LADY   O welaway! what dost thou say? My grief thou dost renew.
A clerk I had as paramour: his love for me was true;
And if we were not soon to meet, no gladsome hour he knew.
I loved him better than my life; I will not lie to you.

CLERK When at the school I was a clerk I garnered much good lore;
    And for thy love have I endured right many wounds and sore
    Out in the wildwood far from men, far from my home of yore.
    Sweet lady, do thou pity me, for now I can no more.

LADY Thou seemest a learnéd man to be; thy speech hath clerkly skill,
    And bitter wounds for loving me thou shalt not suffer still.
    Father, mother and all my kin shall not me work such ill
    But I am thine as thou art mine, and thou shalt do thy will.

*   *   *

Many critics have agreed that William Langland was a poet of the
people, and Chaucer a poet of the court. In temperament the two men
effectively illustrate those two sides of the English character which
came to their most dramatic collision in the war between the sensible,
prosaic Roundhead and the irrational, romantic Cavalier. Langland is
earnest, a plain-speaker (none of your modern fal-lals, such as rhyme,
for him), a flat-footed poet and an almost Tolstoyan moralist. George
Sampson, referring to Langland's long piece *The Vision of Piers Plowman*,
likes it well enough to say that 'it is, in one sense, a beacon light of
farewell. In it the Old English alliterative line, strangely rekindled,
blazes up to a glorious end, and is seen no more'. W. J. Entwistle,
another laudator, observed somewhat damagingly, 'we have no right to
demand from it any other unity than that of a poem one only in temper
and style, and shall be disappointed if we do'.

But why have we 'no right' to ask for shapeliness? Why is Langland
to be uncensured for meandering, for having no clear design in his head,
for leading us wearisomely without definite direction? This on the contrary has always been the typical defect of English writers.

It seems likely that political sympathy has induced many critics to
overpraise this antique eulogy of the Little Man.

4 From *The Vision of Piers Plowman*. *William*
Langland (?1330–1400)

He was born 'somewhere near the Malvern Hills'. Arthur Burrell,
who made the following version of Langland's autobiographical

'chapter', says that he 'lived the precarious, poor, tramping life of a mass or chantry priest, earning little and continually consorting, partly by choice and partly by necessity, in the most intimate way, with friars, theologians, merchants, pilgrims, beggars, drunkards, loose women, and with the honest and hard-working poor'. Mr. Burrell called this section of the poem

The Writer's Life

Thus I woke, God wot, where I dwelt in Cornhill.
Kit my wife and I, dressed like a loller,
And among the London lollers little was I set by,
And among the hermits (trust me for that),
For I made verses on them as my wit taught me.

Once when I had my health, in hot harvest time,
And my limbs to labour with, and loved good fare,
And nothing in life to do, but drink and sleep,
In health of body and mind,
I came on Conscience, and Reason met me,
He met and questioned me, and my memory roamed back,
And Reason reproved me.

'Canst thou serve as a priest or sing in church?
'Make a haycock in the field or pitch the hay?
'Canst mow or stock or bind the sheaves?
'Canst reap or guide the reapers? Canst rise early?
'Canst blow the horn, and keep the kine together,
'Lie out o' nights, and save my corn from thieves?

'Make shoes or clothes or herd the sheep?
'Trim hedge, use harrow, or drive the swine and geese,
'Or do any other work that the people need
'To win some living for them that be bedridden?'

'Nay', said I, 'God help me,
'I am too weak to work with sickle or with scythe.
'I am too long, believe me, to stoop low down,
'Or to last for any time as a true working man'.

'Then hast thou lands to live by or rich lineage
'That findest thee thy food? An idle man thou seemest;
'Thou art a spender and canst spend; thou art a spill-time,
'Or thou beggest thy living at mens buttery hatches;
'Thou art a Friday-beggar, a feast-day beggar in the churches;
'A lollers life is thine, little to be praised.
'Righteousness rewardeth men as they deserve'.
Thou shalt yield to each man after his works.
'Thou art maybe broken in body or limb,
'Maimed maybe through mishap, therefore art thou excused?'

'When I was young', quoth I, 'many a year ago,
'My father and my friends set me to school
'Till I knew throughly what Holy Scripture said,
'What is best for the body, what is safest for the soul.
'Yet never did I find since my friends died
'A life that pleased me save in these long clothes,
'If I must live by labour and earn my living
'I must needs labour at the work I learned'.
Each man in what calling he is called there dwell he.

'I live *in* London and I live *on* London,
'The tools I labour with, to get my living by,
'Are the Lords Prayer, my Primer, my Dirges and my Vespers,
'And sometimes my Psalter and the Seven Psalms;
'I sing masses for the souls of those that give me help,
'And they that find me food, welcome me when I come,
'Man or woman, once a month, into their houses;
'No bag have I nor bottle, only my belly.

'Moreover, my lord Reason, men should, methinks,
'Constrain no cleric to do common work.
'The tonsured clerk, a man of understanding,
'Should neither sweat nor toil, nor swear at inquests,
'Nor fight in the van of battle, nor hurt his foe'.
Render not evil for evil.
'They be the heirs of heaven, all that are ordained,
'And in choir and church Christ's own ministers'.
The Lord is the portion of mine inheritance.

CARNEGIE INSTITUTE
OF TECHNOLOGY LIBRARY

'Clerks it becometh for to serve Christ,
'And for folk unordained to cart and work,
'And no clerk should be tonsured save he be the son
'Of frankleyns and free men and of wedded folk;
'Bondmen and bastards and beggars children,
'*These* are the sons of labour, *these* are to serve lords,
'To serve God and the good as their station asketh.

'But since bondmens sons are made into bishops,
'And bastard bairns are made archdeacons,
'And soap-makers and their sons are knights for silvers sake,
'And lords sons be their labourers and have mortgaged their rents
'And to support this realm have ridden against our foes
'To comfort the Commons and honour the king,
'And monks and nuns that should support the poor
'Have made their own kin knights and paid the fees for it,
'Popes and patrons refuse poor gentle blood,
'And take the sons of Mammon to keep the Sanctuary;
'Holiness of life and love have long to us been strangers,
'And will be till these things wear out, or they be somehow changed.

'Therefore, rebuke me not, Reason, I pray thee,
'For in my conscience I know what Christ would have me do.
'Prayers of a perfect man and his discreet penance,
'These be the dearest work that our Lord loveth'.

Quoth Conscience, 'By Christ, I see not where this tendeth,
'But to beg your life in cities is not the perfect life,
'Save you be in obedience to Prior or to Minster'.

'That's truth', said I, 'I do acknowledge it,
'That I have lost my time, mis-spent my time,
'And yet I hope that even as one who oft hath bought and sold
'And always lost and lost and at the last hath happened
'To buy him such a bargain that he is better for ever
'And all his loss is at the last only as a leaf,
'Such a winning is his, under Gods grace',
The Kingdom of heaven is like treasure . . . etcetera,
A woman who found a piece of silver . . . etcetera

'Even so hope I to have of Him that is Almighty
'A gobbet of His grace; and then begin a time
'That shall turn to profit all the days of my life'.

'I counsel thee', quoth Reason, 'hurry to begin
'The life that is commendable and dear to the soul';
'*Aye, and continue in it*', quoth Conscience.

So to the kirk I went to honour my Lord;
Before the Cross upon my knees I knocked my breast,
Sighing for my sins, saying my prayer,
Weeping and wailing till again I was asleep.

*   *   *

Turning from Langland to Chaucer we exchange the company of a moralist for that of an artist. Without the self-disciplined moralist we should, I surmise, not have constructed an Empire, a many-branching oak-tree whose stem is England and whose ancient root is London; but our strong preoccupation with morals, a tendency which was over-poweringly reinforced by association with the Scots, has continuously over many generations made art-work more difficult for Englishmen. Chaucer, humorous and tender-hearted, looked at the pageant of the world (or the little of it which he could observe) with the fascinated and uncensorious gaze of a child who witnesses a Punch and Judy show.

The Wife of Bath would have seemed to Langland a regrettable example of lust and self-indulgence. To Chaucer she was a jolly figure, a figure of fun. Langland could never have stooped to the schoolboy obscenity of *The Miller's Tale*: nor would he have regarded the Prioress (whom you are about to meet) with Chaucer's twinkling eye. Langland, like our puritan reviewers, would have disliked her pleasant fastidious-ness. Perhaps he was even so conscious of sin and of social injustice that, unlike Chaucer, he could not have spared a glance for the mere daisy—'who so much loves the light'.

Now, innumerable readers have taken one look at Chaucer and have instantly shied away from his archaic English, and never learned how charming a friend he is. In the hope that the present reader will progress from my modernisations to Chaucer's lovely Norman-English, I cheerfully take my place in the Fleet Street stocks. Consider how even George Sampson exclaims, 'Modernise Chaucer, and his verse falls to pieces': but what did that admirable poet Edmund Waller say in the time of Charles the Second? Something very much to the point:

> 'Poets, that lasting marble seek,
> Must carve in *Latin* or in *Greek*:
> We write in sand; our language grows;
> And like the tide, our work o'erflows.
> *Chaucer* his sense can only boast,
> The glory of his numbers lost!
> Years have defac'd his matchless strain,
> And yet he did not write in vain'.

We gain much if we read Chaucer with imagination: with a visual sense of the world in which he worked. What could be better than this background, painted by the Scottish essayist and poet, Alexander Smith?

'And, with his noticing eyes, into what a brilliant, many-tinted world was Chaucer born. In his day life had a certain breadth, colour, and picturesqueness which it does not possess now. It wore a braver dress, and flaunted more in the sun. Five centuries effect a great change on manners. A man may now-a-days, and without the slightest suspicion of the fact, brush clothes with half the English peerage on a sunny afternoon in Pall Mall. Then it was quite different. The fourteenth century loved magnificence and show. Great lords kept princely state in the country; and when they came abroad, what a retinue, what waving of plumes, and shaking of banners, and glittering of rich dresses! Religion was picturesque, with dignitaries and cathedrals, and fuming incense, and the Host carried through the streets. The franklin kept open house, the city merchant feasted kings, the outlaw roasted his venison beneath the greenwood tree. There was a gallant monarch and a gallant court. The eyes of the Countess of Salisbury shed influence; Maid Marian laughed in Sherwood. London is already a considerable place, numbering, perhaps, two hundred thousand inhabitants, the houses clustering close and high along the river banks; and on the beautiful April nights the nightingales are singing round the suburban villages of Strand,

Holborn, and Charing. It is rich withal; for after the battle of Poitiers, Harry Picard, wine-merchant and Lord Mayor, entertained in the city four kings,—to wit, Edward, king of England, John, king of France, David, king of Scotland, and the king of Cyprus,—and the last-named potentate, slightly heated with Harry's wine, engaged him at dice, and being nearly ruined thereby, the honest wine-merchant returned the poor king his money, which was received with all thankfulness. . . .

The Crusades are now over, but the religious fervour which inspired them lingered behind; so that, even in Chaucer's day, Christian kings, when their consciences were oppressed by a crime more than usually weighty, talked of making an effort before they died to wrest Jerusalem and the sepulchre of Christ from the grasp of the infidel. England had at this time several holy shrines, the most famous being that of Thomas à Becket at Canterbury, which attracted crowds of pilgrims. The devout travelled in large companies; and, in the May mornings, a merry sight it was, as, with infinite clatter and merriment, with bells, minstrels, and buffoons, they passed through thorp and village, bound for the tomb of St. Thomas. The pageant of events, which seems enchantment when chronicled by Froissart's splendid pen, was to Chaucer contemporaneous incident: the chivalric richness was the familiar and everyday dress of his time. Into this princely element he was endued, and he saw every side of it—the frieze as well as the cloth of gold. In the *Canterbury Tales* the fourteenth century murmurs, as the sea murmurs in the pink-mouthed shells upon our mantelpieces'.

Geoffrey Chaucer: 1340–1400

was the son of a London vintner. In boyhood he became a page in the entourage of Elizabeth de Burgh, Duchess of Clarence and wife of Edward the Third's second son. In early manhood he was taken prisoner in Brittany, and fortunately was ransomed by King Edward. Perhaps he became familiar with French poetry, especially with Le Romaunt de la Rose (which he translated into English verse), while waiting to be ransomed. He married a lady whose name was Philippa.

In 1372 (being then at the best age for a man) he travelled in, Italy and at Florence he certainly met Boccaccio and probably Petrarch. They would surely have looked upon him as an uncouth foreigner, Italy being at that period so much more cultured than England. On April the 23rd (St. George's Day), 1374, the King gave the poet a pitcher of wine—possibly the origin of that 'keg of sherry' which, given formerly to the reigning Poet Laureate, was reputed (by *Punch*) 'to keep him merry'. In April, 1388, Chaucer made the pilgrimage to the tomb of St. Thomas à Becket at Canterbury. His fellow-pilgrims little knew that the shrewdest poet-humorist in English literature was gently immortalising them.

The poet was buried in Westminster Abbey, but we should not suppose that this in his far-off day was a national honour. A monument to Chaucer was set up in the Abbey in 1555, and his collected Works were printed in 1578. His curious name comes, we are told, 'from a French form of the Latin *calcearius*, a shoemaker'.

5 The Prioress

From the *Prologue to The Canterbury Tales*

There likewise was a Nun, a Prioress
Who when she smiled was coy and simple both;
And 'By Saint Louis' was her strongest oath.
Her name was Madame Eglantyne, and well
She sang the Holy Service, truth to tell
Intoning through her nose delightfully.
She could speak French both well and winsomely—
After the school of Stratford near to Bow,
For, soothly, Paris French she did not know.
Well taught she was to sit at meat withal:
No morsel from her lips would she let fall
Or wet her fingers though the sauce were deep.
A titbit she could deftly steer and keep
So that no scrap e'er dropped upon her breast.
Courtesy of all graces liked she best.
She always wiped her upper lip so clean
That in her cup no smirch was ever seen
To show that she had newly tasted there.
And after meals her manners were full fair.

Delightful, and a friend to everyone,
She also had a lively sense of fun,
And hated to assume that pompous port
And stately manner which is used at Court,
Or ev'n to be too reverently addressed.
Her inner self, too, fitted with the rest:
So kind and so compassionate she was
That she would weep if e'er she saw a mouse
Caught in a trap, and either maimed or dead.
She kept some little dogs, and these she fed
On white bread, milk or roast flesh, and would cry
Most pitiably if one of them should die
Or some man with a strong stick made it smart:
So tender was her conscience and her heart.
Her wimple delicately pleated was;
Her nose well-shaped; her eyes as grey as glass;
Her mouth was small and thereto soft and red;
And certainly a most fair brow she had,
Almost a span in breadth, as I surmised;
And, truly, no way was she undersized.
Her cloak, I saw, was elegantly fair,
And on her arm she wore a little pair
Of coral beads enringed about with green,
From·which there hung a brooch of golden sheen
And on it graven first a crownéd A
And, after, *Amor Vincit Omnia.*

6 Daisies

From *The Legend of Good Women*

As for me, though my learning be but slight,
To read in books I do me much delight
And fully I believe in all they tell,
Studying them devoutly and so well
That there's no game, no pastime ever tried,
Could cozen me to lay my book aside,
Unless perchance on some high holiday;

And yet, assuredly, when the month of May
Is come and I do hear the birds again
And see the new flowers everywhere, why then
Farewell my book, farewell the earnest mind!
My nature, too, was formed in such a kind
That of all flowers which in the fields are spread
I most do love the small ones white and red
Which are called 'daisies' in our town and tongue;
And for them my affection is so strong
That never Maytime comes, as I have said,
Nor ever creeps a May dawn to my bed
But I am up, and to the meads I run
To watch that flower spread out against the sun
As soon as ever morning gilds the air,—
A blissful sight that softeneth all my care. . . .
And when at eve the sun is in the West,
I speed to watch how she will take her rest,
Who so much hates the dark and fears the night
And so much joys to face the early light
That then she will immediately unclose.
Would that in English, were it rhyme or prose,
I could express and rightly praise that flower,—
But woe is me, it lies not in my power!

7   A Roundel

Merciless Beauty : A Triple Roundel

I CAPTIVITY

Your two eyes will destroy me suddenly:
I can the beauty of them not sustain;
It sendeth through my heart a wound so keen.

And if you will not succour hastily
That stricken heart while yet the wound is green,
  Your two eyes will destroy me suddenly
  I can the beauty of them not sustain.

Upon the truth I tell you honestly
That of my life or death you are the queen;
And should I die, that truth will then be seen.
Your two eyes will destroy me suddenly:
I can the beauty of them not sustain;
It sendeth through my heart a wound so keen.

II REJECTION

So hath your beauty rid your heart of rue
That all my lamentations are but vain:
For your proud mind holds pity on a chain.

Thus you decree a guiltless death my due;
And that is truth,—I have no need to feign;
So hath your beauty rid your heart of rue
That all my lamentations are but vain.

Alas, that nature should have formed in you
Beauty so great that no man may attain
To mercy, though he starve away for pain.
So hath your beauty rid your heart of rue
That all my lamentations are but vain;
For your proud mind holds pity on a chain.

III ESCAPE

Since I from Love escapéd am so fat
I'll never enter more his prison lean!
Since I am free, I count him not a bean.

Let him reply, and tell me this or that:
I do not care; I speak out what I mean.
Since I from Love escapéd am so fat,
I'll never enter more his prison lean!

Love has struck out my name from off his slate,
And from my own book his have I struck clean
For evermore: the only way, I ween.
Since I from Love escapéd am so fat,
I'll never enter more his prison lean;
Since I am free, I count him not a bean!

8   A Slender Wench

Full fair was this young wife, and therewithal
Her body, like a weasel's, slim and small.
She wore a girdle which was barred with silk:
An apron, that was white as morning milk
And gussetted, upon her loins she bore.
White was her smock; the collar—both before
And at the back embroidered all about—
Was of a coal-black silk inside and out.
The little tapes that tied her white cap, too,
Were like her collar—of the selfsame hue.
Broad was her silken fillet, set full high,
And certainly she had a lecherous eye.
Fine-plucked were her two brows and like a bow
Bended they were, and black as any sloe.
She was, in sooth, more blissful for to see
Than is the earliest-ripening pear-tree,
And softer than the wool is of a wether.
And by her girdle hung a purse of leather
Silk-tasselled and with pinchbeck pieces pearled.
Although he might go up and down the world
There's no wise man whose fancy could conceive
So gay a poppet or such another Eve.
Full brighter was the shining of her hue
Than in the Tower a 'noble' [1] minted new;
And her full voice, that made the hearer yearn,
Was like a swallow's sitting on a barn.
Moreover, she could skip and play a game
Like any kid or calf following its dame.
Her mouth was sweet as honeyed ale or mead
Or apples laid in loft or hay for need.
Skittish she was as is a pretty colt,
Tall as a mast and upright as a bolt.
On her low collar, too, a brooch there was
As great in girth as any buckler's boss.

---

[1] A noble was a gold coin worth six shillings and eightpence.

Upon her legs the shoes were laced-up high:
She was a primrose, a dear piggy's-eye [1]
That any lord might lay upon his bed
Or any stout young yeoman gladly wed.

When Chaucer was a small boy, perhaps already a page at Court, England was so violently assailed by the Black Death, a plague which came from the East, that 'of the three or four millions who then formed the population of England, more than one-half were swept away'. The result was that the value and price of labour increased enormously. Now it was that John Ball, 'a mad priest of Kent', as Froissart calls him, preached his levelling doctrine; now that the working class took up the famous tag,

'When Adam delved and Eve span,
Who was then the nobleman?'

—lines which are a variant of earlier lines ascribed to Richard Rolle, the thirteenth-century hermit:

'When Adam delf and Eve span, spir, if thou wil spede,
Whare was than the pride of man that now marres his mede?'

And yet, despite this extreme suffering and the social discontent of the period, Chaucer has a better claim than William Morris to Yeats's phrase, 'The Happiest of the Poets'. True, in his own day and for a further hundred years he seems to have been most honoured for his pathetic verse-tale of *Troilus and Criseyde*, a long and admirably sustained work; but there can be no doubt that by temperament he found life gay enough and humanity amusing.

His influence was immediate. Like Giotto, he had freed his art from archaic stiffness and so had made it more tempting and more delightful to practice. No one will be surprised to find that so genial a poet was remembered with glowing affection, as in this 'Lament' by one of his early disciples. . . .

---

[1] 'Piggy's-eye' was a current term of endearment; a little pretty lively object. . . . The class-distinction drawn in the final couplet will be resented by many, but they should struggle to smile at it,—as a touch of temporal colour.

C

9 Lament for Chaucer. *Thomas Hoccleve* (?1370–?1450)

(A Clerk in the Privy Seal, granted an annuity by Henry the Fourth.)

Alas, my worthy master honourable,
   This landë's very treasure and richesse!
Death by thy death hath harm irreparable
   Unto us done. Her vengeable duresse
   Despoiléd hath this land of the sweetness
Of rhetoric; for never amongst us
Was there a man so like to Tullius.[1]

Who else was true heir in philosophy
   To Aristotle, in our tongue, but thou?
And in the steps of Virgil's poesy
   Thou followedst eke, as men wot well enow.
   That world-tormentor who my master slew
(Would I were slain!) was all too hasty—Death,
Who ran on thee and reft thee of thy breath.

She might have stayed her vengeance for a while
   Till that some man might equal to thee be:
Nay, let be that! She knew well that this isle
   Should never man forth bring like unto thee,
   And to fulfil her office needs must she:
God bade her so—I trust as for the best.
O master, master, God thy soul give rest!

*   *   *

Another and equally reverent disciple was the King of Scotland. His poem *The King's Quair* was 'discovered' (perhaps we should say, rediscovered) 'and printed in 1783'. The word quair signifies a poem or pamphlet which could be contained in twenty pages—that is to say, a quire of paper. The meaning of the third stanza certainly calls for the interpretation supplied by a much earlier editor. His reading is, 'Thus endeth my story, caused by the governance of the Almighty, who reigns in heaven; to whom we think that all we have written was couthed (or known) in the high heaven for ages before'. The poem is written, as the reader will notice, in a seven-line stanza which Chaucer had invented.

[1] Marcus Tullius Cicero.

24

10 Godspeed to his Book. *King James (the First) of Scotland* (1394–1437)

Born at Dunfermline in July, 1394. When he was eleven or twelve he was sent for safety to France, but on his way there he was captured at sea by the English. Henry the Fourth was not willing to ransom so valuable a captive and the King (he became King of Scotland in 1406) was held prisoner in the Tower, in Nottingham Castle and at Evesham. Though 'short and stout', he was also supple and strong, and a fine athlete. Moreover he 'became perhaps more cultured than any other prince of his age',—high praise from that austere authority, the *Encyclopædia Britannica*.

It is pleasant to learn that Henry the Fifth treated him in a friendly and handsome manner. In 1423 the Scots ransomed him for 60,000 marks. Early in February, 1424, he married Lady Joan Beaufort, daughter of the Earl of Somerset, whom he had seen from his prison windows while she was walking in the garden. Green says of him that 'in the thirteen years of a short but wonderful reign, justice and order were restored (in Scotland) for a while, the Scotch Parliament organised, the clans of the Highlands assailed in their own fortresses and reduced to swear fealty' to the King.

> Go, little Treatise, naked of eloquence,
>   The offspring of a poor and simple wit;
> And pray the reader to have patience
>   Of thy defect, and to supporten it,
>   And in his goodness thy weak joints to knit,
> And his tongue so to rule and so to steer
> That thy defects may all be healéd here.
>
> But if, alas, thou com'st in that presénce
>   Whereas from blame fainest thou would be quit,
> And she should hear thy crude, crabb'd eloquence,—
>   Who shall be there thy pardon to entreat?
>   None,—unless she in mercy will admit
> Thee from good-will, who is thy guide and star:
> To whom for me beseech her to give ear.

So endeth that predestined influence,
  Willed from high heaven, (where all power is commit'
Of governance), by the magnificence
  Of Him that highest in the heavens doth sit:
  From Whom, we think, comes all that we have writ:
Who might have conned it long since, many a year,
High in the heavens' figure circular.

To all the offspring of my masters dear—
  Gower and Chaucer, who on the stairway sate
Of rhetoric, when they were living here,
  Superlative as poets laureate
  For morals and for eloquence ornate,—
I recommend my book in its lines seven;
And eke their souls unto the bliss of heaven.

For us it is startling to hear that 'in the University Library not more than 122 volumes were recorded in 1424'. A man or a woman caught in the act of reading must have been a really uncommon sight; and the Wars of the Roses, which lasted from 1450 to 1471, cannot have made a distraught nation more book-minded. They may, however, have reduced French influence upon England by keeping Englishmen at home. Certainly our literature now lost much of Chaucer's grace, and became, for the most part, burlier and more boisterous. At the same time men were building some of the loveliest and most majestic chapels, and even homes, which the genius of England has evolved, as, for example, the fan-vaulted Chapel of Henry the Seventh at Westminster, the King's Chapel at Cambridge, Great Chalfield Manor House in Wiltshire, and the George Inn at Norton-St. Philip.

Houses, windows, arches and even costumes become ampler. It is as though England under the later Henries were a well-loaded apple-tree, or had achieved self-confidence, as a man should do in his thirties: but the only writer of this period who has what we might call a fan-vaulted style, and who writes as its masons built, is, so far as I know, Sir Thomas Malory. Of course a gigantic change in the English mind was effected when Caxton, a Kent man, set up his 'emprynting' press in the Almonry at Westminster, for here was an alteration of living conditions comparable in its effect with the invention of gunpowder, the cinematograph or the aeroplane. Caxton started his great work late in life. He was printing only between 1477 and 1491: and Richard the Third, let us charitably recall, was one of his most enthusiastic patrons.

The best-known verseman of this period is Skelton. He has the somewhat rare distinction of, as it were, owning a metre. 'Skeltonic' verse, with its castanet-like quick-firing rhymes, is certainly his 'signature tune', but his writing is perilously close to doggerel. He is still at the stage of being so pleased when he hits on a chain of rhymes, as a juvenile juggler will be excited when he can keep three or four plates in motion, that time and again he chases a rhyme though it takes him over the edge of nonsense. He is a vigorous knockabout rhymester— hardly more.

11.   On the Death of a Sparrow, named Philip.
John Skelton (?1460–?1529)

Cumberland has claimed him, but most authorities believe that he came from Norwich. He graduated at Oxford, and it was there that he was locally acclaimed as Poet Laureate. It was not a royal or a national recognition. In early manhood he became tutor to the accomplished young prince whom history knows as Henry the Eighth. The Countess of Surrey, mother of the poet whose name will soon be in front of us, was one of Skelton's patrons. In later life he was imprisoned by Cardinal Wolsey, probably because with more daring than discretion he had written (about the Cardinal)

> 'Like Mahound (Mahomet) in a play,
> No man dare him withsay'.

Skelton died in sanctuary at Westminster.

In 1566 *The Merie Tales of Skelton* were published, and it was now customary to make up jest-books under a best-selling name: much as, later, various plays were sold by attributing them to William Shakespeare or, with a touch of conscience, to "W.S." Some of the 'merie tales' would not please delicate nostrils, but nearly all of them show the persistence of Skelton's *legend* as that of a wild fellow of rough and hearty behaviour. It was early said of him that 'he did love wel a cup of good wyne', which is not likely to astound anybody; and he himself declared that 'all wines must be strong, and fayre, and well coloured; it must have a redolent savour; it must be cold, and sprinkling in the piece or in a glasse'. That all wine should be cold may provoke comment from a modern connoisseur.

> *Do mi nus,*
> Help now, sweet Jesús!
> *Levavi oculos meos in montes:*
> Would God I had Xenophontes,
> Or Socrates the wise,
> To show me their devise,
> Moderately to take
> This sorrow that I make
> For Philip Sparrow's sake!
> So fervently I shake,
> I feel my body quake;
> So urgently I am brought
> Into careful thought.
> Like Andromach, Hector's wife,
> Was weary of her life,
> When she had lost her joy,
> Noble Hector of Troy;
> In like manner alsó
> Encreaseth my deadly woe,
> For my sparrow is go(ne).
>   It was so pretty a fool,
> It would sit on a stool,
> And learn'd after my school(ing)
> For to keep his cut,
> With 'Philip, keep your cut!'
>   It had a velvet cap,
> And would sit upon my lap,
> And seek after small worms,
> And sometimes white bread crumbs;

And many times and oft,
Between my breasties soft
It would lie and rest;
It was proper and pressed.
  Sometimes he would gasp
When he saw a wasp;
A fly or a gnat,
He would fly at that:
And prettily he would pant
When he saw an ant;
Lord, how he would pry
After the butterfly!
Lord, how he would hop
After the grass-hop'!
And when I said 'Phyp, Phyp',
Then would he leap and skip,
And take me by the lip.
Alas, it will me slo (slay),
That Philip is gone me fro(m).

* * *

Thomas Burke says that in the Middle Ages, 'the ale-houses or "ale-stakes" were just cottages, or huts, usually kept by widows, and distinguished from their neighbours by nothing more than a pole bearing a few leafy boughs. It was on this, the earliest inn-sign, that the old proverb was based—Good wine needs no bush'. Here we have a well-caught snapshot of just such a wayside ale-house.

12   About Eleanor Rumming

And this comely dame,
I understand her name
Is Eleanor Rumming,
At home in her wonning;
And, as men say,
She dwells in Sothray,
In a certain stead
Beside Leatherhead.

She is a tonnish gib;
The devil and she be sib.
   But to make up my tale,
She breweth nappy ale,
And maketh thereof port sale (poor?)
To travellers, to tinkers,
To sweaters, to swinkers,
And all good ale drinkers,
That will nothing spare,
But drink till they stare
And bring themselves bare,
With 'Now, away the mare!'
And 'Let us slay care,
As wise as a hare!'
   Come whoso will
To Eleanor on the hill,
With 'Fill the cup, fill',
And sit there by still,
Early and late:
Thither cometh Kate,
Cicely, and Sare,
With their legs bare,
And also their feet
Hardly full unsweet:
With their heels dagg'd,
Their kirtles all to-jagg'd,
Their smocks all to-ragg'd,
With titters and tatters,
Bring dishes and platters,
With all their might running
To Eleanor Rumming,
To have of her tunning:
She leaneth them on the same,
And thus beginneth the game.
   Some wenches come unlaced,
Some hussifs come unbraced,
With their naked paps,
That flips and flaps;

It wigs and it wags,
Like tawny saffron bags;
A sort of foul drabs
All scurvy with scabs:
Some be flea-bitten,
Some skewed as a kitten;
Some with a short clout
Bind their heads about;
Some have no hair-lace,
Their locks about their face,
Their tresses untrussed,
All full of unlust;
Some look strawny,
Some cawny-mawny;
Full untidy tegs,
Like rotten eggs.
Such a lewd sort
To Eleanor resort
From time to tide:
Abide, abide,
And to you shall be told
How her ale is sold
To Mawte and to Molde. . . .

* * *

Across the border, poetry retained its courtliness. Dunbar, one of the earliest poets of that long line which, not very convincingly, laments the obduracy of a lady, probably studied no work later than Chaucer's. He is a gifted executant, hardly a creator.

13   To a Lady. *William Dunbar* (?1465–?1530)

He was, for a time, a Franciscan friar. Some say that he was killed at Flodden in 1513, when James the Fourth was defeated and slain; but it seems unlikely that he would be a fighting man at the age of forty-eight.

Sweet Rose of virtue and of gentleness,
Delightsome Lily of every loveliness,
  Richest in goodness and in beauty clear
  And every virtue that is held most dear,—
Excepting only that you are merciless!

Into your bower this day I did pursue.
There saw I flow'rs that were all fresh of hue.
  Both white and red most lovely were there seen,
  And wholesome herbs, too, set in their stalks green . . .
But leaf or flow'r find could I none—of rue!

I think that March, with his blasts cold and keen,
Hath slain this gentle herb, the which I mean,
  Whose piteous death gives to my heart such pain
  That I would set the plant to root again,—
So comforting his leaves unto me been.

*   *   *

Long ago had Italy taken the lead in Europe. English noblemen and gentry, aided by the steady advance of printing, were mostly becoming literate. We must not imagine that books even now were common. We must, on the contrary, accept Mr. Walter de la Mare's belief that, even in Elizabethan times, a house with twelve books in it would have been regarded as awe-inspiring. Nevertheless the New Learning was coming in apace from Italy. There was yeast in all Western Europe, and men lived in an exciting atmosphere. Cabot had, for example, landed in America (1497). Colet, who founded St. Paul's School, and Erasmus were fellow-students at Oxford in 1499. Sir Thomas More in his garden and house at Chelsea provided an example of the cultured and charitable life which has never been surpassed, though it may have been equalled by Chinese mandarins long ago. In 1517 'grand old Martin Luther', as the protestant Browning termed him, inaugurated that anti-mediæval movement which, unconsciously affected by the scientific curiosity of the Renaissance, inevitably expanded into complete scepticism. And only a few years earlier Henry the Eighth came to the throne of England and, in the mysterious way of royalty, imparted to his country much of his own temperament and character.

We are far away from the illiterate barons demonstrating 'toughness' in their strongholds or in their wives' 'bowers'. It had now become praiseworthy to practise the arts of music and verse. In the barber's shop, we are told, there was always a lute—waiting for the customer whose beard came next for attention. England was musical, and ready within another generation to listen with enthusiasm to dramas written in elaborate verse.

Our next two poets are, as you will discern, still struggling to keep their metres tidy. Rhyme is still a fascinating and difficult toy. They are at much the same stage as the Italian painters (of a somewhat earlier date) who strove so enthusiastically to represent true perspective.

14   The Unsatisfactoriness of Dream-Love. *Sir Thomas Wyatt* (1503–1542)

Wyatt was of Yorkshire stock on the helmet side, but he was born at Maidstone. At twelve he took his Bachelor's degree at St. John's College, Cambridge. At twenty-one he became Clerk of the King's Jewels. His marriage (to Elizabeth Brooke, daughter of Lord Cobham) was luckless.

It was for this reason, perhaps, that he became enamoured of his magnetic young cousin, Anne Boleyn. In a sonnet he says of her

> 'I leave off, therefore;
> Since in a net I seek to hold the wind'.

Moreover, mindful of the King's overwhelming personality he stated that Anne wears a diamond necklace and that on it

> 'There is written, her fair neck round about:
> *Noli me tangere*, for Cæsar's I am
> And wild for to hold, though I seem tame'.

Even these fragments produce a brilliant impression of Anne Boleyn's ill-starred temperament. When her adultery was discovered, 'Cæsar' imprisoned the poet. Later, in 1541, he was arrested for antipapistry, and on that occasion was befriended by a valiant, but also ill-starred, girl named Kathryn Howard. Wyatt, rather surprisingly, died a natural death. We should think of his poetry as brave pioneering.

THE LOVER HAVING DREAMED ENJOYING OF HIS LOVE, COMPLAINETH THAT THE DREAM IS NOT EITHER LONGER OR TRUER

Unstable dream, according to the place,
Be steadfast once, or else at least be true:
By tasted sweetness make me not to rue
The sudden loss of thy false feignéd grace.
By good respect, in such a dangerous case,
Thou broughtest not her into these tossing seas;
But madest my sprite to live, my care t'encrease,
My body in tempest her delight t'embrace,
The body dead, the spirit had his desire;
Painless was th'one, th'other in delight.
Why then, alas, did it not keep it right,
But thus return to leap into the fire;
   And where it was at wish, could not remain?
   Such mocks of dreams do turn to deadly pain.

15 The Lover Forsaketh his Unkind Love

My heart I gave thee, not to do it pain,
But to preserve, lo, it to thee was taken.
I served thee, not that I should be forsaken;
But, that I should receive reward again,
I was content thy servant to remain;
And not to be repayed after this fashion.
Now, since in thee there is none other reason,
Displease thee not, if that I do refrain.
Unsatiate of my woe, and thy desire;
Assured by craft for to excuse thy fault:
But, since it pleaseth thee to feign default,
Farewell, I say, departing from the fire.
   For he that doth believe, bearing in hand,
   Plougheth in the water, and soweth in the sand.

16 A Vow to Love Faithfully, Howsoever he be Rewarded. *Henry Howard, Earl of Surrey* (1518–1547)

Just as Wyatt was a cousin of Anne Boleyn, so was Henry Howard a cousin of Kathryn Howard, whom Henry the Eighth at first called his 'Rose Without a Thorn'. The poet was a scion of the Norfolks, and the title of Earl was given him as a courtesy. By temperament this poet was a violent man. He became fast friends with 'Mr. Wyatt', son of the preceding poet; and on a February day in 1543, when he was twenty-four, he and Mr. Wyatt beguiled their leisure by breaking the windows of various London citizens. Not all poets, let us perceive, are meek and mild. As a result of this jollification, the Earl was clapped into prison. Later, he returned to prison for having eaten meat in Lent.

Unfortunately, he claimed that as a descendant of the Mowbrays he had a right to use the Arms of King Edward the Confessor. The Howards, we must bear in mind, were then, as they still are, among the noblest and most ancient families of England. Henry Tudor was comparatively an upstart, and he did not intend to let any man talk about being descended from a pre-Conquest King of England. Howard was charged with high treason at the Guildhall on January 13th, 1547. He was condemned, by a packed jury, to the gruesome sentence of being hanged, drawn (disembowelled while living) and quartered. His rank, however, caused him merely to be beheaded—on Tower Hill, January 19th, 1547.

> Set me whereas the sun doth parch the green,
> Or where his beams do not dissolve the ice;
> In temperate heat, where he is felt and seen;
> In presence prest of people, mad, or wise;
> Set me in high, or yet in low degree;
> In longest night, or in the shortest day;
> In clearest sky, or where clouds thickest be;
> In lusty youth, or when my hairs are gray:
> Set me in heaven, in earth, or else in hell,
> In hill, or dale, or in the foaming flood;

Thrall, or at large, alive whereso I dwell,
Sick, or in health, in evil fame or good,
  Her's will I be; and only with this thought
  Content myself, although my chance be nought.

* * *

In this next poem we have an early specimen of the innumerable poems inspired by Horace.

17   The Means to Attain Happy Life

Martial, the things that do attain
The happy life, be these, I find:
The riches left, not got with pain;
The fruitful ground, the quiet mind:

The equal friend, no grudge, no strife;
No charge of rule, nor governance;
Without disease, the healthful life;
The household of continuance:

The mean diet, no delicate fare;
True wisdom join'd with simpleness;
The night dischargèd of all care,
Where wine the wit may not oppress:

The faithful wife, without debate;
Such sleeps as may beguile the night:
Contented with thine own estate;
No wish for death, ne fear his might.

* * *

This part of the book may fitly close with three ballads. The word 'ballad' comes from a word which meant 'to dance', and it is therefore surprisingly connected with the giving of a 'ball'; for the earliest ballads were actually dancing-songs. The chief singer, it is surmised, stood in the centre of a ring of country-dancers. He it was who told whatever simple story the ballad commemorated, while the dancers, moving all the time to the rhythm of the song, enjoyed themselves by joining-in with the easily-remembered refrain. These refrains, reverently imitated by Rossetti and mockingly by Calverley ('Butter and eggs and a pound of cheese' is one of his fabrication), may well be maddening to a modern reader who is taking no part in a happy unsophisticated country-game. It seems in fact that, as the dancing fell away and only the singing of a ballad continued to collect listeners, the refrain was often discarded and forgotten.

Ballads, like folk-tales, were common property. Some striking action occurred. A man of invention started to 'make a song about it', just as miners or pioneers in remote places still do (especially if they are Irishmen); and then other men with a talent for story-telling take up the song-tale and inevitably add their own touches to it, just as theatre-managers of to-day set about improving the text of a dramatist. These ballads, then, have no author. They are as anonymous as all early art is, even from the days of pre-Roman Egypt. This anonymity accounts for (a) the impersonality of a ballad—it bears no 'guinea-stamp', and (b) for its admirable characteristic of getting on with the story. The old ballad-mongers, like the modern playwright, dared not risk a yawn. Any dull bits, therefore, dropped off because people were seen to wander home when the monger came to those bits. So, too, irrelevancies were soon forgotten. Sometimes in these old communal-poems we find what may be called 'stock-phrases'. One of them is 'when leaves were large and long'; and it has been proposed that these phrases gave the singer a moment or two in which to invent, or to remember, the next lines.

Only eleven ballads, we learn, 'are extant in manuscripts older than the seventeenth century'. It is therefore impossible to date any ballad, because it may be the accretion of four or five hundred years. Every literate person should pray for the soul of Bishop Percy, the esteemed friend of Dr. Johnson, whose collection of 'Reliques', made in the latter half of the eighteenth century, is by far the greatest of all efforts in ballad-salvage.

The Robin Hood ballads are, unfortunately, too long for a book of this compass.

18   As Ye Came from the Holy Land. (*Anonymous*)

The beginning suggests a very early date; and an effective opening is
precisely what would make a ballad popular and consequently be the
part of it which would suffer least modification. 'Nymph' and 'viewless
vestals', however, are obviously words too sophisticated to have been
current before the time of Elizabeth. The last two verses may well be
late additions.

'As ye came from the holy land
    Of blessed Walsingham,
O met you not with my true love
    As by the way ye came?'

'How should I know your true love,
    That have met many a one,
As I came from the holy land,
    That have both come, and gone?'

'My love is neither white nor browne,
    But as the heavens faire;
There is none hath her form divine,
    Either in earth, or ayre'.

'Such an one did I meet, good sir,
    With an angellicke face,
Who like a nymphe, a queene appeard
    Both in her gait, her grace'.

'Yes: she hath clean forsaken me,
    And left me all alone,
Who some time loved me as her life,
    And calléd me her owne'.

'What is the cause she leaves thee thus,
    And a new way doth take,
That some times loved thee as her life,
    And thee her joy did make?'

'I, that loved her all my youth,
    Growe old now as you see;
Love liketh not the falling fruite,
    Nor yet the withered tree.

'For love is like a carelesse childe,
    Forgetting promise past;
He is blind, or deaf, whenere he list;
    His faith is never fast.

'His fond desire is fickle found,
    And yieldes a trustlesse joye;
Wonne with a world of toil and care,
    And lost ev'n with a toye.

'Such is the love of womankinde,
    Of LOVES faire name abusde,
Beneathe which many vaine desires
    And follyes are excusde.

'But true love is a lasting fire,
    Which viewless vestals tend,
That burnes for ever in the soule,
    And knowes nor change, nor end'.

19   Barbara Allen's Cruelty. (*Anonymous*, no date)

This ballad must have been unusually popular, for Mr. Pepys tells
posterity that his actress-friend, Mistress Knipp, used to call him
Dapper Dicky and he to call her Barbary Allen. Scarlet Town is said to
mean Scarborough. If 'The Nut-Brown Maid', current in 1503, were
not a great deal more resourceful in its rhyming, we might think that
the many rhymes to 'Allen' condemn this poem as being no simple,
ancient and communal production.

In Scarlet towne, where I was borne,
    There was a faire maid dwellin,
Made every youth crye, Wel-awaye!
    Her name was Barbara Allen.

All in the merrye month of May,
    When greene buds they were swellin,
Yong Jemmye Grove on his death-bed lay,
    For love of Barbara Allen.

He sent his man unto her then,
   To the town where shee was dwellin;
'You must come to my master deare,
   Giff your name be Barbara Allen.

'For death is printed on his face,
   And ore his hart is stealin:
Then haste away to comfort him,
   O lovelye Barbara Allen'.

'Though death be printed on his face,
   And ore his harte is stealin,
Yet little better shall he bee
   For bonny Barbara Allen'.

So slowly, slowly, she came up,
   And slowly she came nye him;
And all she sayd, when there she came,
   'Yong man, I think y'are dying'.

He turned his face unto her strait,
   With deadlye sorrow sighing;
'O lovely maid, come pity mee,
   Ime on my death-bed lying'.

'If on your death-bed you doe lye,
   What needs the tale you are tellin?
I cannot keep you from your death;
   Farewell', sayd Barbara Allen.

He turnd his face unto the wall,
   As deadlye pangs he fell in:
'Adieu! adieu! adieu to you all,
   Adieu to Barbara Allen!'

As she was walking ore the fields,
   She heard the bell a knellin;
And every stroke did seem to saye,
   'Unworthy Barbara Allen!'

She turned her bodye round about,
   And spied the corps a coming:
'Laye down, laye down the corps', she sayd,
   'That I may look upon him'.

With scornful eye she lookèd downe,
 Her cheeke with laughter swellin,
Whilst all her friends cryd out amaine,
 'Unworthye Barbara Allen!'

When he was dead, and laid in grave,
 Her harte was struck with sorrowe;
'O mother, mother, make my bed,
 For I shall dye to-morrowe.

'Hard-harted creature, him to slight,
 Who lovèd me so dearlye:
O that I had been more kind to him,
 When he was alive and neare me!'

She, on her death-bed as she laye,
 Beg'd to be buried by him,
And sore repented of the daye,
 That she did ere denye him.

'Farewell', she sayd, 'ye virgins all,
 And shun the fault I fell in:
Henceforth take warning by the fall
 Of cruel Barbara Allen'.

20 The Bailiff's Daughter of Islington. (*Anonymous, no date*)

To a romantic Londoner it is a blow to hear that 'Islington in Norfolk is probably the place here meant'. Bishop Percy states that he reproduced this tale from 'an ancient black-letter copy in the Pepys Collection, with some improvements communicated by a lady as she heard the same recited in her youth'.

There was a youthe, and a well-belovèd youthe,
 And he was a squires son:
He loved the bayliffes daughter deare,
 That lived in Islington.

Yet she was coye, and would not believe
　　That he did love her soe,
Noe nor at any time would she
　　Any countenance to him showe.

But when his friendes did understand
　　His fond and foolish minde,
They sent him up to faire London,
　　An apprentice for to binde.

And when he had been seven long yeares,
　　And never his love could see,—
'Many a teare have I shed for her sake,
　　When she little thought of mee'.

Then all the maids of Islington
　　Went forth to sport and playe,
All but the bayliffes daughter deare;
　　She secretly stole awaye.

She pullèd off her gowne of greene,
　　And put on ragged attire,
And to faire London she would go
　　Her true love to enquire.

And as she went along the high road,
　　The weather being hot and drye,
She sat her downe upon a green bank,
　　And her true love came riding bye.

She started up, with a colour soe redd,
　　Catching hold of his bridle-reine;
'One penny, one penny, kind sir', she sayd,
　　'Will ease me of much paine'.

'Before I give you one penny, sweet-heart,
　　Praye tell me where you were borne'.
'At Islington, kind sir', sayd shee,
　　'Where I have had many a scorne'.

'I prythee, sweet-heart, then tell to mee,
　　O tell me, whether you knowe
The bayliffes daughter of Islington'.
　　'She is dead, sir, long agoe'.

'If she be dead, then take my horse,
  My saddle and bridle alsó;
For I will into some farr countrye,
  Where noe man shall me knowe'.

'O staye, O staye, thou goodlye youthe,
  She standeth by thy side;
She is here alive, she is not dead,
  And readye to be thy bride'.

'O farewell griefe, and welcome joye,
  Ten thousand times therefore;
For nowe I have founde mine owne true love,
  Whom I thought I should never see more'.

'It was Horace Walpole', murmured my old friend as we crossed the garden of Leicester Square, 'who bequeathed to us that profound phrase "Life is a comedy to those who think, a Tragedy to those who feel". Believe me, dear fellow, the soul is not clever: and it is from the soul, not from mere intelligence, that masterpieces arise'.

(*The Old Man from Somerset*, p. 84.)

PART TWO
1550–1650

Part Two

1550–1650

IT IS MORE than mere fancy to say that Chaucer's poetry is like Spring-time, that in Spenser there is the lushness of early Summer, and that in Shakespeare we find the magnificence of mid-June and the electrical storms of July. By the time that he has finished this book the reader will, I hope, have perceived that our poetry has twice repeated the pattern of the four seasons. It is likely to repeat that pattern for ever. And seeing that the Elizabethan Age is one of the two midsummers which our poetry has at present experienced, this seems not an inapt point at which to find out, if we can, what poetry really is.

* * *

We should think of it under two aspects which, nevertheless, cannot be separated. We must consider, I mean, the content and the form. In other words, poetry is an expression of emotional experience but is also an elaborate fine art. A dog's growl is an expression of emotion, and so are the optimistic jingles in a penny newspaper. Obviously, then, art is necessary if the growl is to become a poem, as it does in several speeches in *Lear* and *Othello*; but we must also concede, however hazardously, that not all emotions are the potential substance of poetry. It is not a matter of morals, as the Victorians believed, for morality is both temporal and geographical. Moreover, fine poetry might well be made, like many of Beardsley's drawings, from perverse emotions or exotic sensations, and perhaps has already been made by, for example, Baudelaire. But neither is the emotional field to be limited by an assumption that many emotions are not sufficiently noble, for this was a conception of poetry which blighted most of the verse written in the Eighteenth Century. Poetry does not need to be either respectable or 'elevated' although, clearly, it may be either. I suggest that the touchstone of poetic emotion, as also of appreciation of poetry, is a high degree of sensibility. A poem may be coarse but may not be

46

vulgar. Nor may it arise from a crude sensation or emotion. The emotion in poetry *need not be noble but must not be ignoble*: and to this we may add that poetry is essentially incompatible with a matter-of-fact outlook on the world. For the rest, it may reside in one of Herrick's fanciful word-toys, or in Chaucer's humorous liking of humanity, or in the wild young passion of 'Romeo', or the titanic mental anguish of 'Lear', or the tender melancholy of Gray's *Elegy*, or the stately lamentation of Tennyson's great ode, or even in the delicate pains and pleasures of the decadent in the 'nineties. This vast range of emotions that are fit matter for poetry will be seen, nevertheless, to imply—from end to end of the spectrum—a certain intensity or subtlety of feeling or, in one word,—sensibility.

And when we turn to consider poetry as an art, as versecraft, we shall see that without sensibility nothing can be attained. The purpose of this art is precisely to communicate shades of emotion with subtle exactness. What then are some of the principles in versecraft which, like certain valuable rules in an art-school, can be taught and learned? We might say to a poet, 'First catch your emotion' and, next, find a metre or rhythmic pattern which fits what you desire to say. It is surprisingly often that we meet with sad sentiments phrased in a hopping measure, or a slow-moving metre chosen to express a moment of rapture. In a true poet the emotion spontaneously finds an appropriate rhythm, even if at first the poet captures only three or four lines. The pulse in that fragment will set the rhythmic pattern for all that is to follow.

Let us imagine, then, that the poem is going to form itself into stanzas or at least into several distinct parts. Each stanza is a shaped emotion, as a stone is shaped by a mason; but here we come at once upon the commonest defect in all English literature, whether prose or verse; for the many or several stanzas of a poem ought to build up into a form of beauty which is perceptible only when we can review the poem as a whole, and it is in this architectural feeling that our writers, and their English critics also, are astonishingly defective. Even when architecture is present in a poem, a play or a novel, not one Englishman in ten millions can perceive it. There is architectural beauty in all the odes that Keats left us, in Matthew Arnold's *The Scholar Gipsy*, and in a fair number of small poems, where of course it is the more easily achieved: but you may hardly find it anywhere in the voluminous work of Browning or Swinburne.

The design or plan of a poem having thus been projected, the artist will concern himself with making his work pleasant to read and, if possible, so seductive that it 'reads itself', as we say, and winds its way imperceptibly into our memory. Supreme poetry is always easily memorised. And this quality of seduction is to be obtained by contriving a continuous verbal music; and verbal music, again, consists of rhythmical charm, a delicate management of vowels and consonants, and perhaps also of rhyme. Now there is a vague though perceptible rhythm in all good prose; but sometimes the rhythmic beat becomes so definite as to obliterate the boundaries of prose. The prose becomes hybrid; but there can also be hybrid verse, verse not rhythmic enough to enchant. Listen, for example, to the opening of Whitman's noble dirge for Abraham Lincoln. In order to bring out more emphatically the alternating use of phrases which contain four or three beats (accented syllables), let us slightly alter Whitman's arrangement of the lines . . .

'When lílacs lást in the dóoryard blóom'd,	4
And the gréat stár eárly dróop'd	4
In the wéstern ský in the níght,	3
I moúrn'd, and yét shall móurn	3
With éver-retúrning spríng,	3
Evér-retúrning spríng,	3
Trínity súre to mé you bríng,	4
Lílac blóoming perénnial	3
And dróoping stár in the wést,	3
And thóught of hím I lóve'.	3

Whitman supposed that he had defiantly broken away from the effete verse-patterns of old Europe, but observe how, at his best, he unconsciously begins to use *Repeated Rhythm*, for here is the vital separation between poetry and even poetic prose. Under emotional pressure, prose-writers who, like Dickens, have no ear for rhythm, often flounder into blank-verse of the flattest kind; and the reason is that they are instinctively struggling to get up into the intenser atmosphere of poetry and so, automatically, begin to repeat a rhythm as the heart reiterates its beat. From the dawn of human experience Repeated Rhythm, inducing a very mild hypnosis, has offered men a forgetfulness of superficial life and troubled the wide waters of the subconscious mind. Repeated Rhythm is literally a mode of enchantment. It is the element in poetry which in ancient times made people regard a poet as a half-sacred person. The bard was a spellbinder. He could stir up the subconscious, the depth of mind at which we become at least a little more than our workaday selves; and if the most modern of those who are now called poets have renounced this mode of enchantment, and have therefore in reality taken to writing crumbled prose, we may easily perceive that they have never apprehended the origin or the purpose of poetry.

But a rhythm repeated for a long time without variation becomes a maddening monotony, like the dripping of water or the shriek of a neglected telephone. This, indeed, was the defect of early English attempts (in *Gorboduc*) to write verse without rhyme. There must be, as architects put it, variety in unity. There must be a basic pattern, a rhythmic norm, within which variations of accent will be used only in order that the ear may not drop off to sleep. In fine versecraft, therefore, the normal run of accented syllables will be judiciously interrupted. Every first-rate poet thus keeps his verse alive by introducing small variations.

And of that part of verbal music, the management of vowels and consonants, the reader will soon detect that the poems which most delight his ear are those in which the same vowel-sound is never quickly repeated, and in which on the contrary the poet, whether by art or by instinct, has continually varied the vowels. A keen student may learn to admire 'this side idolatry' the versecraft of Milton if he tries to keep count of the number of vowel-sounds in the lines:

49

> 'I did but prompt the age to quit their clogs
> By the known rules of ancient liberty,
> When straight a barbarous noise environed me
> Of owls and cuckoos, asses, apes and dogs;
> As when those twain that were transform'd to frogs
> Rail'd at Latona's twin-born progeny,
> Which, after, held the sun and moon in fee;
> But this is got by casting pearl to hogs. . . .'

You will very seldom hear so many sounds within the compass of eight lines. And it will be obvious that the pleasure of hearing the rhyme-chimes would be ruined if vowel-sounds similar to those of the rhyme-words were to occur midway within the lines. Again, the sensitive artist will strive to limit his use of dental-sounds (t and d) and to see that they collide as rarely as possible. Above all, he will do desperate battle with the letter s, which infests our language as though it were bindweed in a flower-bed. Sibilants ought never to swallow one another, like symbolic serpents.

Oddly enough, it is Milton himself, a master in the delightful use of rhyme, who most severely attacks it, saying that 'it is no necessary adjunct or true ornament of a poem', and again that it is 'to all judicious ears, trivial and of no musical delight'. Still, what would remain of Shakespeare's best lyrics if he had 'abjured rhyme'? But if rhyme is to be used, it must on no account be a will-o'-the-wisp misleading the poet into unintended errancies. The rhyme-pair must seem to occur as naturally as fillipines in a nutshell. In fact, the poet as artist has failed if we can be certain which of his rhymes precipitated the other; and of this we shall hear something further anon.

All these are matters of craft, anxieties of the workshop. A busy man —a shepherd, a sailor, a doctor, a Cabinet Minister, a 'bus-conductor— may come to love certain poems so intensely that their beauty acts as a talisman throughout a long life; and such a man may never have time enough to investigate the minutiæ of wordcraft; but his delight, nevertheless, will be due partly to the poet's conscientious and delicate artistry. No sensible reader will suppose that the most expert work-manship can, in itself, produce the rare moods of great poetry. The most deeply poetic passages in our literature occur when, as if by a miracle, the words chosen to express the poet's meaning contrive somehow to set overtones of emotion vibrating in the reader's profoundest self. This effect—the effect for which all serious poetry strives—cannot be analysed or explained. Where it exists, it can be instantly recognised: or if it is not recognised, then the reader is destined to go through life without understanding why poetry is so highly esteemed by nearly all the best minds in any age. No one can explain what happens within us when we repeat such words as

> 'Old unhappy far-off things,
> And battles long ago',

or

> 'Alas, that Spring should vanish with the Rose,
> That Youth's sweet-scented Manuscript should close',

or that magnificently terrible line,

> 'Frantic-mad with evermore unrest'. . . .

Change the word 'Manuscript' in Fitzgerald's couplet, or translate the lines into any other tongue, and the sad syringa fragrance of the passage, with its 'dying fall', will at once evaporate.

From this we see how 'it' could *not* be 'just as well said in plain prose': and perhaps we may fitly end this portion of our enquiry with a suggestion that the difference between prose and poetry is the difference between letting words walk and letting them dance. We must remember that once upon a time there was ceremonial dancing, and religious dancing, and that no one would have trod a pavane or a forlana if he or she could have derived the same fine happiness from the sensible prac-tice of walking. Perhaps, too, we should reflect that much of the so-called poetry of our time may correspond to the so-called dancing in our night-clubs.

* * *

We have come, then, to a time when English versecraft is mature. And I have marked the period as lying between 1550 and 1650 because soon after 1550 Elizabeth became Queen of England, an event which coincided with an immense liberation of mind, and because the death of Charles the First in 1649 coincided with a distinctive change of mood in our literature. This is not the right place at which to comment at length upon the mysterious way in which our monarchs epitomise the temper of their times, how Restorational was Charles the Second, how massively Eighteenth Century were the Hanoverian Georges, how Regency was George the Fourth, how solidly Victorian was Queen Victoria, just as though they were predestined personalities and avatars of the national being; but at least we may acknowledge the debt which literature owes to the personality of Elizabeth. When she came to the throne, in 1558, England, we learn, was still about equally divided between Catholics and Protestants. The new Queen, fortunately, had not the fanaticism of her sister, the late Queen Mary, and there was no burning of Catholics to make up for the recent burning of Protestants. Elizabeth was a typical prince of the Renaissance. Her tastes were secular. She was much more interested in England than in Heaven or Hell. Indeed, her lack of religious feeling probably developed into the complete scepticism of Leonardo da Vinci, and in this we were exceedingly fortunate because, had the Queen shared more of her sister's nature, many of our writers might have wasted their genius in sectarian controversy and, at best, no writer would have felt free to delineate the hurly-burly of immediate life without reference to theological doctrines concerning the life to come. We were also lucky in having for our principal enemy the perfervidly Catholic land of Spain. The peril of having to endure a Spanish government united English Catholics and Protestants in a common patriotism; and it is worth noting that although everybody is aware of Shakespeare's patriotism, nobody can tell whether he had some religious conviction or none at all.

Social reformers may shake their heads over this, that or the other aspect of the Elizabethan Era but, judging by its architecture and its literature, there can be no doubt that most of its inhabitants lustily enjoyed it and that a modern writer may well look back on it with envy. Men had a keen appetite for the strongest, fullest experience which life could yield them, and this necessarily meant that they were not afraid of emotion. In other words, the typical Elizabethan was romantic. British phlegm in fact was imported, together with double or treble chins, by the Hanoverians. The Earl of Essex was neither phlegmatic nor reasonable when he tossed his bonnet into the harbour as the ship triumphantly rode in upon Cadiz; and neither Falstaff nor Hamlet conforms to the ideal of a strong silent Englishman. The writers, too, exuberantly enjoyed the manipulation of a language that was still young, vigorous, unexplored, undimmed. They had also the exhilaration of living in an age of genius when the man of moderate talent inevitably catches fire from the men of first magnitude who are at work in the same atmosphere, and so contrives to produce better work than he could have achieved by himself.

In European culture Italy still led the field. There is no evidence, I believe, that the Elizabethans knew much, if anything, about Dante, but nearly all of them (like Wyatt and Surrey aforetime) were profoundly influenced by the mellifluous and lachrymose genius of Petrarch. Many were also influenced by Poliziano, Tasso and Guarini, particularly in setting up a long-lasting fashion in pastoral poetry. Court-ladies and tavern-haunting poets begin to figure in literature as nymphs and shepherds. Even Shakespeare addresses his friend Kit Marlowe as 'Dead shepherd'; even Milton (so much later) says that he and his friend Lycidas 'fed the same flock'. Spenser was a confirmed pastoralist, although in *The Faerie Queene* he concerned himself less with shepherds than with knights. Nevertheless, during this period Shakespeare and a few of his fellows broke free from all affectations and achieved sonnets that burn with sincerity and passion. The songs of this mighty age are innumerable and, if we pick out the best, have never been equalled in their perfect fitting of sound to sense. It is as though the words were translucent and so permitted the author's original emotion to shine through them without obstacle: or as though exactly those words in that particular arrangement had miraculously alighted on the page from the tip of the poet's quill.

Despite the prestige of Italy, English character has now become so definite that it easily transformed its models. There is a last lingering Petrarchan influence in those of Shakespeare's sonnets (assuredly the earlier group) which a well-meaning contemporary called 'sugar'd', but there is nothing in all Italian literature, with the exception of some lines by the much later Leopardi, comparable with the naked agony of the sonnet by Shakespeare which will presently come to the reader's eye. What would have happened if there had been a superb written, highly sophisticated, Italian drama at this time? There were, in fact, only semi-operatic pastoral plays and the brilliant charades of the Commedia dell' Arte. In any circumstances English genius would soon have forced its way to *King Lear* and *A Midsummer Night's Dream*; but Italian models might have delayed the supreme glory of English literature.

Nature cannot exceed midsummer, the moon cannot become more than a full moon; and in the same way, in accordance with the same law, every art comes now and again as near to perfection as is possible. No one can improve on the Temple of Neptune at Pæstum, the widest-winged of Plato's Dialogues, Titian's portrait of grey-sleeved Ariosto, Beethoven's deepest music or Shakespeare's mightiest verse. Only the rebellion and impatience of youth misleads each new generation into supposing that the arts inevitably progress. Science, the accumulation of knowledge, must progress,—if it is not obliterated by a tidal wave of barbarism; but art, the expression of human delight, hope and sorrow, no more progresses than a fruit tree which yields a new crop every year but never a different fruit and not necessarily a better example. 'In literature', said Swinburne, 'there is no Past', and it was nobly said.

Edward de Vere, Earl of Oxford: 1550–1604

The de Veres came over with the Conqueror, and the poet, when twelve years of age, became seventeenth Earl of Oxford. He was a Royal ward. He studied at Cambridge, going to Queen's College and, like so many future poets, to 'John's'.

At twenty-one he married Anne Cecil, daughter of Lord Burghley, the Queen's most trusted counsellor. In 1575–76 the poet travelled in Italy: and came home somewhat 'italianated'. He formed a Company of Players which in 1584 visited Stratford-on-Avon. In the following year Shakespeare betook himself to London. Anne died in 1588, and Oxford afterwards married Elizabeth Trentham. He died at Newington, near London.

By temperament he was moody, quarrelsome and eccentric, spending much of his leisure with the 'players'. An ingenious attempt has been made to establish him as the true author of the Shakespearean plays. The date of his death seems fatal to this theory, but there is more than a possibility that he may have written some of the detachable soliloquies or even Mercutio's Queen Mab speech and, like Hamlet in relation to the players, have charged Shakespeare to weave them into the dramatic text. We must remember that a gentleman might compose poetry with credit to himself, but that actors were regarded then as prizefighters or professional cricketers are regarded now, and that even a bohemian Earl could not admit to writing for the public stage.

The theme of the following poem is pleasantly unhackneyed. It is a pity that the seventh line should contain the assonance of 'make' and 'change'.

21   Of Women

If women could be fair, and yet not fond,
Or that their love were firm, not fickle, still,
I would not marvel that they make men bond
By service long to purchase their good will:
But when I see how frail those creatures are,
I muse that men forget themselves so far.

To mark the choice they make, and how they change,
How oft from Phœbus they do flee to Pan,
Unsettled still, like haggards wild, they range,
These gentle birds that fly from man to man;
Who would not scorn and shake them from the fist,
And let them fly, fair fools, which way they list?

Yet, for disport, we fawn and flatter both,
To pass the time when nothing else can please;
And train them to our lure with subtle oath,
Till, weary of their wiles, ourselves we ease:
And then we say, when we their fancy try,
To play with fools, O what a fool was I!

* * *

Let us pass from this somewhat formal, though elegant, versecraft to the work of a major poet. . . .

E

Edmund Spenser: 1552–1599

Born at East Smithfield, whither his father had migrated from the Burnley district of Lancashire (but we must imagine a rural Burnley). He was educated at The Merchant Taylor's School, and he matriculated from Pembroke Hall, Cambridge, in 1576. Soon afterwards he became Secretary to the fourteenth Lord Grey de Wilton.

When he was twenty-eight Spenser went as Lord-Deputy to Ireland, where he seems to have been conscientious but ill at ease. He compiled a prose work called *A View of the Present State of Ireland*.

At the age of forty-two he married Elizabeth Boyle, who has the high distinction of having inspired two rich and stately poems *Prothalamion* and *Epithalamion*, which are not only examples of Spenser at his greatest as a poet but are also among the finest of all those poems in our language which have been inspired by joy.

In 1598 the O'Neils and other Irishmen burned Spenser's castle at Kilcolman. The poet returned to London and seems to have lived, hard hit by poverty, in King Street, Westminster, but he endured only for a month longer. He was buried near to Chaucer in Westminster Abbey, and so splendid was his fame among his peers that the principal poets of the time, including the thirty-five-year-old Shakespeare, cast manuscript poems of tribute into his grave. It was on this account that in 1938 an attempt was made to open the grave—when, apparently, the wrong grave was broached.

Throughout this anthology I have tried to avoid using portions of any poem which achieves beauty of shape as a whole. To have printed a half of any Ode by Keats would be like reproducing a photograph which has not recorded the upper half of the face photographed: but shape is so rarely present in English poetry that not many bones have been broken. *The Faerie Queene*, for example, is an immense work, containing many hundreds of 'Spenserian' stanzas and consequently many thousands of lines, and yet even so it is a mere fragment of the scheme in the poet's mind. Any page, however, can be detached without injury to the whole.

No man should be so foolish as to cavil without much care at a poetical work which was deeply loved by a poet so finely perceptive as

56

John Keats; but what Keats admired must have been the full-toned, never-failing music of the almost endless stanzas and the great lengths of rich brocaded fancies that stretch onward, page after page. There is no interest, and could never have been any, in the cumbrous allegorical story inside that multitudinous decoration. Moreover, just as there is no metrical variety to be found though we continue to read the poem for several days, so is there practically no change of beauty. Open the huge poem at any page and you find the same elaborate slow beauty which enfolded and delighted you as you perused the first fifty stanzas. If, as seems likely, Spenser was stimulated by Ariosto's long-drawn adagio narrative—*Orlando Furioso*—it is noteworthy that the English poet, a wholly serious person, caught nothing of the Italian poet's light-hearted mockery.

Spenser's poetry is for a leisurely reader who can sensitively relish the music of words. It would yield its full value to one lying in a punt beneath motionless willows on a midsummer afternoon, not unaccompanied by a busyness of bees. We must keep in mind that whenever words like 'crisped' or 'seemed' or 'scattered' are thus written, containing the final letters 'ed', those letters are a separate syllable.

2 2   Stanzas from *The Faerie Queene*

> Her face so faire as flesh it seeméd not,
> But heavenly pourtraict of bright Angels hew,
> Cleare as the skye, withouten blame or blot,
> Through goodly mixture of complexions dew:
> And in her cheekes the vermeill red did shew
> Like roses in a bed of lillies shed,
> The which ambrosiall odours from them threw,
> And gazers sence with double pleasure fed,
> Hable to heale the sicke, and to revive the ded.
>
> In her faire eyes two living lamps did flame,
> Kindled above at th'hevenly makers light,
> And darted fyrie beames out of the same,
> So passing persant, and so wondrous bright,
> That quite bereav'd the rash beholders sight:

In them the blinded god his lustfull fyre
To kindle oft assayd, but had no might;
For, with dredd Majestie and awfull yre,
She broke his wanton darts, and quenchéd bace desyre.

Her yvorie forhead, full of bountie brave,
Like a broad table did it selfe dispred,
For Love his loftie triumphes to engrave,
And write the battailes of his great godhed;
All good and honour might therein be red,
For there their dwelling was. And, when she spake,
Sweete wordes like dropping honny she did shed;
And twixt the perles and rubins softly brake
A silver sound, that heavenly musicke seemd to make.

Upon her eyelids many Graces sate,
Under the shadow of her even browes,
Working belgardes and amorous retrate,
And everie one her with a grace endowes,
And everie one with meekenesse to her bowes.
So glorious mirrhour of celestiall grace,
And soveraine moniment of mortall vowes,
How shall frayle pen descrive her heavenly face,
For feare, through want of skill, her beauty to disgrace?

So faire, and thousand thousand times more faire,
She seemd, when she presented was to sight;
And was yclad, for heat of scorching aire,
All in a silken Camus lilly whight,
Purfled upon with many a folded plight,
Which all above besprinckled was throughout
With golden aygulets, that glistred bright
Like twinckling starres; and all the skirt about
Was hemd with golden fringe.

Below her ham her weed did somewhat trayne,
And her streight legs most bravely were embayld
In golden buskins of costly Cordwayne,
All bard with golden bendes, which were entayld
With curious antickes, and full fayre aumayld:

Before, they fastned were under her knee
In a rich jewell, and therein entrayld
The ends of all the knots, that none might see
How they within their fouldings close enwrapped bee;

Like two faire marble pillours they were seene,
Which doe the temple of the Gods support,
When all the people decke with girlands greene,
And honour in their festival resort;
Those same with stately grace and princely port
She taught to tread, when she herselfe would grace;
But with the woody Nymphes when she did play,
Or when the flying Libbard she did chace,
She could then nimbly move, and after fly apace.

And in her hand a sharpe bore-speare she held,
And at her backe a bow and quiver gay,
Stuft with steele-headed dartes, wherewith she queld
The savage beastes in her victorious play,
Knit with a golden bauldricke, which forelay
Athwart her snowy brest, and did divide
Her daintie paps; which, like young fruit in May,
Now little gan to swell, and being tide
Through her thin weed their places only signifide.

Her yellow lockes, crispéd like golden wyre,
About her shoulders weren loosely shed,
And, when the winde emongst them did inspyre,
They wavéd like a penon wyde dispred,
And low behinde her backe were scatteréd:
And, whether art it were or headlesse hap,
As through the flouring forrest rash she fled,
In her rude heares sweet flowres themselves did lap,
And flourishing fresh leaves and blossoms did enwrap.

* * *

The first English theatre, built in Shoreditch, was opened in 1576:
a tremendous event in the story of our literature. The building of that

theatre proves the avid desire of Londoners for better drama than the strolling fit-up companies could provide. A sense of drama must have been in the air. Now, Spenser reveals no dramatic instinct, and as he was a grave young secretary, twenty-five years old, when the theatre at last flew a flag from its topmost point, he was probably not influenced at all by the upcoming movement. In the same year, however, Michael Drayton was a lad of thirteen, Shakespeare (in far-away Stratford) was twelve, Marlowe (in Canterbury) was the same age, Nashe was only nine, and Ben Jonson an infant of three. A dozen years later, the mighty Elizabethan drama is in full sail. Drayton, it is true, wrote no plays, but much of his work is vividly dramatic. There is, in fact, no more dramatic sonnet in the language than his famous and much-quoted 'Since there's no help, come let us kiss and part'; but indeed, his sonnet-sequence called *Idea* seems never yet to have been extolled within even measurable distance of its high merit. There is at least as much vitality in those sonnets as in the Shakespearean sequence up to the moment when the impact of the Dark Lady puts a stop to all prettification. Moreover, in *Idea* we are in touch with a quite definite personality, a robustly poetic man.

Drayton's *Battle of Agincourt* is thought to have been written *circa* 1605. What inspired this vigorous and technically-original poem? Can Drayton have recently witnessed his friend's patriotic drama—*Henry the Fifth*? The reader will be astonished, I hope, time after time by the electrical force of phrase in this poem. He may also be surprised by Drayton's complete mastery of rhyme. How he made his words ring! 'Lopp'd the French lilies', 'Trumpet to trumpet spake Thunder to thunder', and 'The English archery Stuck the French horses'. . . . Not for another two hundred years did an English poet inject quite such energy into patriotic verse. And then too, let us give Drayton all praise for finding so triumphant a final stanza to a poem already sustained at so high a pitch.

The Battle of Agincourt occurred in 1415. Seeing how vivid the memory of it was, after so long a stretch of time, to Shakespeare and Drayton, both of whom had seen the Armada loom up and vanish away, we may well wonder whether the great events of a nation's youth do not remain always the most permanent of that nation's memories. A man will remember his first success or first anguish more keenly than the larger triumphs or deeper troubles of middle-age; and no subsequent deeds of heroism and fortitude have obliterated from the mightier memory of Europe the archetypal happenings at Salamis and Marathon.

Michael Drayton: 1563–1631

Born at Hartshill, Warwickshire. In youth he was page to Sir Henry Goodere of Powlesworth, and he seems afterwards to have studied at Oxford. He is known to have been a friend (as he was a fellow-Warwickshireman) of Shakespeare with whom, in Ben Jonson's company, he is said to have drunk deep at Stratford shortly before Shakespeare's death. Drayton was buried in Westminster Abbey.

23 Agincourt

Fair stood the wind for France
When we our sails advance,
Nor now to prove our chance
    Longer will tarry;
But putting to the main,
At Caux, the mouth of Seine,
With all his martial train
    Landed King Harry.

And taking many a fort,
Furnish'd in warlike sort,
Marcheth tow'rds Agincourt
    In happy hour;
Skirmishing day by day
With those that stopp'd his way,
Where the French gen'ral lay
    With all his power.

Which, in his height of pride,
King Henry to deride,
His ransom to provide
   Unto him sending;
Which he neglects the while
As from a nation vile,
Yet with an angry smile
   Their fall portending.

And turning to his men,
Quoth our brave Henry then,
'Though they to one be ten
   Be not amazèd:
Yet have we well begun;
Battles so bravely won
Here ever to the sun
   By fame been raisèd.

'And for myself (quoth he)
This my full rest shall be:
England ne'er mourn for me
   Nor more esteem me:
Victor I will remain
Or on this earth lie slain,
Never shall she sustain
   Loss to redeem me.

'Poitiers and Cressy tell,
When most their pride did swell,
Under our swords they fell:
   No less our skill is
Than when our grandsire great,
Claiming the regal seat,
By many a warlike feat
   Lopp'd the French lilies'.

The Duke of York so dread
The eager vaward led;
With the main Henry sped
   Among his henchmen.

Excester had the rear,
A braver man not there;
O Lord, how hot they were
    On the false Frenchmen!

They now to fight are gone,
Armour on armour shone,
Drum now to drum did groan,
    To hear was wonder;
That with the cries they make
The very earth did shake:
Trumpet to trumpet spake,
    Thunder to thunder.

Well it thine age became,
O noble Erpingham,
Which didst the signal aim
    To our hid forces!
When from a meadow by,
Like a storm suddenly
The English archery
    Stuck the French horses.

With Spanish yew so strong,
Arrows a cloth-yard long
That like to serpents stung,
    Piercing the weather;
None from his fellow starts,
But playing manly parts,
And like true English hearts
    Stuck close together.

When down their bows they threw,
And forth their bilbos drew,
And on the French they flew,
    Not one was tardy;
Arms were from shoulders sent,
Scalps to the teeth were rent,
Down the French peasants went—
    Our men were hardy.

This while our noble king,
His broadsword brandishing,
Down the French host did ding
   As to o'erwhelm it;
And many a deep wound lent,
His arms with blood besprent,
And many a cruel dent
   Bruisèd his helmet.

Gloster, that duke so good,
Next of the royal blood,
For famous England stood
   With his brave brother;
Clarence, in steel so bright,
Though but a maiden knight,
Yet in that furious fight
   Scarce such another.

Warwick in blood did wade,
Oxford the foe invade,
And cruel slaughter made
   Still as they ran up;
Suffolk his axe did ply,
Beaumont and Willoughby
Bare them right doughtily,
   Ferrers and Fanhope.

Upon Saint Crispin's Day
Fought was this noble fray,
Which fame did not delay
   To England to carry.
O when shall English men
With such acts fill a pen?
Or England breed again
   Such a King Harry?

* * *

Only a typical Elizabethan could have felt and phrased the ample
seventh and eighth lines of this sonnet. . . .

24   Sonnet

How many paltry foolish painted things,
That now in coaches trouble every street,
Shall be forgotten, whom no poet sings,
Ere they be well wrapped in their winding-sheet!
Where I to thee eternity shall give,
When nothing else remaineth of these days,
And queens hereafter shall be glad to live
Upon the alms of thy superfluous praise.
Virgins and matrons, reading these my rhymes,
Shall be so much delighted with thy story,
That they shall grieve thy lived not in these times,
To have seen thee, their sex's only glory:
   So shalt thou fly above the vulgar throng,
   Still to survive in my immortal song.

Christopher Marlowe: 1564–1593

Son of a Canterbury shoemaker. He was educated at the King's
School, Canterbury, and at Corpus Christi College, Cambridge. When
he had 'gone down', he attached himself as player and playwright to
the Earl of Nottingham's Company of Actors, and it was by this Company that his richly-coloured resonant plays were presented. Most
scholars believe that he was part-author of *Titus Andronicus* and of *Henry
the Sixth, Parts 2 and 3*. His translations from Ovid were issued *circa* 1597.
Swinburne said of him, 'He is the greatest discoverer, the most daring
and inspired pioneer, in all our poetic literature'.

He was an incautious atheist, and he is now thought to have been a
double-crossing spy. A warrant for his arrest was issued in 1593, and in
May of that year at an inn in Deptford he quarrelled with a man named
Archer, who stabbed him to death. In *As You Like It*, written soon after
this tragedy, there is a sudden and touching tribute from the young
Shakespeare,—

    'Dead shepherd, now I know thy saw of might:
    Who ever loved that loved not at first sight?' . . . . .

the latter line being a quotation from Marlowe, and a line typical of Marlowe's headstrong, enthusiastic soul. From first to last, ardour was the keynote of Marlowe's nature.

When Ben Jonson minted the famous phrase 'Marlowe's mighty line', he was probably remembering the full-lung'd rhetoric of *Tamburlaine*, but in the following passage from the end of *The Tragical History of Dr. Faustus* we find many lines which a powerful actor would rejoice to speak. Dr. Faustus, a great scholar, has, of course, sold his soul to Mephistopheles and Lucifer in exchange for a period of worldly power: and now is the night of reckoning. These lines should be read aloud.

25 The End of Dr. Faustus

The clock strikes eleven.

Faustus: Ah Faustus,
Now hast thou but one bare hour to live,
And then thou must be damn'd perpetually:
Stand still you ever-moving spheres of heaven,
That time may cease, and midnight never come:
Fair Nature's Eye, rise, rise again, and make
Perpetual day, or let this hour be but
A year, a month, a week, a natural day,
That Faustus may repent, and save his soul,
O lente, lente curite noctis equi :
The stars move still, time runs, the clock will strike,
The devil will come, and Faustus must be damn'd.
O I'll leap up to my God: who pulls me down?
See, see where Christ's blood streams in the firmament!
One drop would save my soul, half a drop, ah my Christ!
Ah rend not my heart for naming of my Christ,
Yet will I call on him: oh spare me, Lucifer!
    Where is it now? tis gone. And see where God
Stretcheth out his arm, and bends his ireful brows:
Mountains and hills, come, come, and fall on me,
And hide me from the heavy wrath of God.
    No, no. . . .
Then will I headlong run into the earth:

Earth gape! O no, it will not harbour me:
You stars that reigned at my nativity,
Whose influence hath alloted death and hell,
Now draw up Faustus like a foggy mist,
Into the entrails of yon labouring cloud,
That when you vomit forth into the air,
My limbs may issue from your smoky mouths,
So that my soul may but ascend to heaven.

The clock strikes.

Ah half the hour is past:
'Twill all be past anon. . . .
Oh God,
If thou wilt not have mercy on my soul,
Yet for Christ's sake, whose blood hath ransom'd me,
Impose some end to my incessant pain.
Let Faustus live in hell a thousand years,
A hundred thousand, and at last be saved.
O, no end is limited to damnéd souls,
Why wert thou not a creature wanting soul?
Or, why is this immortal that thou hast?
Ah, Pythagoras' metempsychosis,—were that true,
This soul should fly from me, and I be chang'd
Unto some brutish beast. . . . All beasts are happy,
For when they die,
Their souls are soon dissolved in elements,
But mine must live still to be plagued in hell.
Curst be the parents that engendered me,—
No, Faustus, curse thyself, curse Lucifer
That hath depriv'd thee of the joys of heaven.

The clock strikes twelve.

O it strikes, it strikes! Now, body, turn to air,
Or Lucifer will bear thee quick to hell. . . . .

Thunder and lightning.

O soul, be chang'd into little water-drops,
And fall into the ocean,—ne'er be found.
My God, my God, look not so fierce on me.

Enter devils.

Adders and serpents, let me breathe a while. . . . .

Ugly hell, gape not, come not Lucifer,—
I'll burn my books,—ah Mephistopheles!

Faustus is carried out.

CHORUS

Cut is the branch that might have grown full straight,
And burnèd is Apollo's laurel bough
That sometimes grew within this learnèd man.
Faustus is gone; regard his hellish fall
Whose fiendful fortune may exhort the wise,
Only to wonder at unlawful things,
Whose deepness doth entice such forward wits
To practise more than heavenly power permits.

The play ends.

* * *

There is in Shakespeare the most powerful and the most delicate poetry ever written. Almost the whole world acknowledges his supremacy over all other poets of any land and any age. It seems therefore unnecessary to do more in so slight a collection than to present one sonnet, because the real passion in it makes most sonnets of the time look pale and artificial, and one song which might well be chosen as the most entirely beautiful lyric that ever was penned. Examine this tiny piece in detail, remembering that the movement of the first two lines clearly shows that the poet was matching words to a tune in his head. The fourth and fifth lines are equal in pith and charm, but we cannot guess which of them came first to his mind. This is also true of the seventh and eighth lines, and again of the tenth and eleventh. This intense and equal beauty of every line in the poem makes it a sheer miracle.

The student should notice, too, the twelfth line of the sonnet,—how much nervous movement is expressed by the irregular accent of '*vainly expressed*'.

Ben Jonson in a poem 'to the Memory of my Beloved Master William Shakespeare, and What he hath Left us', says that he would

'tell how far thou didst our Lyly outshine,
Or sporting Kyd, or Marlowe's mighty line',

but critics long ago pointed out that Shakespeare would not rank nearly so high as Marlowe if he had died, like Marlowe, at the age of twenty-nine. Jonson also addresses the poet as 'My gentle Shakespeare', and it is strange to realise that not for some eighty years did the world seem aware of the titanic aspect of Shakespeare's genius. Even Milton refers to him as

> 'Sweetest Shakespeare, fancy's child,
> Warbling his native woodnotes wild',

as though he had written nothing more violent than *As You Like It* and *A Midsummer Night's Dream*. In due course Dryden, that wholly admirable critic, forestalled posterity by saying, 'He was the man who of all modern and perhaps ancient poets, had the largest and most comprehensive soul'.

William Shakespeare: 1564–1616

He was the third child and eldest son of John Shakespeare, who in 1565 was a Stratford alderman, and of Mary Arden, daughter of a well-to-do farmer at Wilmcote, a neighbouring village. His father, after rising to the office of bailiff, went downhill by reason of debt, and became a butcher.

The poet had his schooling under Walter Roche at Stratford Grammar School, but when he was about thirteen he left school and worked with his father. Evidently—and as everyone would suppose—of an extremely amorous nature, he wanted when he was eighteen to marry a girl named Anne Whateley, but he had already got with child a young woman named Anne Hathaway, who was then twenty-four. Her relatives forced a marriage. Had he achieved lasting happiness with Anne Whateley, we might have missed all or many of his masterpieces: but it seems unlikely that the author of the tragedies could have lived a smooth life.

Shakespeare arrived in London *circa* 1586, and he soon became a member of the Earl of Leicester's theatrical company. He acted in at least two of Ben Jonson's plays (*Every Man in his Humour*, 1598, and *Sejanus*, 1603), and is said to have brought Jonson into the world of the theatre.

In 1611 he retired to Stratford, a man of substance, and here he died, and was buried, in 1616. His granddaughter sold the poet's substantial house—New Place—in 1675: and at about that time his direct line became extinct.

26   Sonnet

My love is as a fever, longing still
For that which longer nurseth the disease;
Feeding on that which doth preserve the ill,
The uncertain sickly appetite to please.
My reason, the physician to my love,
Angry that his prescriptions are not kept,
Hath left me, and I desperate now approve
Desire is death, which physic did except.
Past cure I am, now reason is past care,
And frantic-mad with evermore unrest;
My thoughts and my discourse as madmen's are,
At random from the truth vainly express'd;
    For I have sworn thee fair, and thought thee bright,
    Who art as black as hell, as dark as night.

27   Sweet-and-Twenty

O mistress mine, where are you roaming?
O, stay and hear! your true love's coming,
    That can sing both high and low:
Trip no further, pretty sweeting:
Journeys end in lovers meeting,
    Every wise man's son doth know.

What is love? 'tis not hereafter:
Present mirth hath present laughter;
    What's to come is still unsure:
In delay there lies no plenty;
Then come kiss me, sweet-and-twenty!
    Youth's a stuff will not endure.

*   *   *

Sometimes in a piece of woodland there seem suddenly to be bluebells
everywhere; and sometimes we walk into a meadow half silver with
daisies, half golden with buttercups. It is with much the same astonished

delight that a man first realises what a multitude of light-footed, fragrant, truly singable lyrics this great age thrust forth. We have book after book of these 'songs' and 'glees' and 'madrigals', nearly all of them charming in some degree, nearly all of them marked by that slightly hesitant movement of the word-rhythm which usually means that the words were fitted to music or were twin-born with it. There has been no other period which had a comparable instinct for hitting upon singable sentences—a term which implies shortness (no singer can uphold the meaning of a four-line sentence), fewness of sibilants, and a large proportion of open vowels. Thomas Hood, in a treatise on verse-technique, quotes as unsingable a line from Shelley—

> 'The fresh earth in new leaves dressed'

where, as he points out, there is no vowel which would make a round note possible. Before we snatch a handful of delicious anonymous lyrics, let us look at a famous outburst of happiness, a tiny poem which would alone suffice to keep alive and to endear the memory of the man who made it.

Thomas Nashe: 1567–1601

Another of the poets from St. John's College, Cambridge. He was a pronounced hater of Puritanism. He was also a pungent controversialist, as we see in the pages of *Have with You to Saffron-Walden!* where he baits the pedantic Gabriel Harvey who, he says, goes about 'ruffling it in hufty-tufty'. In *The Isle of Dogs* he attacked some of the abuses of the age, and consequently spent several months in the Fleet Prison.

A great measure of life-experience lies packed into the line, in the following lyric, which begins 'Young lovers meet' . . . . .

28   Spring Song

Spring, the sweet Spring, is the year's pleasant king:
Then blooms each thing, then maids dance in a ring,
Cold doth not sting, the pretty birds do sing,
　　Cuckoo, jug-jug, pu-we, to-witta-woo!

The palm and may make country houses gay,
Lambs frisk and play, the shepherds pipe all day,
And we hear aye birds tune this merry lay,
   Cuckoo, jug-jug, pu-we, to-witta-woo!

The fields breathe sweet, the daisies kiss our feet,
Young lovers meet, old wives a-sunning sit,
In every street these tunes our ears do greet,
   Cuckoo, jug-jug, pu-we, to-witta-woo!
      Spring, the sweet Spring!

* * *

Take first a pair of pastoral idylls, noting—for later comparison—
their lack of grossness. Love-play between the sexes is still treated as an
innocent and clean delight. The air to which *Amorous Silvy* was sung is
typically gallant and engaging, nor is it reasonable to think sourly of a
time which could find so fair a melody for such fair words.

29   The Never-Certain Male

Thyrsis and Milla, arm in arm together,
In merry may-time to the green garden walked,
Where all the way they wanton riddles talked;
The youthful boy, kissing her cheeks so rosy,
Beseech'd her there to gather him a posy;
She straight her light green silken coats uptucked,
And may for Mill and thyme for Thyrsis plucked;
Which when she brought, he clasped her by the middle
And kiss'd her sweet, but could not read her riddle.
'Ah, fool!' with that the nymph set up a laughter,
And blush'd, and ran away, and he ran after.

30   Parting at Dawn

On a time the amorous Silvy
Said to her shepherd, 'Sweet, how do you?
Kiss me this once, and then God be wi' you,
                    My sweetest dear!

Kiss me this once and then God be wi' you,
For now the morning draweth near'.

With that, her fairest bosom showing,
Opening her lips, rich perfumes blowing,
She said, 'Now kiss me and be going,
                  My sweetest dear!
Kiss me this once and then be going,
For now the morning draweth near'.

With that the shepherd waked from sleeping,
And, spying where the day was peeping,
He said, 'Now take my soul in keeping,
                  My sweetest dear!
Kiss me, and take my soul in keeping,
Since I must go, now day is near'.

* * *

Take now two flawless examples of the keep-your-distance theme.
The second is not strictly anonymous, the words being by 'Robert
Heath', but I can find no reference to him anywhere. His lyric may well
have been written a good many years before 1660—a date at which he
is known to have "flourished".

31   The Wise Virgin

'Art thou that she than whom no fairer is;
  Art thou that she, Desire so strives to kiss?'
    'Say I am: how then?
      Maids may not kiss
    Such wanton-humour'd men'.

'Art thou that she the world commends for wit?
  Art thou so wise and makest no use of it?'
    'Say I am: how then?
      My wit doth teach me shun
    Such foolish foolish men'.

32   The Sceptical Lady

You say you love me, nay, can swear it too;
But stay, sir, 'twill not do.
I know you keep your oaths
Just as you wear your clothes,
While new and fresh in fashion;
But once grown old,
You lay them by,
Forgot like words you speak in passion.
I'll not believe you, I.

*   *   *

All great ages are predominantly serious, for not to recognise the tragic basis of life is to remain immature,—like a brain-bright undergraduate. The Elizabethans and their sons and daughters were spiritually real enough to take love seriously and to learn the glories and griefs of it. In all our literature we have no intenser expression of idealistic first-passion, no more

'loyal canton of contemnéd love',

than in the unknown poet's 'Fain would I change that note'. Moreover, few lyrics mount so steadily to their climax. Here is one of those rare poems which can never go out because it was lighted by an everlasting emotion.

In the second of these serious love-poems the poet reveals his emotional situation much more definitely than is at all usual in poetry. Almost he outlines the very story in which he was living a part. This we shall appreciate if we repeat several times the sadly-courageous line which contains the phrase 'I that loved and you that liked' (they epitomise many a love-distress) or the phrase which begins 'I asked your leave. . . .' It is a thousand pities that the penultimate line should jingle with so many 'i' sounds.

33 'Fain would I change . . .'

Fain would I change that note
To which fond love hath charm'd me
Long long to sing by rote,
Fancying that that harm'd me:
Yet when this thought doth come,
'Love is the perfect sum
Of all delight',
I have no other choice
Either for pen or voice
To sing or write.

O Love, they wrong thee much
That say thy sweet is bitter,
When thy ripe fruit is such
As nothing can be sweeter.
Fair house of joy and bliss,
Where truest pleasure is,
I do adore thee;
I know thee what thou art,
I serve thee with my heart,
And fall before thee.

34 'Since first I saw your face . . .'

Since first I saw your face I resolved to honour and renown you;
If now I be disdained I wish my heart had never known you.
What? I that loved and you that liked shall we begin to wrangle?
No, no, no, my heart is fast, and cannot disentangle.

If I admire or praise too much, that fault you may forgive me,
Or if my hands had strayed a touch, then justly might you leave me.
I asked you leave, you bade me love; is't now a time to chide me?
No, no, no, I'll love you still what fortune e'er betide me.

The sun whose beams most glorious are, rejecteth no beholder,
And your sweet beauty past compare made my poor eyes the bolder:
Where beauty moves, and wit delights and signs of kindness bind me,
There, O there! where'er I go I'll leave my heart behind me.

In any collection of poems the tone of the one which now follows would be certain to startle the reader. It belongs, in fact, to a mystically religious phase which was to become pronounced a little later—in the verse of Vaughan, Herbert, Bishop King, Traherne and a few others. This poem is presumably a fragment, but it contains an image so elaborately worked out and so admirably completed that no previous lines could have enriched it. The almost colloquial ease of phrasing suggests a practised poet; the vivid imagery suggests a Welshman; and the grave tone suggests that the writer may have been a mystically-minded clergyman. I cannot discover the meaning of 'Spanish tables'.

35   The King's Visit

Yet if his majesty our sovereign lord
Should of his own accord
Friendly himself invite,
And say 'I'll be your guest to morrow night',
How should we stir ourselves, call and command
All hands to work! 'Let no man idle stand.
Set me fine Spanish tables in the hall,
See they be fitted all;
Let there be room to eat,
And order taken that there want no meat.
See every sconce and candlestick made bright,
That without tapers they may give a light.
Look to the presence: are the carpets spread,
The dais o'er the head,
The cushions in the chairs,
And all the candles lighted on the stairs?
Perfume the chambers, and in any case
Let each man give attendance in his place'.
Thus if the king were coming would we do,
And 'twere good reason too;
For 'tis a duteous thing
To show all honour to an earthly king,
And after all our travail and our cost,
So he be pleased, to think no labour lost.

But at the coming of the King of Heaven
All's set at six and seven:
We wallow in our sin,
Christ cannot find a chamber in the inn.
We entertain him always like a stranger,
And as at first still lodge him in the manger.

* * *

Skill in the writing of verse that has an 'air' about it, as of a man stylishly dressed, becomes fairly common when the century turns. Many poets continue to write not so much *for* music as *to* it, and the strange courtly movement of 'Kind are her answers' is a clear example. The other poem by the same author must have been set to music, for it appears in his *Book of Airs* (1613), but if the music had existed before the poem we should not have found such adroit shiftings of accent at the line-beginnings. Musical accentuation is always at odds to some extent with the variations of stress which a poet would give his verse if he were left free. The reader is likely to relish the happy, wholesome, and not over-fantasticated picture which the poet gives us of country life in the days of James the First. We have come a long way from the nymphs and shepherds of fifty years earlier.

Thomas Campion: 1567–1619

As a poet he speaks rather with the tones of the seventeenth than of the sixteenth century. He is thought to have been educated on the Continent. Certainly he was a Doctor of Medicine; and as a musical composer (of small-scale work) he almost equalled himself as a song-poet. Between 1607 and 1617, Campion devised court-masques, a form of entertainment which was threatening to outmode the true drama. It was this fashion which caused Shakespeare to supply *The Tempest* with a masque: perhaps one that he did not write himself.

36   Song of Pleasure and Pain

Kind are her answers,
But her performance keeps no day;
Breaks time, as dancers
From their own music when they stray.
All her free favours
And smooth words wing my hopes in vain.
O did ever voice so sweet but only feign?
Can true love yield such delay,
Converting joy to pain?

Lost is our freedom,
When we submit to women so:
Why do we need them
When, in their best they work our woe?
There is no wisdom
Can alter ends, by Fate prefixt.
O why is the good of man with evil mixt?
Never were days yet calléd two,
But one night went betwixt.

It will be clear that Campion should not have used in one verse end-words so near in sound as 'stray', 'favours', 'vain' and the rhymes to the first and third of these. For once he forgot the whole purpose of rhyme.

37   A Happy Marriage

Jack and Joan, they think no ill,
But loving live, and merry still:
Do their week-days' work, and pray
Devoutly on the holy day:
Skip and trip it on the green,
And help to choose the Summer Queen;
Lash out at a country feast
Their silver penny with the best.

Well can they judge of nappy ale,
And tell at large a winter tale;
Climb up to the apple loft,
And turn the crabs till they be soft.
Tib is all the father's joy,
And little Tom the mother's boy.
All their pleasure is Content;
And care, to pay their yearly rent.

Joan can call by name her cows
And deck her windows with green boughs;
She can wreaths and tutties [1] make,
And trim with plums a bridal cake.
Jack knows what brings gain or loss;
And his long flail can stoutly toss:
Makes the hedge which others break,
And ever thinks what he doth speak.

Now, you courtly dames and knights,
That study only strange delights;
Though you scorn the homespun gray
And revel in your rich array;
Though your tongues dissemble deep,
And can your heads from danger keep;
Yet, for all your pomp and train,
Securer lives the silly swain.

* * *

In most generations there is one dominant Personality, be he maker or critic or both, who rules the literary world. These Personalities are often by no means the men of highest talent in their times, but they are necessarily self-confident and assertive persons. Nobody refers to Ben Jonson as 'gentle' or 'sweet', and it is probable that Shakespeare was the better listener, Jonson the more effective talker. At least we know that he is one of the very few English writers who actually had a School of followers, they who called themselves The Tribe of Benjamin. In all his work, dramatic or lyrical, there are strong sinews. It is, if anything, excessively masculine, and a little lacks grace.

[1] Nosegays.

79

Benjamin Jonson: 1573–1631

Although of Border descent, Jonson was probably born in Westminster. He was educated at Westminster School, under William
Camden, and at St. John's College, Cambridge—that Laureate College.
He served as a foot-soldier in Flanders; and is said to have worked as a
bricklayer, and, indeed, to have repaired a part of old London Wall.

He wrote for the Admiral's Company, and at least in 1597 also tried
his luck as an actor. He killed a fellow-actor during a brawl, but escaped
death by Benefit of Clergy. For a few years he was a Roman Catholic.

In 1618 he walked to Scotland, a tremendous undertaking in those
days of vile roads, and in Scotland he stayed with the poet William
Drummond. One of the most not-to-be-expected treasures in our
literature is the account, set down by Drummond, of his burly guest's
fascinating table-talk. Jonson was buried in the Abbey.

38   To Celia

Come, my Celia, let us prove,
While we may, the Sports of Love;
Time will not be ours, for ever:
He, at length, our good will sever.
Spend not then his Gifts in vain:
Suns, that set, may rise again,
But, if once we lose this light
'Tis, with us, perpetual Night.
Why should we defer our Joys?
Fame and Rumor are but Toys.
Cannot we delude the eyes
Of a few poor household Spies?
Or his easier Ears beguile,
So removéd by our wile?
'Tis no Sin, Love's Fruit to steal,
But the sweet Theft to reveal:
To be taken, to be seen,—
These have Crimes accounted been.

There is often in Jonson a flourish, as it were, of Cavalier feathers.
We find it in his famous *Drink to me only with thine eyes*, and again in
these robust lines. . . . .

39   He teaches her to kiss

For Love's sake, kiss me once again:
I long, and should not beg in vain.
  Here's none to spy, or see.
    Why do you doubt, or stay?
    I'll taste as lightly as the Bee
That doth but touch his Flower, and flies away.
  Once more and, faith, I will be gone:
  Can he that loves, ask less than one?
Nay, you may err in this, and all your Bounty wrong:
  This could be call'd but half a Kiss:
What we're but once to do, we should do long.
  I will but mend the last, and tell
  Where, how, it would have relished well:
    Join Lip to Lip, and try . . . . .
  Each suck the other's breath,
  And whilst our Tongues perplexéd lie,
Let who will think us dead, or wish our death.

It is always a delight to find a poet speaking in his own person, and
not as if he were an impersonal purveyor of poetry. In this amusing
poem we can almost hear the belly-laughs of Big Ben as he came to the
lines which describe his appearance in full middle-age. The words cut
on his gravestone (O Rare Ben Jonson) have made posterity think kindly
of this learned, combative, jealous, abundant man. The proposal that
'O Rare' was meant for 'Orare' will not convince a Latinist.

40   Middle Age overtakes him

I now think Love is rather deaf than blind,
  For else it could not be
        That she,
  Whom *I* adore so much, should so slight *me*,
    And cast my love behind.

I'm sure my Language to her was as sweet,
 And every close did meet
 In Sentence, of as subtle Feet,
  As hath the youngest He
That sits in shadow of Apollo's Tree.
Oh, but my conscious Fears,
 That fly my Thoughts between,
 Tell me that she hath seen
 My Hundreds of Gray Hairs,
 Told Seven and Forty Years.
Read so much waste, as she cannot embrace
My Mountain Belly, and my Rocky Face,
And all these through her Eyes, have stopt her Ears.

*　*　*

Drummond reports of Ben Jonson's talk that 'he esteemeth John Donne the first poet in the World, in some things. . . . . Affirmeth Donne to have written all his best pieces ere he was 25 years old'. Earlier, however, Jonson had said 'That Donne, for not keeping of accent, deserved hanging',—an example of æsthetic enthusiasm which ought to have all our approbation. Donne died before the Civil War broke out, and therefore makes a suitable poet with whom to close this part of the book. Interesting, ingenious and vital though he is, he may have been overvalued in the between-war years when so many intellectual persons were more at home with the minor than with the major poets, and when verbal music and a smooth surface were out of fashion.

John Donne: 1573–1631

He was admitted to Lincoln's Inn in 1592. In 1596, he sailed with Essex's expedition to Cadiz. After this, he became Secretary to Sir Thomas Egerton, Keeper of the Great Seal, but in 1601 he was dismissed for having contracted an imprudent marriage.

He took Holy Orders in 1615 and became Chaplain to James the First. He was Rector of Keyston, Huntingdonshire, and, subsequently (1621–1631), Dean of St. Paul's. His son, a ribald scribbler, was tried in 1633 for the manslaughter of an eight-year-old child but was acquitted.

The following poem is much less tortured than are most of his verses.

41　Song ('Feignéd deaths')

Sweetest love, I do not go
　　For weariness of thee,
Nor in hope the world can show
　　A fitter love for me;
　　　　But since that I
　　At the last must part, 'tis best
　　Thus to use myself in jest
　　　　By feignéd deaths to die.

Yesternight the sun went hence,
　　And yet is here to-day;
He hath no desire nor sense,
　　Nor half so short a way:
　　　　Then fear not me,
　　But believe that I shall make
　　Speedier journeys, since I take
　　　　More wings and spurs than he.

O how feeble is man's pow'r!
　　That if good fortune fall,
Cannot add another hour,
　　Nor a lost hour recall;
　　　　But come bad chance,
　　And we join to it our strength,
　　And we teach it art and length
　　　　Itself o'er us to advance.

When thou sigh'st thou sigh'st not wind,
　　But sigh'st my soul away;
When thou weep'st, unkindly kind,
　　My life's blood doth decay.
　　　　It cannot be
　　That thou lovest me as thou say'st
　　If in thine my life thou waste,
　　　　That art the best of me.

Let not thy divining heart
  Forethink me any ill;
Destiny may take thy part
  And may thy fears fulfil;
    But think that we
Are but turned aside to sleep.
They who one another keep
    Alive, ne'er parted be!

PART THREE

Part Three

THE WARS IN which Englishmen had hitherto taken part were inspired by this or that person's passion for ruling other people. No Englishman can have cared a row of pins for King Stephen or Queen Matilda, and very few can have minded much whether the Red Rose or the White Rose should come out victorious. Men went to the wars as they might have joined in a dangerous sport; and although it was, no doubt, a high adventure to fight for the King of England's claim to rule Frenchmen, there can have been no wildfire martial enthusiasm among our ancestors until the King of Spain desired to rule Englishmen. But the Civil War of 1642–1648 was not an enterprise of ambition. It was a spiritual contest. It projected into the world of bones and flesh, of swords and cannonballs, a conflict which is inherent in the English temperament. Even now, three hundred years later, it is significantly easy to stir up a lively debate on the quarrel between Puritan and Cavalier; and the shortest cut to some knowledge of a new acquaintance would be to ask him on which side he would have fought.

The Puritans had been growing in numbers and influence for a long time. It was because they controlled the City of London that the first playhouses (and the bear-pits too) were built on the south bank of the Thames, where the City had no jurisdiction. Not all Puritans were like Zeal-of-the-Land Busy, not all of them were canting killjoys, as the dramatists liked to pretend. Cromwell, for instance, did not disapprove of plays, and Milton of course actually composed dramatic works which were performed. But it is fair to say that the Puritan is intent rather upon self-discipline than self-fulfilment, and aims at a moral perfection which is largely negative. Because a desire for pleasure may degenerate into a spineless or a debauched life, he tends to suspect pleasure and to decry it; and from this to a suspicion of happiness itself is no great step. Beauty, therefore, being a principal promoter of human happiness, became perilous and then wicked. By temperament, moreover, the Puritan is a plain man. Having no mystical sense, he regards ritual and all ceremony as so much mumbo-jumbo. A king or a queen is for him

86

simply an ordinary man or woman who has dressed-up. At his best, he becomes a rugged and austerely noble character, such as Abraham Lincoln or perhaps Oliver Cromwell; at his worst, he is one who persecutes joy and beauty because the first is wicked and the second is worthless. It is the Puritan who develops into the rationalist, for he is always quite certain that a spade is only a spade, a crown a mere metal hoop, and poetry an affected manner of saying what a sensible man would say in prose.

This half of the English temperament, then, became strong enough during the Civil War to challenge and to lay low the other half. Its actual sovereignty over Britain lasted only ten years; but, having once established itself in the national life, Puritanism never again became merely mockable, and it powerfully reasserted itself during the long reign of Queen Victoria.

The Cavalier at his worst was a tippling wencher and roisterer, but even in his cups he apprehended that there is some strange value in the ideas represented by a king, a crown and a sceptre; and the emotion of loyalty so glowed within him that he not only hazarded his life for the king but also recklessly melted down the family silver and gold. At his best, he developed a mystical sense, and could see that ritual and ceremony are an attempt to make the poor foolish body partake of the soul's experience, to raise it up a little instead of telling it that it is incurably disgusting. The Cavalier did not stay to consider whether Hampden had just cause for defying King Charles: he recognised that Kingship stood for a way of life which seemed to him right, natural and happy; and following a pattern of society which he liked rather than one which he might have agreed to be more reasonable, the Cavalier behaved as an Irrationalist.

The typical Cavalier—Sir John Suckling—shows in the fascinating poem which reappears in this book that he and his type were gay, gallant, sensual but not muddy-minded men. Muddiness, as Touchstone might have predicted, was to come hereafter. Herrick is probably the lightest of all real poets, and the easiest of all introductions to the delight which verse-fashioning can give us: he, and perhaps Edgar Allen Poe, with his simple, drum-beat, exaggerated rhythms. For us the

G

point is that this next group of poets is mostly made up of obvious Cavaliers, ending with poets whose irrationality had progressed to a profoundly interesting mysticism: but also that the two finest poets in this section were Parliament men, Puritans—Milton and Marvell.

Edward Thomas, himself a true poet and a fine-fingered critic, says of Herrick that 'he liked women as he might like fruits or cakes. They are all tiny, childish things, and at their best when he compares them with flowers. . . . His task was to write lyrics for marionettes. . . .' And, again, 'No more wonderful proof of the power of style can be found than the survival of the work of this trivial vicar'. Let the reader pause to see what 'style' can achieve on behalf of extreme triviality in the lyric *To Electra*. It is so pearl-like, so roundly perfect, that not to memorise it must be a difficult feat: but it is an imitation pearl.

Robert Herrick: 1591–1674

Another poet who went to St. John's College, Cambridge, but he graduated from Trinity Hall, in 1617. In 1629 he became vicar of Dean Pryor, Devonshire. In 1647, when the Puritans were in the saddle, he was ejected. In 1662, with Charles the Second on the throne, Herrick was restored to his incumbency, but he seems to have found Devonshire as dismal as Spenser had found Ireland.

Let us first look at a poem which links the new and smaller age with the stronger age that has passed away,—Herrick to Ben Jonson.

42   His Prayer to Ben Jonson

When I a verse shall make,
    Know I have prayed thee,
For old religion's sake,
    Saint Ben, to aid me.

Make the way smooth for me,
    When I, thy Herrick,
Honouring thee, on my knee
    Offer my lyric.

Candles I'll give to thee,
And a new altar,
And thou, Saint Ben, shalt be
Writ in my Psalter.

43   Delight in Disorder

A sweet disorder in the dress
Kindles in clothes a wantonness:
A lawn about the shoulders thrown
Into a fine distraction,
An erring lace, which here and there
Enthrals the crimson stomacher,
A cuff neglectful, and thereby
Ribbons to flow confusedly;
A winning wave, deserving note,
In the tempestuous petticoat;
A careless shoe-string, in whose tie
I see a wild civility;—
Do more bewitch me, than when art
Is too precise in every part.

44   Chop-Cherry

Thou gav'st me leave to kiss,
  Thou gav'st me leave to woo;
Thou mad'st me think, by this
  And that, thou lov'dst me too.

But I shall ne'er forget
  How, for to make thee merry,
Thou mad'st me chop, but yet
  Another snapped the cherry.

45   To Electra

I dare not ask a kiss,
  I dare not beg a smile,
Lest having that or this
  I might grow proud the while.

> No! no! the utmost share
> Of my desire shall be,
> Only to kiss that air
> That lately kissed thee.

Herrick was a maker of toy-poems, and none of these Cavalier poets retained the grandeur and the high seriousness which usually character-ised Elizabethan poetry. During the reign of Charles the First no great dramas were written, and in place of drama there were only court-masques. It is in the same way that the moods of poetry become lighter, perhaps even shallower, and the Cavalier is now, as we shall see, not more than gallant and gay. At the same time his sensuality is still simple and clean. Consider, for example, the last verse (often omitted) of Suckling's brilliant *Landscape with Figures*.

Thomas Carew: (?)1595–(?)1639

He studied at Merton College, Oxford. He led a dissipated life, never married, admitted that no fair woman could come near him but he must court her, and declares in one poem that long life, children, honour, friends or a good wife are 'nothing to a wench about thirteen, already voted to the queen of lust and lovers'. He staged a deathbed repentance.

46   Epitaph on The Lady Mary Villiers

> The Lady Mary Villiers lies
> Under this stone: with weeping eyes
> The parents that first gave her birth,
> And their sad friends, laid her in earth.
> If any of them, reader, were
> Known unto thee, shed a tear;
> Or if thyself possess a gem
> As dear to thee as this to them,
> Though a stranger to this place,
> Bewail in theirs thine own hard case;
> For thou perhaps at thy return
> May'st find thy darling in an urn.

James Shirley: 1596–1666

He was educated at Merchant Taylors'; St. John's College, Oxford; and St. Catherine's, Cambridge. He was a fairly successful—and meritorious—playwright who had the misfortune to be at work a generation too late for help from the strong gale of Elizabethan genius. He died from miseries caused by the Great Fire of London.

The following poem is indeed a 'Crown Jewel'. It is said to have 'terrified Cromwell'. Here we have an example of poetic miracle. The vowels and consonants of the poem, especially of the first stanza, glow and burn, nor should it be possible to miss the grave and stately music of this 'Dirge'. Dryden, in his satirical poem *MacFlecnoe*, states with complacence that the works of 'Heywood, Shirley and Ogleby' have become, as it were, waste-paper: but the soundest of all England's literary critics could not conceivably have underrated this marvellous threnody. Perhaps he did not come across it.

47   Death the Leveller

The glories of our blood and state
    Are shadows, not substantial things;
There is no armour against Fate;
    Death lays his icy hand on kings:
        Sceptre and Crown
        Must tumble down,
And in the dust be equal made
With the poor crookèd scythe and spade.

Some men with swords may reap the field,
    And plant fresh laurels where they kill:
But their strong nerves at last must yield;
    They tame but one another still:
        Early or late
        They stoop to fate,
And must give up their murmuring breath
When they, pale captives, creep to death.

> The garlands wither on your brow:
>   Then boast no more your mighty deeds!
> Upon Death's purple altar now
>   See where the victor-victim bleeds.
>   Your heads must come
>   To the cold tomb:
> Only the actions of the just
> Smell sweet and blossom in their dust.

* * *

At one time—fifty or sixty years ago—it was modish to maintain that Waller's *Go, Lovely Rose* was the perfect short poem, the Kohinoor of English lyrics. In his own age he enjoyed a dizzy reputation. No verse-lover could deny that he moves with attractive grace within metre and rhyme, or that he had an uncommonly sensitive ear for language. Nor should anybody think less of his versecraft because nobody can think highly of his character.

Edmund Waller: 1606–1687

These dates manifest that he flourished like a baytree. He was born in the purple and possibly with a bay-wreath round his head. Waller 'inherited Beaconsfield', the Buckinghamshire village. He was educated, characteristically, at 'Eton and King's'. He married a London heiress, Anne Banks, who left him a widower at the age of twenty-eight.

He was asked to parley with King Charles at Oxford in 1643. Three months later, in May, he was the ringleader in a plot to 'seize London for the King', but in order to save his life he informed against his associates. He escaped with an imprisonment in the Tower. He then married Mary Bracey, and in 1644 (probably foreseeing that the King's cause would be lost) he 'withdrew to Paris'. In 1651 Cromwell 'pardoned' him, and Waller came back to England. In 1655 he published laudatory verses about the Protector. In 1658 he published verses of delight because the Protector had just died. Mary, his second wife, did not die until the poet was seventy-one.

In 1661 Waller was Member of Parliament for Hastings.

48   Of the Last Verses in the Book

When we for age could neither read nor write,
The subject made us able to indite;
The soul, with nobler resolutions decked,
(The body stooping), does herself erect.
No mortal parts are requisite to raise
Her that, unbodied, can her Maker praise.

The seas are quiet when the winds give o'er;
So, calm are we when passions are no more!
For then we know how vain it was to boast
Of fleeting things, so certain to be lost.
Clouds of affection from our younger eyes
Conceal that emptiness which age descries.

The soul's dark cottage, battered and decayed,
Lets in new light through chinks that time has made;
Stronger by weakness, wiser men become,
As they draw near to their eternal home.
Leaving the old, both worlds at once they view,
That stand upon the threshold of the new.

*   *   *

We might reasonably have supposed that no splendid poetic blooms could spring from the sour soil of Puritanism. The truth was that the Cavalier Spirit had degenerated into triviality, and that only the opposition could restore poetry to deep and serious use.

A posturing American poetaster named Ezra Pound who had in Fleet Street the usual success of the self-advertiser, though his parade of scholarship was as ludicrous as his verses were uncouth, proclaimed in the nineteen-twenties that 'Milton was a pompous ass'. It was unwise to belittle a poet who had received the homage of Landor, Keats, Tennyson, Bridges, and the Good Readers of almost three hundred years.

Here, in Milton's work, we have poetic artistry—versecraft—at its very finest. There was to be no comparable poetic art-work until the flourishing of Tennyson—two centuries later. These poems by Milton are the best of all possible models and are subjects for microscopic study by anyone who dreams of some day bequeathing 'great verse unto a little clan'. Over and over again we find here beautiful, familiar phrases which could not have been bettered: 'Bosom'd high in tufted trees', 'Storied windows richly dight, casting a dim religious light' (a memory, doubtless, of King's Chapel, Cambridge); and dozens of equally miraculous lines written down with an immortal ink.

Examine the vowel-variations in the ensuing sonnets. Examine, in one of these sonnets, the brilliant technique with which Milton triumphs over so unacceptable a rhyme-word as 'bench'. He does not allow the few and awkward rhymes to deflect his meaning.

Lycidas, a supreme example of what language can achieve to the credit of Man's mind, may be slightly spoiled by Milton's introduction of a religious-political issue, urgent at the time but dead wood to us, in the lines which begin with 'Next, Camus, reverend sire. . . .' and yet no one could ever find a more magnificent success in versecraft than *Lycidas*, or spend too much time examining and appreciating its literary texture. Notice that 'such as for their bellies' sake', an over-sibilant line, is followed by a line without a sibilant.

John Milton: 1608–1674

It is significant that this poet was an accomplished organ-player, and that his father was a composer of motets and madrigals. Musically he is the most knowledgeable of our poets until the arrival of Browning: although Campion has a place of some honour at the wedding of music and poetry.

Milton is the tremendous glory of St. Paul's School. He graduated from Christ's College, Cambridge. After this, he travelled in Italy—1637–1639: and his poems in Italian are better than mere exercises in a foreign tongue. He intended to take Holy Orders; but he was a Puritan only in his brain and, by instinct, he was decidedly sexual. At Cambridge, Milton was nicknamed 'the lady'.

In 1643 (early in the Civil War) he married Mary Powell. She returned within a month to her father. In 1656 he married Catherine Woodcock. Two years later she died. In 1662, after six celibate years, he married Elizabeth Minshull. It is clear, from a passage in *Paradise Lost*, that Milton looked upon Eve as decidedly inferior to Adam. He expected his wife to be his servant: and some people, it is true, believe that an artist should marry his cook.

He became Latin Secretary to Oliver Cromwell. Everybody has heard that 'he received £10 for *Paradise Lost*', but it is not so well known that his wife 'afterwards settled all subsequent claims for £8'. By 1688 thirteen hundred copies had been sold. The reader may indulge in his own reflections.

This faultless word-artist died of 'gout struck in' (? gout at the heart); and was buried in St. Giles's, Cripplegate.

Despite his stern Puritanism, here is an immortal poem which shows that the poet was at least not sour.

49   L'Allegro

Hence, loathéd Melancholy,
   Of Cerberus and blackest Midnight born
In Stygian cave forlorn
   'Mongst horrid shapes, and shrieks, and sights unholy!
Find out some uncouth cell,
   Where brooding Darkness spreads his jealous wings,
And the night-raven sings;
   There, under ebon shades and low-browed rocks,
As ragged as thy locks,
   In dark Cimmerian desert ever dwell.
But come, thou Goddess fair and free,
In heaven yclept Euphrosyne,
And by men heart-easing Mirth;
Whom lovely Venus, at a birth,
With two sister Graces more,
To ivy-crownéd Bacchus bore:
Or whether (as some, sager, sing)
The frolic wind that breathes the spring,

Zephyr, with Aurora playing,
As he met her once a-Maying,
There, on beds of violets blue,
And fresh-blown roses washed in dew,
Filled her with thee, a daughter fair,
So buxom, blithe, and debonair.
Haste thee, Nymph, and bring with thee
Jest, and youthful Jollity,
Quips and cranks and wanton wiles,
Nods and becks and wreathéd smiles,
Such as hang on Hebe's cheek,
And love to live in dimple sleek;
Sport that wrinkled Care derides,
And Laughter holding both his sides.
Come, and trip it, as you go,
On the light fantastic toe;
And in thy right hand lead with thee
The mountain-nymph, sweet Liberty;
And, if I give thee honour due,
Mirth, admit me of thy crew,
To live with her, and live with thee,
In unreprovéd pleasures free;
To hear the lark begin his flight,
And, singing, startle the dull night,
From his watch-tower in the skies,
Till the dappled dawn doth rise;
Then to come, in spite of sorrow,
And at my window bid good-morrow,
Through the sweet-briar or the vine,
Or the twisted eglantine:
While the cock, with lively din,
Scatters the rear of darkness thin:
And to the stack, or the barn-door,
Stoutly struts his dames before:
Oft listening how the hounds and horn
Cheerly rouse the slumbering morn,
From the side of some hoar hill,
Through the high wood echoing shrill:

Sometime walking, not unseen,
By hedgerow elms, on hillocks green,
Right against the eastern gate
Where the great Sun begins his state,
Robed in flames and amber light,
The clouds in thousand liveries dight;
While the ploughman, near at hand,
Whistles o'er the furrowed land,
And the milkmaid singeth blithe,
And the mower whets his scythe,
And every shepherd tells his tale
Under the hawthorn in the dale.
Straight mine eye hath caught new pleasures,
Whilst the landskip round it measures:
Russet lawns, and fallows grey,
Where the nibbling flocks do stray;
Mountains on whose barren breast
The labouring clouds do often rest;
Meadows trim, with daisies pied;
Shallow brooks, and rivers wide;
Towers and battlements it sees
Bosomed high in tufted trees,
Where perhaps some beauty lies,
The cynosure of neighbouring eyes.
Hard by, a cottage chimney smokes
From betwixt two aged oaks,
Where Corydon and Thyrsis met
Are at their savoury dinner set
Of herbs and other country messes,
Which the neat-handed Phyllis dresses;
And then in haste her bower she leaves,
With Thestylis to bind the sheaves;
Or, if the earlier season lead,
To the tanned haycock in the mead.
Sometimes, with secure delight,
The upland hamlets will invite,
When the merry bells ring round,
And the jocund rebecks sound

To many a youth and many a maid
Dancing in the chequered shade,
And young and old come forth to play
On a sunshine holiday,
Till the livelong daylight fail:
Then to a spicy nut-brown ale,
With stories told of many a feat,
How Faery Mab the junkets eat,
And was pinched and pulled, she said:
And he, by Friar's lantern led,
Tells how the drudging goblins sweat
To earn his cream-bowl duly set,
When in one night, ere glimpse of morn,
His shadowy flail hath threshed the corn
That ten day-labourers could not end;
Then lies him down, the lubber fiend,
And, stretched out all the chimney's length
Basks at the fire his hairy strength,
And crop-full out of doors he flings,
Ere the first cock his matin rings.
Thus done the tales, to bed they creep,
By whispering winds soon lulled asleep.
Towered cities please us then,
And the busy hum of men,
Where throngs of knights and barons bold,
In weeds of peace, high triumphs hold,
With store of ladies, whose bright eyes
Rain influence, and judge the prize
Of wit or arms, while both contend
To win her grace whom all commend.
There let Hymen oft appear
In saffron robe, with taper clear,
And pomp, and feast, and revelry,
With mask and antique pageantry;
Such sights as youthful poets dream
On summer eves by haunted stream.
Then to the well-trod stage anon,
If Jonson's learnèd sock be on,

Or sweetest Shakespeare, Fancy's child,
Warble his native wood-notes wild.
And ever, against eating cares,
Lap me in soft Lydian airs
Married to immortal verse,
Such as the meeting soul may pierce
In notes with many a winding bout
Of linkéd sweetness long drawn out
With wanton heed and giddy cunning,
The melting voice through mazes running,
Untwisting all the chains that tie
The hidden soul of harmony;
That Orpheus' self may heave his head
From golden slumber on a bed
Of heaped Elysian flowers, and hear
Such strains as would have won the ear
Of Pluto to have quite set free
His half-regained Eurydice.
These delights if thou canst give,
Mirth, with thee I mean to live.

Milton is sufficiently sure of himself, let us notice, to abandon the simpler Shakespearean form of the sonnet and to undertake the writing of sonnets in the Italian style—with two rhymes only in the octet (or first eight lines): nor was 'clogs' an easy rhyme to set himself. . . .

50   On the detraction which followed upon my writing certain treatises

I did but prompt the age to quit their clogs
    By the known rules of ancient liberty,
    When straight a barbarous noise environs me
    Of owls and cuckoos, asses, apes, and dogs;
As when those hinds that were transformed to frogs
    Railed at Latona's twin-born progeny,
    Which after held the Sun and Moon in fee,
    But this is got by casting pearl to hogs

That bawl for freedom in their senseless mood,
    And still revolt when Truth would set them free.
    Licence they mean when they cry Liberty;
For who loves that must first be wise and good:
    But from that mark how far they rove we see,
    For all this waste of wealth and loss of blood.

51   To the Lord General Cromwell, May 1652, on the Proposals of Certain Ministers at the Committee for Propagation of the Gospel

Cromwell, our chief of men, who through a cloud
    Not of war only, but detractions rude,
    Guided by faith and matchless fortitude,
    To peace and truth thy glorious way hast ploughed,
And on the neck of crownéd Fortune proud
    Hast reared God's trophies, and his work pursued,
    While Darwen stream, with blood of Scots imbrued,
    And Dunbar field, resounds thy praises loud,
And Worcester's laureate wreath: yet much remains
    To conquer still: Peace hath her victories
    No less renowned than War: new foes arise,
Threatening to bind our souls with secular chains.
    Help us to save free conscience from the paw
    Of hireling wolves, whose Gospel is their maw.

Here again we should note how confidently the master-metrist accepts the exceedingly unpromising rhyme-word 'bench', and admire his ability not to be led astray while he pursues it.

52   To Cyriack Skinner

Cyriack, whose grandsire on the royal bench
    Of British Themis, with no mean applause,
    Pronounced, and in his volumes taught, our laws,
    Which others at their bar so often wrench,

To-day deep thoughts resolve with me to drench
  In mirth that after no repenting draws;
  Let Euclid rest, and Archimedes pause,
  And what the Swede intend, and what the French.
To measure life learn thou betimes, and know
  T'wards solid good what leads the nearest way;
  For other things mild Heaven a time ordains,
And disapproves that care, though wise in show,
  That with superfluous burden loads the day,
  And, when God sends a cheerful hour, refrains.

And next we come to one of the high peaks of English poetry,—language superbly controlled by a brain of great strength and resolution. Moreover, here—and with how much advantage—there is architectural form.

53 Lycidas

In this Monody the Author bewails a learned Friend, unfortunately drowned in his passage from Chester on the Irish Seas, 1637; and, by occasion, foretells the ruin of our corrupted Clergy, then in their height.

Yet once more, O ye laurels, and once more,
Ye myrtles brown, with ivy never hoar,
I come to pluck your berries harsh and crude,
And with forced fingers rude
Shatter your leaves before the mellowing year.
Bitter constraint and sad occasion dear
Compels me to disturb your season due;
For Lycidas is dead, dead ere his prime,
Young Lycidas, and hath not left his peer.
Who would not sing for Lycidas? he knew
Himself to sing, and build the lofty rhyme.
He must not float upon his watery bier
Unwept, and welter to the parching wind,
Without the meed of some melodious tear.

Begin, then, Sisters of the sacred well
That from beneath the seat of Jove doth spring;
Begin, and somewhat loudly sweep the string.
Hence with denial vain and coy excuse:
So may some gentle Muse
With lucky words favour *my* destined urn,
And as he passes turn,
And bid fair peace be to my sable shroud!
     For we were nursed upon the self-same hill,
Fed the same flock, by fountain, shade, and rill;
Together both, ere the high lawns appeared
Under the opening eyelids of the Morn,
We drove a-field, and both together heard
What time the grey-fly winds her sultry horn,
Battening our flocks with the fresh dews of night,
Oft till the star that rose at evening bright
Toward heaven's descent had sloped his westering wheel.
Meanwhile the rural ditties were not mute;
Tempered to the oaten flute,
Rough Satyrs danced, and Fauns with cloven heel
From the glad sound would not be absent long;
And old Damoetas loved to hear our song.
     But, oh! the heavy change, now thou art gone,
Now thou art gone and never must return!
Thee, Shepherd, thee the woods and desert caves,
With wild thyme and the gadding vine o'ergrown,
And all their echoes, mourn.
The willows, and the hazel copses green,
Shall now no more be seen
Fanning their joyous leaves to thy soft lays.
As killing as the canker to the rose,
Or taint-worm to the weanling herds that graze,
Or frost to flowers, that their gay wardrobe wear,
When first the white-thorn blows;
Such, Lycidas, thy loss to shepherd's ear.
     Where were ye, Nymphs, when the remorseless deep
Closed o'er the head of your loved Lycidas?
For neither were ye playing on the steep

Where your old bards, the famous Druids, lie,
Nor on the shaggy top of Mona high,
Nor yet where Deva spreads her wizard stream.
Ay me! I fondly dream
'Had ye been there', . . . for what could that have done?
What could the Muse herself that Orpheus bore,
The Muse herself, for her enchanting son,
Whom universal nature did lament,
When, by the rout that made the hideous roar,
His gory visage down the stream was sent,
Down the swift Hebrus to the Lesbian shore?
　　Alas! what boots it with incessant care
To tend the homely, slighted, shepherd's trade,
And strictly meditate the thankless Muse?
Were it not better done, as others use,
To sport with Amaryllis in the shade,
Or with the tangles of Neaera's hair?
Fame is the spur that the clear spirit doth raise
(That last infirmity of noble mind)
To scorn delights and live laborious days;
But the fair guerdon when we hope to find,
And think to burst out into sudden blaze,
Comes the blind Fury with the abhorréd shears,
And slits the thin-spun life. 'But not the praise',
Phœbus replied, and touched my trembling ears:
'Fame is no plant that grows on mortal soil,
Nor in the glistening foil
Set off to the world, nor in broad rumour lies,
But lives and spreads aloft by those pure eyes
And perfect witness of all-judging Jove;
As he pronounces lastly on each deed,
Of so much fame in heaven expect thy meed'.
　　O fountain Arethuse, and thou honoured flood,
Smooth-sliding Mincius, crowned with vocal reeds,
That strain I heard was of a higher mood:
But now my oat proceeds,
And listens to the Herald of the Sea,
That came in Neptune's plea.

He asked the waves, and asked the felon winds,
What hard mishap hath doomed this gentle swain?
And questioned every gust of rugged wings
That blows from off each beakéd promontory.
They knew not of his story;
And sage Hippotades their answer brings,
That not a blast was from his dungeon strayed:
The air was calm, and on the level brine
Sleek Panope with all her sisters played.
It was that fatal and perfidious bark,
Built in the eclipse, and rigged with curses dark,
That sunk so low that sacred head of thine.

Next, Camus, reverend sire, went footing slow,
His mantle hairy, and his bonnet sedge,
Inwrought with figures dim, and on the edge
Like to that sanguine flower inscribed with woe.
'Ah! who hath reft', quoth he, 'my dearest pledge?'
Last came, and last did go,
The Pilot of the Galilean Lake;
Two massy keys he bore of metals twain
(The golden opes, the iron shuts amain).
He shook his mitred locks, and stern bespake:—
'How well could I have spared for thee, young swain,
Enow of such as, for their bellies' sake,
Creep, and intrude, and climb into the fold!
Of other care they little reckoning make
Than how to scramble at the shearers' feast,
And shove away the worthy bidden guest.
Blind mouths! that scarce themselves know how to hold
A sheep-hook, or have learnt aught else the least
That to the faithful herdman's art belongs!
What recks it them? What need they? They are sped;
And, when they list, their lean and flashy songs
Grate on their scrannel pipes of wretched straw;
The hungry sheep look up, and are not fed,
But, swoln with wind and the rank mist they draw,
Rot inwardly, and foul contagion spread;
Besides what the grim wolf with privy paw
Daily devours apace, and nothing said;

But that two-handed engine at the door
Stands ready to smite once, and smite no more'.
  Return, Alpheus; the dread voice is past
That shrunk thy streams; return Sicilian Muse,
And call the vales, and bid them hither cast
Their bells and flowerets of a thousand hues.
Ye valleys low, where the mild whispers use
Of shades, and wanton winds, and gushing brooks,
On whose fresh lap the swart star sparely looks,
Throw hither all your quaint enamelled eyes,
That on the green turf suck the honeyed showers,
And purple all the ground with vernal flowers.
Bring the rathe primrose that forsaken dies,
The tufted crow-toe, and pale jessamine,
The white pink, and the pansy freaked with jet,
The glowing violet,
The musk rose, and the well-attired woodbine,
With cowslips wan that hang the pensive head,
And every flower that sad embroidery wears;
Bid amaranthus all his beauty shed,
And daffadillies fill their cups with tears,
To strew the laureate hearse where Lycid lies.
For so, to interpose a little ease,
Let our frail thoughts dally with false surmise.
Ay me! whilst thee the shores and sounding seas
Wash far away, where'er thy bones are hurled,
Whether beyond the stormy Hebrides,
Where thou perhaps under the whelming tide
Visit'st the bottom of the monstrous world;
Or whether thou, to our moist vows denied,
Sleep'st by the fable of Bellerus old,
Where the great Vision of the guarded mount
Looks toward Namancos and Bayona's hold.
Look homeward, Angel, now, and melt with ruth:
And, O ye dolphins, waft the hapless youth.
  Weep no more, woeful shepherds, weep no more,
For Lycidas, your sorrow, is not dead,
Sunk though he be beneath the watery floor.

So sinks the day-star in the ocean bed,
And yet anon repairs his drooping head,
And tricks his beams, and with new-spangled ore
Flames in the forehead of the morning sky;
So Lycidas sunk low, but mounted high,
Through the dear might of him that walked the waves,
Where other groves and other streams along,
With nectar pure his oozy locks he laves,
And hears the unexpressive nuptial song,
In the blest kingdoms meek of joy and love.
There entertain him all the Saints above,
In solemn troops, and sweet societies,
That sing, and singing in their glory move,
And wipe the tears for ever from his eyes.
Now, Lycidas, the shepherds weep no more;
Henceforth thou art the Genius of the shore,
In thy large recompense, and shalt be good
To all that wander in that perilous flood.

Thus sang the uncouth swain to the oaks and rills,
While the still morn went out with sandals grey:
He touched the tender stops of various quills,
With eager thought warbling his Doric lay:
And now the sun had stretched out all the hills,
And now was dropt into the western bay
At last he rose, and twitched his mantle blue;
To-morrow to fresh woods, and pastures new.

* * *

Generations have delighted in Suckling's *Ballad Upon A Wedding*. No poet, since Theocritus, had so vividly caught the scene and mood of a happy simple event. Here is no sense of another and subtler world which interpenetrates the world of farmyards and of human couplings. Here is a picture of healthy English life in the earlier days of the Stuarts.

Sir John Suckling: 1609–1642

He came of an old Norfolk family; his father was Secretary of State. The poet studied at Trinity College, Cambridge. He 'professed to live for pleasure and to despise all else'. Not only did he write plays—of merit—but so fastidious was he that he bought all the dresses used in their performance and would have only real gold and silver lace, 'no tinsel'. In 1639 he raised a company of troopers to aid the King's cause in Scotland, and he so luxuriously attired his men as to make himself a laughing-stock. The diarist Aubrey tells of a magnificent entertainment provided by Suckling for a great number of young and beautiful ladies of quality in London. He gave them 'all the rarities that this part of the world could afford, and the last service was silk stockings and garters', says Aubrey, 'and I think also gloves'.

His love-poems, said Edward Thomas with fine perception, 'suggest a society where women were over-flattered and under-valued'. He was so reckless a gambler that 'his sisters came crying to the bowling-green for fear lest he should lose all their portions'. He was the inventor of cribbage.

Aubrey states that he committed suicide in Paris.

54   A Ballad Upon A Wedding

I tell thee, Dick, where I have been:
Where I the rarest things have seen,
    O, things without compare!
Such sights again cannot be found
In any place on English ground,
    Be it at wake or fair.

At Charing Cross, hard by the way
Where we (thou know'st) do sell our hay,
    There is a house with stairs;
And there did I see coming down
Such folk as are not in our town,
    Forty at least, in pairs.

Amongst the rest, one pest'lent fine
(His beard no bigger though than thine)
   Walkt on before the rest:
Our landlord looks like nothing to him:
The King (God bless him!), 'twould undo him,
   Should he go still so drest.

At Course-a-Park, without all doubt,
He should have first been taken out
   By all the maids i' th' town:
Though lusty Roger there had been,
Or little George upon the Green,
   Or Vincent of the Crown.

But wot you what? the youth was going
To make an end of all his wooing;
   The parson for him staid:
Yet by his leave (for all his haste)
He did not so much wish all past
   (Perchance) as did the maid.

The maid—and thereby hangs a tale;
For such a maid no Whitson-ale
   Could ever yet produce;
No grape, that's kindly ripe, could be
So round, so plump, so soft as she,
   Nor half so full of juice.

Her finger was so small, the ring
Would not stay on, which they did bring;
   It was too wide a peck:
And to say truth (for out it must)
It lookt like the great collar (just)
   About our young colt's neck.

Her feet beneath her petticoat,
Like little mice, stole in and out,
   As if they fear'd the light:
But O, she dances such a way!
No sun upon an Easter-day
   Is half so fine a sight.

He would have kist her once or twice;
But she would not, she was so nice,
    She would not do't in sight:
And then she lookt as who should say,
'I will do what I list to-day,
    And you shall do 't at night'.

Her cheeks so rare a white was on,
No daisy makes comparison
    (Who sees them is undone);
For streaks of red were mingled there,
Such as are on a Katherne pear
    (The side that's next the sun).

Her lips were red; and one was thin,
Compar'd to that was next her chin
    (Some bee had stung it newly)
But, Dick, her eyes so guard her face,
I durst no more upon them gaze
    Than on the sun in July.

Her mouth so small, when she does speak,
Thou 'dst swear her teeth her words did break,
    That they might passage get;
But she so handled still the matter,
They came as good as ours, or better,
    And are not spent a whit.

If wishing should be any sin,
The parson himself has guilty been
    (She lookt that day so purely);
And, did the youth so oft the feat
At night, as some did in conceit,
    It would have spoil'd him surely.

Just in the nick the cook knockt thrice,
And all the waiters in a trice
    His summons did obey:
Each serving-man, with dish in hand,
Marcht boldly up, like our train'd band,
    Presented, and away.

When all the meat was on the table,
What man of knife or teeth was able
   To stay to be intreated?
And this the very reason was—
Before the parson could say grace,
   The company was seated.

The bus'ness of the kitchen's great,
For it is fit that man should eat;
   Nor was it there deni'd—
Passion o' me, how I run on!
There's that that would be thought upon
   (I trow) besides the bride.

Now hats fly off, and youths carouse,
Healths first go round, and then the house:
   The bride's came thick and thick;
And, when 'twas nam'd another's health,
Perhaps he made it hers by stealth;
   (And who could help it, Dick?)

O' th' sudden up they rise and dance;
Then sit again and sigh, and glance;
   Then dance again and kiss;
Thus several ways the time did pass,
Whilst ev'ry woman wished her place,
   And every man wished his.

By this time all were stol'n aside
To counsel and undress the bride;
   But that he must not know;
And yet 'twas thought he guess'd her mind,
And did not mean to stay behind
   Above an hour or so.

When in he came, Dick, there she lay
Like new-fall'n snow melting away
   ('Twas time, I trow, to part):
Kisses were now the only stay,
Which soon she gave, as who would say,
   God b' w' ye, with all my heart.

But, just as Heav'ns would have, to cross it,
In came the bridesmaids with the posset:
   The bridegroom eat in spite;
For, had he left the women to 't,
It would have cost two hours to do 't,
   Which were too much that night.

At length the candle's out; and now
All that they had not done they do;
   What that is, who can tell?
But I believe it was no more
Than thou and I have done before
   With Bridget and with Nell.

But it is not fair to represent Suckling only by his one familiar success.
Here is another specimen of his work which again shows the tendency
in the Cavalier toward the merely frivolous.

55   Lutea Allison

Si sola es, nulla es

Though you, Diana-like, have liv'd still chaste,
Yet must you not (fair) die a maid at last;
The roses on your cheeks were never made
To bless the eye alone, and so to fade;
Nor had the cherries on your lips their being,
To please no other sense than that of seeing;
You were not made to look on, though that be
A bliss too great for poor mortality:
In that alone those rarer parts you have,
To better uses sure wise nature gave
Than that you put them to: to love, to wed,
For Hymen's rights, and for the marriage-bed
You were ordain'd, and not to lie alone;
One is no number, till that two be one.
To keep a maidenhead but till fifteen,
Is worse than murder, and a greater sin
Than to have lost it in the lawful sheets
With one that should want skill to reap those sweets:

But not to lose 't at all—by Venus, this,
And by her son, inexpiable is:
And should each female guilty be o' th' crime,
The world should have its end before its time.

Abraham Cowley: 1618–1667

Cowley was a King's Scholar at Westminster School, and afterwards a scholar of Trinity College, Cambridge. In or about 1647, when the Civil War was going badly for the King, he became cipher-secretary to the Queen,—Henrietta Maria. In 1656, when the Puritans had the country well under control, he acted in England as a royalist spy. He was a Fellow of the Royal Society.

His poem *The Wish* has a refreshing note of sincerity. It is a sharp self-photograph. He was, they say, 'much in love with his Leonora, who married someone else, and never was in love with anybody after'. No earlier poet had sagaciously wished for 'a Mistress moderately fair'. The romantic instinct has, by this time, fallen low.

56   The Wish

Well then! I now do plainly see
This busy world and I shall ne'er agree.
The very honey of all earthly joy
Does of all meats the soonest cloy;
    And they, methinks, deserve my pity
Who for it can endure the stings,
The crowd, and buzz, and murmurings,
    Of this great hive, the City.

Ah! yet ere I descend to the grave,
May I a small house and large garden have;
And a few friends, and many books, both true,
Both wise, and both delightful too!
    And, since Love ne'er will from me flee,
A Mistress moderately fair,
And good as guardian angels are,
    Only beloved and loving me.

O fountains! when in you shall I
Myself eased of unpeaceful thoughts espy?
O fields! O woods! when, when shall I be made
The happy tenant of your shade?
   Here's the spring-head of pleasure's flood;
Here's wealthy Nature's treasury,
Where all the riches lie that she
   Has coined and stamped for good!

Pride and ambition here
Only in far-fetched metaphors appear;
Here nought but winds can hurtful murmurs scatter
And nought but Echo flatter.
   The gods, when they descended, hither
From heaven, did always choose their way:
And therefore we may boldly say
   That 'tis the way too thither.

How happy here should I
And one dear She live, and embracing die!
She who is all the world, and can exclude
In deserts solitude.
   I should have then this only fear:
Lest men, when they my pleasures see,
Should hither throng to live like me;
   And make a City here!

*   *   *

Except in an epicene age, sex-joy is recognised to be as fine a motive for song in men as it is in birds: but the Cavaliers trifled with the thought of woman, and the Puritans regarded her as the inferior half of humanity. It is with happiness that most readers come at this point in their literary exploration to poems which arose out of a mystical religious feeling. Religion was the most violent concern of the seventeenth century: but it is obvious that very few men have a genius for religion as very few men have a genius for poetry. Mystical experience—which might almost be described as falling in love with God or with the Spirit who projected Space and Time—is the only true religion, and is high above any quarrel of East and West, of Roman or Anglican.

CARNEGIE INSTITUTE
OF TECHNOLOGY LIBRARY

Now—in the midst of that psychological upheaval which we term the Civil War,—several Anglican churchmen, of a type very different from Herrick, used poetry for the expression of spiritual longing. Anyone who studies the poems of this period,—the period which came after the execution of King Charles,—should be able to determine whether he is a Puritan-Scientist or a Cavalier-Mystic.

Henry Vaughan: 1622–1695

An Oxford graduate—from Jesus College. He then studied law in London and medicine, strangely enough, in Brecknock. The lovely poem which follows appeared in 1655, when the literal-minded Puritans were, as it must have seemed, permanently in charge of our national interests.

Aldous Huxley took from this poem the words 'The World of Light' as a title for an anti-spiritualist play. Vaughan might have been saddened. 'Pérspective' in this poem means 'telescope'.

57   They are all gone

They are all gone into the world of light,
    And I alone sit lingering here;
Their very memory is fair and bright,
    And my sad thoughts doth clear.

It glows and glitters in my cloudy breast,
    Like stars upon some gloomy grove,
Or those faint beams in which this hill is dressed
    After the sun's remove.

I see them walking in an air of glory,
    Whose light doth trample on my days:
My days, which are at best but dull and hoary,
    Mere glimmering and decays.

O holy hope, and high humility!
    High as the heavens above!
These are your walks, and you have showed them me,
    To kindle my cold love.

Dear, beauteous death! the jewel of the just,
    Shining no where but in the dark;
What mysteries do lie beyond thy dust,
    Could man outlook that mark!

He that hath found some fledged bird's nest may know,
    At first sight, if the bird be flown;
But what fair well or grove he sings in now,
    That is to him unknown.

And yet, as angels in some brighter dreams
    Call to the soul when man doth sleep,
So some strange thoughts transcend our wonted themes,
    And into glory peep.

If a star were confined into a tomb,
    Her captive flames must needs burn there;
But when the hand that locked her up gives room,
    She'll shine through all the sphere.

O Father of eternal life, and all
    Created glories under Thee!
Resume Thy spirit from this world of thrall
    Into true liberty.

Either disperse these mists, which blot and fill
    My perspective still as they pass,
Or else remove me hence unto that hill,
    Where I shall need no glass.

*   *   *

Before the coming—from men who had been exiled in France—of cynicism, satire, cleverness and dexterity of word-usage, pause for one more moment with the mystics: with a man whose voice speaks to us, better than from any gramophone record, in the words 'You never enjoy the world aright till the sea itself floweth in your veins, till you are clothed with the heavens, and crowned with the stars'.

To all natural Puritans his ringing sentence will seem absurd. To an English minority those words not only make sense but also make the materialistic point of view look indistinguishably like nonsense.

Thomas Traherne: 1637–1674

Like Vaughan and Herbert, another poet finely inspired by religion, Traherne was of Welsh engendering. His father was a Hereford shoemaker. The poet, they think, may have been born in Ledbury. In 1652 he became a Commoner at Brasenose. In 1656 he became a Bachelor of Arts; in 1661, a Master of Arts; in 1669, a Bachelor of Divinity and private chaplain to the Keeper of the Seals.

The discovery of Traherne's poetry is a strange story. Until 1888 his manuscripts rusted in the negligence of a Ledbury family named Skipp. In 1896 these manuscripts were 'on the bookstalls', and a Mr. W. T. Brooke 'bought them for a few pence'. This Mr. Brooke parted with the marvellous manuscript volumes ('one folio, two octavo') to Dr. Grosart, a pundit of the period: but the pundit supposed that the poems were by Vaughan. The high credit of having rescued Traherne from the threepenny bookstall must go to the poet-bookseller, Dobell.

Traherne's prose-memories of Intimations Received During Childhood (though he does not call them so) are even more startling-true to the mystic than the poet's verse-work.

Technique has now little farther to go. It has only to master the quick-running metres,—the use of dactyl or anapæst.

58   The Preparative

My body being dead, my limbs unknown;
 Before I skill'd to prize
 Those living stars mine eyes,
Before my tongue or cheeks were to me shown,
 Before I knew my hands were mine,
Or that my sinews did my members join,
 When neither nostril, foot nor ear
As yet was seen, or felt, or did appear:
  I was within
A house I knew not, newly cloth'd with skin.

Then was my soul my only all to me,
 A living endless eye,
 Just bounded with the sky.
Whose power, whose act, whose essence, was to see:
 I was an inward Sphere of Light,
Or an interminable Orb of Sight,
 An endless and a living day,
A vital Sun that round about did ray
  All life, all sense,
A naked simple pure Intelligence.

I then no thirst nor hunger did perceive,
 No dull necessity,
 No want was known to me;
Without disturbance then I did receive
 The fair ideas of all things,
And had the honey even without the stings.
 A meditating inward eye
Gazing at quiet did within me lie,
  And every thing
Delighted me that was their heavenly King.

For sight inherits beauty, hearing sounds,
 The nostril sweet perfumes;
 All tastes have hidden rooms
Within the tongue; and feeling feeling wounds
 With pleasure and delight; but I
Forgot the rest, and was all sight or eye:
 Unbodied and devoid of care,
Just as in Heaven the holy Angels are,
  For simple sense
Is Lord of all created excellence.

Being thus prepared for all felicity,
 Not prepossest with dross,
 Nor stiffly glued to gross
And dull materials that might ruin me,
 Nor fettered by an iron fate
With vain affections in an earthly state

To any thing that might seduce
My sense, or else bereave it of its use,
     I was as free
As if there were not sin, nor misery.

Pure empty powers that did nothing loath,
    Did like the fairest glass,
    Or spotless polished brass,
Themselves soon in their object's image clothe.
    Divine impressions when they came
Did quickly enter and my soul inflame.
    'Tis not the object, but the light
That maketh Heaven: 'tis a purer sight.
        Felicity
Appears to none but them that purely see.

A disentangled and a naked sense,
    A mind that's unpossest,
    A disengagèd breast,
An empty and a quick intelligence
    Acquainted with the golden mean,
An even spirit pure and serene,
    Is that where beauty, excellence,
And pleasure keep their Court of Residence.
        My soul retire,
Get free, and so thou shalt even all admire.

PART FOUR

I

Part Four

NOW SUMMER IS over and even August is gone, with its jaded leaves that were fresh once and its dusty mockeries of midsummer glory, and here is that decay of autumn for which the attentive reader has long been looking. 'When Marvell died at the age of fifty-seven, in 1678, poetry', said Edward Thomas, 'had entered an age when it was to reflect less of the influence of women than at any other. It was an age of clubs and coffee-houses, of a purely masculine tone in society and in literature. . . . Poetry was social; men wrote only what they would say and think in the company of other men—only not alas! in the same language'. We must remember, too, that Waller had already foreshadowed the coarse tone of the Restoration in such lines as

> 'Women enjoyed, whate'er before they've been,
> Are like romances read, or scenes once seen;
> Fruition dulls or spoils the play much more
> Than if one read, or knew, the plot before'.

This weary and uninspiring attitude would have seemed mighty poorspirited to the romantic Elizabethan who could pen lines of pure rapture to the mere wraith of Grecian Helen. Shakespeare's frank sonnet about male lust is hot with passion and remorse, not cold with a cynicism that reduces sex-love to the level of a superficial pleasure. When women and lust and love are not taken seriously, a second-rate age, an autumnal debility, has caught the world.

The truth is that the exiled Cavaliers had been schooling themselves in France, and that here they persuaded themselves to regard wit as of higher importance than passion, and 'love' as a game of Badminton—shuttlecock women and battledore men. To feel deeply was then, as it became during the inter-war years, a sign of uncouthness. In a word, writers became too clever for the creation of first-rate poetry. Poetry cannot arise in a mind which is incapable of wildness, in a mind too neatly trimmed by long sojourn within the closed garden of a University, in a mind which is unhappy if it is naked. Consider, even, how the statues of this long period—the Restoration and the whole of the eighteenth century—are usually bewigged and half-nude gentlemen tricked out to resemble Roman Emperors. John Donne, a belated Elizabethan, could apostrophise his lover's body as 'O my America, my Newfoundland', and chide the sun as a 'busy old fool' for breaking in upon their love-delights; but after the Restoration, nudity became improper, passion somewhat rustical, and flippancy was the only wear. We have witnessed like symptoms in our own time, but have not recognised that, artistically, we live in a damp and foggy season.

Dryden died as the eighteenth century was born. He was a writer of splendid gifts. Indeed, he was not only the first writer to use prose which does not seem to us antiquated, but was also a master of prose which, notwithstanding Addison, Hazlitt and Ruskin, has never been overshot. His highjump remains a record. But it was only because he possessed this magnificent literary sense that he was able, through sheer strength of talent, to compose poems which we can still admire, not for any subtle overtones but for the evidence which they provide of a sinewy mind which could almost, but not quite, override its period and achieve the tremor of poetry. Most anthologists represent Dryden by his massive near-successes. It may be fairer to his genius if we meet him when he is in his element and is hitting the gold, even if he stood only fifty yards away from the target: in satire, that is to say, and in compliment.

'Mrs. Nelly', who speaks the first piece, is Nell Gwyn. She excelled in these direct contacts with the public and was, in fact, the supreme revue-artist, born too soon by some ten generations. Observe (in the lines to his dear friend Mr. Congreve) how, even so early, the New Age is confident that it had the old 'boisterous English wit with art endued': observe this, because most of the eighteenth-century poets and architects are going to be assured that the Tudor past was semi-barbarous and that 'the Age of Reason' was incontestably superior to any age of mere ardour.

John Dryden: 1631–1700

Educated at Westminster School and Trinity College, Cambridge. He seems to have had a vacillating temperament. For instance, in 1658 he wrote an elegy on Cromwell, but in 1661 a panegyric on the

Restoration of Charles the Second; in 1682 he defended the Church of England in his poem *Religio Laici*, but in 1687, having been converted, he championed Roman Catholicism in his allegorical poem *The Hind and the Panther*.

His talent was not lyrical, but so strong was his literary gift that he is among the earliest of our poets to write without discomfort in an anapæstic measure. His dramatic work is powerful and memorable; and, having the sovereign preservative of style, may return to favour with the judicious to-morrow or the day after.

At one stage in his life 'he to be a tearing blade thought fit', and it is amusing to find that his contemporaries were not at all impressed by this ill-judged effort to emulate the court-philistines.

He visited Milton in the greater poet's old age, and asked permission to recast *Paradise Lost* in rhyme. Milton replied, 'You may tag my verses if you wish'.

Nell had at first been cast for tragedy-queen parts, and it is interesting to see that both Dryden and she had now realised that she could not convincingly 'die for love'.

59   Epilogue to 'Tyrannick Love, or the Royal Martyr'

Spoken by Mrs. Ellen when she was to be carried off dead by the Bearers

To the Bearer

Hold! are you mad? you damned, confounded dog!
I am to rise, and speak the epilogue.

To the Audience

I come, kind gentlemen, strange news to tell ye;
I am the ghost of poor departed Nelly.
Sweet ladies, be not frighted; I'll be civil;
I'm what I was, a little harmless devil.
For, after death, we sprites have just such natures
We had, for all the world, when human creatures;
And, therefore, I, that was an actress here,
Play all my tricks in hell, a goblin there.

Gallants, look to 't, you say there are no sprites;
But I'll come dance about your beds at nights;
And faith you'll be in a sweet kind of taking,
When I surprise you between sleep and waking.
To tell you true, I walk, because I die
Out of my calling, in a tragedy.
O poet, damned dull poet, who could prove
So senseless, to make Nelly die for love!
Nay, what's yet worse, to kill me in the prime
Of Easter-term, in tart and cheese-cake time!
I'll fit the fop; for I'll not one word say,
To excuse his godly, out-of-fashion play;
A play, which, if you dare but twice sit out,
You'll all be slandered, and be thought devout.
But farewell, gentlemen, make haste to me,
I'm sure ere long to have your company.
As for my epitaph when I am gone,
I'll trust no poet, but will write my own:—
Here Nelly lies, who, though she lived a slattern,
Yet died a princess, acting in St. Catherine.

The reader will detect at once that when Dryden sat down to write the following elegy he had some music-composer in mind. Not only is this shown by the frequent cues for music, as we may call them, but also by the last line of the first stanza which almost suggests its own musical setting.

60   On the death of Mr. Purcell

Mark how the lark and linnet sing;
With rival notes
They strain their warbling throats
To welcome in the spring.
But in the close of night,
When Philomel begins her heavenly lay,
They cease their mutual spite,
Drink in her music with delight,
And listening and silent, silent and listening, listening
and silent, obey.

So ceased the rival crew, when Purcell came;
They sang no more, or only sung his fame:
 Struck dumb, they all admired
  The godlike man,
 Alas! too soon retired,
  As he too late began.
We beg not Hell our Orpheus to restore;
  Had he been there,
  Their sovereign's fear
 Had sent him back before.
The power of harmony too well they knew;
He long ere this had tuned their jarring sphere,
 And left no Hell below.

The heavenly choir, who heard his notes from high,
Let down the scale of music from the sky;
 They handed him along,
And all the way he taught, and all the way they sung.
Ye brethren of the lyre and tuneful voice,
Lament his lot; but at your own rejoice:
Now live secure, and linger out your days;
The gods are pleased alone with Purcell's lays,
 Nor know to mend their choice.

61 **To my dear friend, Mr. Congreve, on his comedy called The Double Dealer**

Well then, the promised hour is come at last:
The present age of wit obscures the past:
Strong were our sires, and as they fought they writ,
Conquering with force of arms and dint of wit:
Theirs was the giant race before the flood;
And thus, when Charles returned, our empire stood.
Like Janus, he the stubborn soil manured,
With rules of husbandry the rankness cured;
Tamed as to manners, when the stage was rude,
And boisterous English wit with art endued.
Our age was cultivated thus at length,
But what we gained in skill we lost in strength.

Our builders were with want of genius curst;
The second temple was not like the first.
Till you, the best Vitruvius, come at length,
Our beauties equal, but excel our strength.
Firm Doric pillars found your solid base,
The fair Corinthian crowns the higher space;
Thus all below is strength, and all above is grace.
In easy dialogue is Fletcher's praise;
He moved the mind, but had not power to raise.
Great Jonson did by strength of judgment please,
Yet, doubling Fletcher's force, he wants his ease.
In different talents both adorned their age,
One for the study, t'other for the stage,
But both to Congreve justly shall submit,
One matched in judgment, both o'ermatched in wit.
In him all beauties of this age we see,
Etherege his courtship, Southern's purity,
The satire, wit, and strength of manly Wycherly.
All this in blooming youth you have achieved;
Nor are your foiled contemporaries grieved.
So much the sweetness of your manners move,
We cannot envy you, because we love.
Fabius might joy in Scipio, when he saw
A beardless Consul made against the law,
And join his suffrage to the votes of Rome,
Though he with Hannibal was overcome.
Thus old Romano bowed to Raphael's fame,
And scholar to the youth he taught became.
   O that your brows my laurel had sustained!
Well had I been deposed, if you had reigned:
The father had descended for the son,
For only you are lineal to the throne.
Thus, when the State one Edward did depose,
A greater Edward in his room arose:
But now, not I, but poetry is curst;
For Tom the second reigns like Tom the first.
But let them not mistake my patron's part
Nor call his charity their own desert.

Yet this I prophesy,—Thou shalt be seen,
Though with some short parenthesis between,
High on the throne of wit, and, seated there,
Not mine—that's little—but thy laurel wear.
Thy first attempt an early promise made;
That early promise this has more than paid.
So bold, yet so judiciously you dare,
That your least praise is to be regular.
Time, place, and action may with pains be wrought,
But genius must be born, and never can be taught.
This is your portion, this your native store:
Heaven, that but once was prodigal before,
To Shakespeare gave as much; she could not give him more.
   Maintain your post: that's all the fame you need;
For 'tis impossible you should proceed.
Already I am worn with cares and age,
And just abandoning the ungrateful stage:
Unprofitably kept at Heaven's expense,
I live a rent-charge on His providence:
But you, whom every Muse and grace adorn,
Whom I foresee to better fortune born,
Be kind to my remains; and oh, defend,
Against your judgment, your departed friend!
Let not the insulting foe my fame pursue,
But shade those laurels which descend to you:
And take for tribute what these lines express;
You merit more, nor could my love do less.

Most people will agree that these lines have a ring of sincerity; and we must recognise that Congreve is in some ways so expert that Dryden may be pardoned for having expected too much of him. We have already seen a link of admiration connect Hoccleve with Chaucer, Shakespeare with Marlowe, Milton with Shakespeare, Herrick with Jonson, Dryden with Milton, and here, once more, Dryden with Congreve. The older poet wrote in a letter that the ' "Double Dealer" is much censured by the greater part of the town, and is defended only by the best judges, who, as you know, are commonly the bravest. Yet it gains ground daily'. It is pleasant to learn, in view of the last lines in the above poem, that Congreve edited an edition of Dryden's works.

'Tom the first' means Shadwell, Dryden's favourite butt, and 'Tom the second' is thought to mean Thomas Rymer, an exceedingly feeble dramatist.

Lastly, let us savour the grace of Dryden in complimentary or courtly mood. . . .

62   On Mrs. Margaret Paston, of Barningham, in Norfolk

> So fair, so young, so innocent, so sweet,
> So ripe a judgment, and so rare a wit,
> Require at least an age in one to meet.
> In her they met; but long they could not stay,
> 'Twas gold too fine to fix without allay.
> Heaven's image was in her so well exprest,
> Her very sight upbraided all the rest;
> Too justly ravished from an age like this,
> Now she is gone, the world is of a piece.

*   *   *

In the reign of Queen Ann almost everything suddenly became elegant. We find this change, for example, in the houses of the well-to-do, in their furniture, in the ornaments on their mantelpieces, in their tea-cups and their cream-jugs. Everything is less heavy than it used to be. And the same elegance is the outstanding merit of Addison's prose and of Pope's verse. Dryden's verse was like a well-tempered sword: Pope's is like an equally fine stiletto. And it is well to keep in mind that the narrow perfection which Pope showed to be attainable caused him to dominate practically the whole of the eighteenth century. Horace, men thought, was the perfect Latin poet, Pope, the perfect English poet; and the reason must have been that both were sensible unexaggerated souls, not poets at all but exceedingly fine versemen, and that the eighteenth century suspected all poetry, romance, passion and enthusiasm. Indeed, the word 'enthusiasm' came to mean at this time 'foolish', 'uncontrolled', 'ill-bred',—much as the word 'romantic' is now used by reviewers in the sense of 'brainless' or 'silly'.

So powerful was Pope's influence over the century, and even beyond it, that men had the utmost difficulty in breaking away from his style. There has been no literary domination comparable in length of time with that of Pope. His mind was so worldly that even unpoetic readers imagined themselves to be appreciating poetry: and again, he was so skilled a craftsman that any age must in some measure delight in the smooth satinwood surface of his couplets. How consciously he achieved his one kind of perfection we may see if we read *An Essay on Criticism*, itself inspired by Horace. Any young writer must gleefully examine such brilliant lines as:

'Apt alliteration's artful aid'

or

'The needless alexandrine ends the song,
Which like a wounded snake drags his slow length along'.

People now preferred a trim garden to wild nature. Mountains were 'horrid'. No first-rate tragedy was written because men were no longer capable of any 'bee-like ecstacy'. Their intemperance was merely of the bottle, not of the soul. Religion, until John Wesley had been at work for many years, was tepid and formal. It was, in short, a self-conscious age when everybody was afraid of giving himself away; and in such an atmosphere none but a genius of the first magnitude could bring poetry to life again.

Pope's short poems are, for him, so poor that on this occasion I am compelled to break off a fragment from a poem—*The Rape of the Lock*—which has the rare virtue of being a shapely whole. It is impossible for any one in any period to surpass the special kind of verse-craft which this poem displays. It might possibly be equalled, it could no more be bettered than we can improve upon the geometry of a crystal. And yet? 'There are two ways of disliking poetry', said Oscar Wilde, 'one is to dislike it, the other is to like Pope'. Equally well, and with more truth, Lord Alfred Douglas observed, 'He knew how to write poetry, but he had none to write'.

Alexander Pope: 1688–1744

At the time of his birth, his mother and his father were alike forty-six: and in a rare book (*A Study of British Genius*) Havelock Ellis demonstrates that the child of over-mature parents is likely to be defective physically and alert psychically—or, as we say, 'intelligent'. Pope, however, had at the age of twelve a severe illness which left him a hunchback in body and in soul. He quarrelled with almost everybody of literary importance in his time but, so blinding was the brilliance of his technique, especially when the barbs were poisoned with malice, that he ruled the kingdom of English poetry right into the hey-day of Byron. There have been few such literary dominations. What names could we cite? Ben Jonson, Addison, Dryden (doubtfully), Pope (above all others, for generations of good readers assumed that he had achieved the *non plus ultra*), Samuel Johnson, Tennyson, and in our own time Bernard Shaw and, possibly, H. G. Wells. More than any other man of the period, Pope made malice fashionable.

This deformed body, glittering brain and wry soul were buried 'in Twickenham Church'; unless perhaps the soul in him unravelled itself and went marching on. 'Shock' is her ladyship's lapdog.

63   From *The Rape of the Lock*

Ye *Sylphs* and *Sylphids*, to your Chief give ear,
Fays, Fairies, Genii, Elves, and *Demons* hear!
Ye know the Spheres and various Tasks assign'd
By Laws Eternal to th' Aerial Kind.
Some in the Fields of purest *Aether* play,
And bask and whiten in the Blaze of Day.
Some guide the Course of wand'ring Orbs on high,
Or roll the Planets through the boundless Sky.
Some less refin'd, beneath the Moon's pale Light
Pursue the Stars that shoot athwart the Night;
Or suck the Mists in grosser Air below,
Or dip their Pinions in the painted Bow,

Or brew fierce Tempests on the wintry Main,
Or o'er the Glebe distil the kindly Rain.
Others on Earth o'er human Race preside,
Watch all their Ways, and all their Actions guide:
Of these the Chief the Care of Nations own,
And guard with Arms Divine the *British Throne*.

Our humbler Province is to tend the Fair,
Not a less pleasing, tho' less glorious Care.
To save the Powder from too rude a Gale,
Nor let th' imprison'd Essences exhale;
To draw fresh Colours from the vernal Flow'rs,
To steal from Rainbows ere they drop in Show'rs
A brighter Wash; to curl their waving Hairs,
Assist their Blushes, and inspire their Airs;
Nay oft, in Dreams, Invention we bestow,
To change a *Flounce*, or add a *Furbelo*!

This Day, black Omens threat the brightest Fair
That e'er deserv'd a watchful Spirit's Care;
Some dire Disaster, or by Force, or Slight,
But what, or where, the Fates have wrapt in Night.
Whether the Nymph shall break *Diana's* law,
Or some frail *China* jar receive a Flaw,
Or stain her Honour, or her new Brocade,
Forget her Pray'rs, or miss a Masquerade,
Or lose her Heart, or Necklace, at a Ball;
Or whether Heav'n has doom'd that *Shock* must fall.
Haste then ye Spirits! to your Charge repair;
The flutt'ring Fan be *Zephyretta's* Care;
The Drops to thee, *Brillante*, we consign;
And *Momentilla*, let the Watch be thine;
Do thou, *Crispissa*, tend her fav'rite Lock;
Ariel himself shall be the guard of *Shock*.

To Fifty chosen *Sylphs*, of special Note,
We trust th' important Charge, the *Petticoat*:
Oft have we known that sev'nfold Fence to fail,
Tho' stiff with Hoops, and arm'd with Ribs of Whale;
Form a strong Line about the Silver Bound,
And guard the wide Circumference around.

Whatever Spirit, careless of his Charge,
His Post neglects, or leaves the Fair at large,
Shall feel sharp Vengeance soon o'ertake his Sins,
Be stop'd in *Vials*, or transfixt with *Pins*;
Or plung'd in Lakes of bitter *Washes* lie,
Or wedg'd whole Ages in a *Bodkin's* Eye:
Gums and *Pomatums* shall his Flight restrain,
While clog'd he beats his silken Wings in vain;
Or Alom-*Stypticks* with contracting Pow'r
Shrink his thin Essence like a rivell'd Flower.
Or, as *Ixion* fix'd, the Wretch shall feel
The giddy Motion of the whirling Mill,
Midst Fumes of burning Chocolate shall glow,
And tremble at the Sea that froaths below!

He spoke; the Spirits from the Sails descend;
Some, Orb in Orb, around the Nymph extend,
Some thrid the mazy Ringlets of her Hair,
Some hang upon the Pendants of her Ear;
With beating Hearts the dire Event they wait,
Anxious, and trembling for the Birth of Fate.

* * *

Even the poets of this period who managed to write differently from
Pope were liable at any moment to feel that familiar words were unsuit-
able to poetry. A country girl must be a nymph and her lad must be a
swain. The wind is usually a 'gale', sometimes a 'zephyr'. A poet has
always to avoid the dangers either of using familiar phrases with a flat
result or of using heightened language with an effect of mere pom-
posity. In the following poem, for all its dignity and all its verbal music,
the poet, who has obviously admired Milton, seems to be condescending
towards Nature and keeping her at due distance.

James Thomson: 1700–1748

Son of a Scottish minister, he finished his education at Edinburgh
University. *The Seasons*, his most famous and best-liked work, if we
except *Rule, Britannia*, is an early production, having been published in

sections between 1726 and 1730. He achieved some success as a play-wright, but that side of his endeavour is now remembered only for one ludicrous blank-verse line—

'Oh Sophonisba! Sophonisba, oh!'

Thomson, in a period of steadily increasing debauchery and lack of idealism toward women, was faithful to one lady who, unfortunately, was persuaded by an ambitious mother to marry an Admiral. 'It was', says Edward Thomas, 'an age of unmarried poets', and he cites Otway, Pope, Gay, Gray, Swift and Prior.

64   A Shearing Scene

Now swarms the village o'er the jovial mead:
The rustic youth, brown with meridian toil,
Healthful and strong; full as the summer rose
Blown by prevailing suns, the ruddy maid
Half naked, swelling on the sight, and all
Her kindled graces burning o'er her cheek.
Even stooping age is here; and infant-hands
Trail the long rake, or, with the fragrant load
O'ercharged, amid the kind oppression roll.
Wide flies the tedded grain; all in a row
Advancing broad, or wheeling round the field,
They spread their breathing harvest to the sun,
That throws refreshful round a rural smell:
Or, as they take the green-appearing ground,
And drive the dusky wave along the mead,
The russet hay-cock rises thick behind,
In order gay. While heard from dale to dale,
Waking the breeze, resounds the blended voice
Of happy labour, love, and social glee.

Or rushing thence, in one diffusive band,
They drive the troubled flocks, by many a dog
Compell'd, to where the mazy-running brook
Forms a deep pool; this bank abrupt and high,
And that fair-spreading in a pebbled shore.

Urg'd to the giddy brink, much is the toil,
The clamour much, of men, and boys, and dogs,
Ere the soft fearful people to the flood
Commit their woolly sides. And oft the swain,
On some impatient seizing, hurls them in:
Embolden'd then, nor hesitating more,
Fast, fast, they plunge amid the flashing wave,
And panting labour to the farthest shore.
Repeated this, till deep the well-wash'd fleece
Has drunk the flood, and from his lively haunt
The trout is banish'd by the sordid stream;
Heavy, and dripping, to the breezy brow
Slow move the harmless race: where, as they spread
Their swelling treasures to the sunny ray,
Inly disturb'd, and wondering what this wild
Outrageous tumult means, their loud complaints
The country fill; and, toss'd from rock to rock,
Incessant bleatings run around the hills.
At last, of snowy white, the gathered flocks
Are in the wattled pen innumerous press'd,
Head above head: and, rang'd in lusty rows
The shepherds sit, and whet the sounding shears.
The housewife waits to roll her fleecy stores,
With all her gay-drest maids attending round.
One, chief, in gracious dignity enthron'd,
Shines o'er the rest, the pastoral queen, and rays
Her smiles, sweet beaming, on her shepherd king;
While the glad circle round them yield their souls
To festive mirth, and wit that knows no gall.
Meantime, their joyous talk goes on apace:
Some mingling stir the melted tar, and some,
Deep on the new-shorn vagrant's heaving side,
To stamp his master's cypher ready stand;
Others the unwilling wether drag along;
And, glorying in his might, the sturdy boy
Holds by the twisted horns th' indignant ram.
Behold where bound, and of its robe bereft
By needy Man, that all-depending lord,

How meek, how patient, the mild creature lies!
What softness in its melancholy face,
What dumb complaining innocence appears!
Fear not, ye gentle tribes, 'tis not the knife
Of horrid slaughter that is o'er you wav'd;
No, 'tis the tender swain's well-guided shears,
Who having now, to pay his annual care,
Borrowed your fleece, to you a cumbrous load,
Will send you bounding to your hills again.

* * *

Gray's *Elegy* might be starred as the noblest and loveliest poem achieved by any English poet during the eighteenth century. It lives with undimmed lustre because it is formed out of sad and tender emotion sincerely expressed and phrased with flawless music. The same warm-toned word-music sustains the following Ode. Tennyson chose for special admiration the sound of the 'Theban eagle' lines; but indeed we may examine endlessly the superb workmanship of this poem. And here we shall find Gray's link of admiration for Dryden.

Thomas Gray: 1716–1771

It will some day be found that women are, by a vast preponderance, responsible for transmitting artistic genius, or perhaps the physical apparatus of that genius. Gray's father was 'brutal and half-mad'. His mother bore twelve children, but the poet alone survived. Mrs. Gray, working as a milliner, managed to pay her son's way to Eton and to Peterhouse, Cambridge. When she died (he was then thirty-six) the poet wrote, 'I know I am the better for it. We are all idle and thought-less things, and have no sense, no use in the world any longer than that sad impression lasts: the deeper it is engraved, the better'.

Gray was, through most of his life, a Cambridge man. He gained (and was limited) by the strong but narrow culture of the University. It taught him to write as a gentleman should behave; it did not prevent him from indulging an eccentric taste for Icelandic saga-literature; but Cambridge influence precluded him from the experience of tossing his bonnet over the windmill, or into the Bay of Cadiz.

Matthew Arnold, as perceptive a literary critic as our uncritical nation has produced, seizing upon the chance phrase of someone who knew the poet, termed him 'the man who never spoke out'.

65 The Progress of Poesy. A Pindaric Ode

Awake, Aeolian lyre, awake,
And give to rapture all thy trembling strings.
From Helicon's harmonious springs
A thousand rills their mazy progress take;
The laughing flowers, that round them blow,
Drink life and fragrance as they flow.
Now the rich stream of music winds along
Deep, majestic, smooth, and strong.
Thro' verdant vales, and Ceres' golden reign;
Now rolling down the steep amain,
Headlong, impetuous, see it pour;
The rocks, and nodding groves rebellow to the roar.

Oh! Sovereign of the willing soul,
Parent of sweet and solemn-breathing airs,
Enchanting shell! the sullen Cares,
And frantic Passions hear thy soft control.
On Thracia's hills the Lord of War
Has curb'd the fury of his car,
And drop'd his thirsty lance at thy command.
Perching on the scept'red hand
Of Jove, thy magic lulls the feather'd king
With ruffled plumes, and flagging wing:
Quench'd in dark clouds of slumber lie
The terror of his beak, and light'nings of his eye.

Thee the voice, the dance, obey,
Temper'd to thy warbled lay.
O'er Idalia's velvet-green
The rosy-crownéd Loves are seen
On Cytherea's day
With antic Sports, and blue-eyed Pleasures,
Frisking light in frolic measures;

K

Now pursuing, now retreating,
Now in circling troops they meet:
To brisk notes in cadence beating,
Glance their many-twinkling feet.
Slow melting strains their Queen's approach declare:
Where'er she turns the Graces homage pay.
With arms sublime, that float upon the air,
In gliding state she wins her easy way:
O'er her warm cheek, and rising bosom, move
The bloom of young Desire, and purple light of Love.

Man's feeble race what Ills await.
Labour, and Penury, the racks of Pain,
Disease, and Sorrow's weeping train.
And Death, sad refuge from the storms of Fate.
The fond complaint, my Song, disprove,
And justify the laws of Jove.
Say, has he giv'n in vain the heav'nly Muse?
Night, and all her sickly dews,
Her Spectres wan, and Birds of boding cry,
He gives to range the dreary sky:
Till down the eastern cliffs afar
Hyperion's march they spy, and glitt'ring shafts of war.

In climes beyond the solar road,
Where shaggy forms o'er ice-built mountains roam,
The Muse has broke the twilight-gloom
To chear the shriv'ring Native's dull above.
And oft, beneath the od'rous shade
Of Chili's boundless forests laid,
She deigns to hear the savage Youth repeat
In loose numbers wildly sweet
Their feather-cinctured Chiefs, and dusky Loves.
Her track, where'er the Goddess roves,
Glory pursue, and generous Shame,
Th' unconquerable Mind, and Freedom's holy flame.

Woods, that wave o'er Delphi's steep,
Isles, that crown th' Egæan deep,
Fields, that cool Ilissus laves,
Or where Mæander's amber waves

In lingering Lab'rinths creep,
How do your tuneful Echo's languish,
Mute, but to the voice of Anguish?
Where each old poetic Mountain
Inspiration breath'd around:
Ev'ry shade and hallow'd Fountain
Murmur'd deep a solemn sound:
Till the sad Nine in Greece's evil hour
Left their Parnassus for the Latian plains.
Alike they scorn the pomp of tyrant-Power,
And coward Vice, that revels in her chains.
When Latium had her loftly spirit lost,
They sought, oh Albion! next thy sea-encircled coast.

Far from the sun and summer-gale,
In thy green lap was Nature's Darling laid,
What time, where lucid Avon stray'd,
To Him the mighty Mother did unveil
Her aweful face: The dauntless Child
Stretch'd forth his little arms, and smiled.
This pencil take (she said) whose colours clear
Richly paint the vernal year:
Thine too these golden keys, immortal Boy!
This can unlock the gates of Joy;
Of Horror that, and thrilling Fears,
Or ope the sacred source of sympathetic Tears.

Nor second He, that rode sublime
Upon the seraph-wings of Extasy,
The secrets of th' Abyss to spy.
He pass'd the flaming bounds of Place and Time;
The living Throne, the saphire-blaze
Where Angels tremble, while they gaze,
He saw; but blasted with excess of light,
Closed his eyes in endless night.
Behold, where Dryden's less presumptuous car,
Wide o'er the fields of Glory bear
Two Coursers of ethereal race,
With necks in thunder cloath'd, and long-resounding pace,

Hark, his hands the lyre explore!
Bright-eyed Fancy hovering o'er
Scatters from her pictured urn
Thoughts, that breath, and words, that burn.
But ah! 'tis heard no more—
Oh! Lyre divine, what daring Spirit
Wakes thee now? tho' he inherit
Nor the pride, nor ample pinion,
That the Theban Eagle bear
Sailing with supreme dominion
Thro' the azure deep of air:
Yet oft before his infant eyes would run
Such forms, as glitter in the Muse's ray
With orient hues, unborrow'd of the Sun:
Yet shall he mount, and keep his distant way
Beyond the limits of a vulgar fate,
Beneath the Good how far—but far above the Great.

* * *

A poet's style is usually well indicated by the time that he is twenty-five. Cowper, therefore, belongs to the latter half of the century: and soon after the beginning of this latter half, English literature becomes (on the whole) more serious and even at times downright solemn or portentous. The architecture of Dr. Johnson's prime is a great deal more massive than that which appeared in Addison's heyday. Cowper succeeded by sheer sincerity in deflating the too self-consciously impressive style of current verse. His best works are the longest, but the following *Robinson Crusoe* verses, famous to wearisomeness throughout the nineteenth century, are interesting because they are early specimens of anapæstic lines. The Elizabethans could do everything in verse except to write easily in these rushing metres.

William Cowper: 1731–1800

His father was rector of Great Berkhampstead; his mother, to whom he remained utterly devoted although she died in 1737, was a Miss Donne and probably came from the same Welsh family as the poet, John Donne. Cowper was deeply influenced at all times by the affection of women. As a very young man he was articled to a solicitor, and in 1754 he became a barrister of the Middle Temple.

Melancholia first markedly attacked him when he was twenty-two, and subsequently he had long periods of insanity. These were partly induced by a conviction that he would not be 'saved' and could not avoid eternal damnation.

Cowper was a good scholar—a Westminster boy—and late in life translated Homer, using a style less dapper and more suitable than that of Pope.

66   Verses

Supposed to be written by Alexander Selkirk, during his solitary abode in the island of Juan Fernandez

I am monarch of all I survey,
   My right there is none to dispute;
From the centre all round to the sea,
   I am lord of the fowl and the brute.
Oh, solitude! where are the charms
   That sages have seen in thy face?
Better dwell in the midst of alarms,
   Than reign in this horrible place.

I am out of humanity's reach,
   I must finish my journey alone,
Never hear the sweet music of speech;
   I start at the sound of my own.
The beasts, that roam over the plain,
   My form with indifference see;
They are so unacquainted with man,
   Their tameness is shocking to me.

Society, friendship, and love,
   Divinely bestow'd upon man,—
Oh, had I the wings of a dove,
   How soon would I taste you again!
My sorrows I then might assuage
   In the ways of religion and truth,
Might learn from the wisdom of age,
   And be cheer'd by the sallies of youth.

139

Religion! what treasure untold
  Resides in that heavenly word!
More precious than silver and gold,
  Or all that this earth can afford:
But the sound of the church-going bell
  These vallies and rocks never heard;
Ne'er sigh'd at the sound of a knell,
  Or smil'd when a sabbath appear'd.

Ye winds, that have made me your sport,
  Convey to this desolate shore
Some cordial endearing report
  Of a land I shall visit no more.
My friends, do they now and then send
  A wish or a thought after me?
O tell me I yet have a friend,
  Though a friend I am never to see.

How fleet is a glance of the mind!
  Compar'd with the speed of its flight,
The tempest itself lags behind,
  And the swift wingéd arrows of light.
When I think of my own native land,
  In a moment I seem to be there;
But alas! recollection at hand
  Soon hurries me back to despair.

But the sea-fowl is gone to her nest,
  The beast is laid down in his lair,
Ev'n here is a season of rest,
  And I to my cabin repair.
There's mercy in every place;
  And mercy, encouraging thought!
Gives even affliction a grace,
  And reconciles man to his lot.

That *The Stricken Deer* had humour may surprise us, nor will *John Gilpin* seem now so fine a comic poem as it was for generations held to be. Here, however, is a little-known glimpse of Cowper's all too infrequent sense of amusement.

67 On Observing some Names of Little Note

Recorded in The Biographia Britannica

Oh, fond attempt to give a deathless lot
To names ignoble, born to be forgot!
In vain, recorded in historic page,
They court the notice of a future age:
Those twinkling tiny lustres of the land
Drop one by one from Fame's neglecting hand;
Lethæan gulphs receive them as they fall,
And dark oblivion soon absorbs them all.

So when a child, as playful children use,
Has burnt to tinder a stale last year's news,
The flame extinct, he views the roving fire—
There goes my lady, and there goes the squire,
There goes the parson, oh! illustrious spark,
And there, scarce less illustrious, goes the clerk!

* * *

The chief interest of *An Excelente Balade* is probably the fact that here in the self-satisfied mid-eighteenth century a clever lad responds to the beauty of old things, old words, old metres. The reader will detect at once the influence of Spenser who, let us remember, himself quite consciously used archaic words, words out of usage even in his own day.

Thomas Chatterton: 1752–1770

It was to the memory of Chatterton that Keats dedicated *Endymion*. Chatterton was the posthumous son of a poor schoolmaster in Bristol. In his earliest teens he became fascinated by old manuscripts, and indeed at thirteen he actually began to fake supposedly fifteenth-century ballads by a fictitious 'Thomas Rowley'. Skilful and imaginative as they were, he could not impose upon experienced readers such as Horace Walpole and Dr. Johnson. It is significant that his mother had taught him to read by using a black-letter Bible. He came to London, and in a lodging at Brooke Street, Holborn, he committed suicide by swallowing arsenic. D. G. Rossetti, in later life, conceived a high—probably too high—admiration for his genius.

68 An Excelente Balade of Charitie :

AS WROTEN BIE THE GODE PRIEST, THOMAS ROWLEIE,

1464

In Virginè the sultry sun 'gan sheen,
    And hot upon the meads did cast his ray;
The apple ruddied from its paly green,
    And the lush pear did bend the leafy spray;
    And pied chelandry [1] sang the livelong day;
'Twas now the pride, the manhood of the year,
And eke the ground was dight in its most deft aumere.[2]

The sun was gleaming in the mid of day,
    Dead still the air, and eke the welkin blue,
When from the sea arist in drear array
    A heap of clouds of sable sullen hue,
    The which full fast unto the woodland drew,
Shrouding at once the sunnès festive face,
And the black tempest swelled and gathered up apace.

Beneath a holm, fast by a pathway side
    Which did unto Saint Godwin's convent lead,
A hapless pilgrim moaning did abide,
    Poor in his view, ungentle in his weed,
    Long breast-full of the miseries of need.
Where from the hailstone could the palmer fly?
He had no hostel there, nor any convent nigh.

Look in his gloomèd face, his sprite there scan;
    How woe-begone, how withered, shrunken, dead!
Haste to thy church-glebe-house,[3] woe-stricken man!
    Haste to thy grave, thy only sleeping bed.
    Cold as the clay which will grow on thy head,
Are Charity and Love among high elves;
Knightès and barons live for pleasure and themselves.

[1] Goldfinch.   [2] Robe.   [3] Tomb.

The gathered storm is ripe; the big drops fall;
  The sun-burnt meadows smoke, and drink the rain;
The coming ghastness doth the cattle 'pall,
    And the full-flocks are driving o'er the plain;
    Dashed from the clouds the waters sweep again;
  The welkin opes; the yellow lightning flies;
And the hot fiery steam in mighty wreathings dies.

List! now the thunder's rattling noisy sound
  Moves slowly on, and then discharging clangs,
Shakes the high spire, and lost, expended, drowned,
    Still on the frighted ear of terror hangs;
    The winds are up; the lofty elm-tree swangs;
  Again the lightning and the thunder pours,
And the full clouds are burst at once in stony showers.

* * *

It is necessary to take at least a mouthful or two of Crabbe if only
because he was for a long time so much respected and praised. Byron
called him 'Nature's sternest painter but her best', because Crabbe
wrote about village life without sentimentalising it. Late in the nineteenth century, Edward Fitzgerald (the refashioner of *Omar*) strove to
re-establish Crabbe, choosing the second of these two fragments as
a perfect landscape-in-words.

Technically Crabbe goes right back to Pope, but it is as though someone were to serve mild-and-bitter in champagne glasses. The manner is
too genteel for the matter.

George Crabbe: 1754–1832

He was partly of Norfolk stock, and was born at Aldeburgh, Suffolk.
After assisting an apothecary, and 'practising surgery', he studied mid-
wifery and walked the London hospitals. In 1772 he became engaged to
a girl named Sarah Elmy, but his fortunes fell so low that for a time he
worked as a labourer, pushing butter-barrels, and, a little later, might
have starved if Sarah had not helped him with money. Suddenly, in 1781,
he was taken up as a poet by Edmund Burke, the great orator, and

thenceforth his life straightened out. He married Miss Elmy in 1783, having recently taken Holy Orders. He ended as rector of Trowbridge, Wiltshire, and as a poet of such popularity that John Murray paid him three thousand pounds for the copyright of his poetical works. During the last years of his life he became flirtatious, Sarah having died in 1813, and found comfort in opium.

69   The Cathedral (an extract)

In the Cathedral's gloom I pass'd my time,
Much in devotion, much in thought sublime;
There oft I paced the aisles, and watch'd the glow
Of the sun setting on the stones below,
And saw the failing light, that strove to pass
Through the dim coating of the storied glass,
Nor fell within, but till the day was gone
The red faint fire upon the window shone.
I took the key, and ofttimes chose to stay
Till all was vanish'd of the tedious day,
Till I perceived no light, nor heard a sound,
That gave me notice of a world around.

70   An Autumn Day (an extract)

There was a day, ere yet the autumn closed,
When, ere her wintry wars, the earth reposed,
When from the yellow weed the feathery crown,
Light as the curling smoke, fell slowly down;
When the wing'd insect settled in our sight,
And waited wind to recommence her flight;
When the wide river was a silver sheet,
And on the ocean slept th' unanchor'd fleet;
When from our garden, as we look'd above,
There was no cloud, and nothing seem'd to move.

* * *

Blake's loveliest lyrics can now be seen almost everywhere. He flamed like a comet across the Age of Reason and the poetic empire of

Pope. The *Song* was written in boyhood. Notice the 'Phœbus' line, one of the most excruciating examples of the eighteenth century at its worst. Obviously the boy-poet had difficulty in rhyming to 'cage' and fell back on a period-line which presumably did not seem to him out of tone with the rest of his unperiod lyric. The largest of these three poems is a magnificent specimen of that mood in which a poet feels, like the Hebrew prophets, that his burning ideas must be flung at the stupid world, whether or not it cares to meditate them. These are glowing lines.

William Blake: 1757–1827

Son of a London hosier. Even as a boy, William Blake 'took to' drawing, and at an early age he was apprenticed to a well-known engraver. In 1782 he married Catherine Boucher, who was the daughter of a Battersea market-gardener. His first poems were published, without success, during the next year.

The unique imaginative power of his work both as designer and as poet made it almost wholly foreign to his contemporaries. He was able to get a moderate living as an artist, but very few persons took any interest in his verse until, forty years after his death, Swinburne and the Rossetti brothers perceived and acclaimed his fiery genius. He died singing, and surrounded, he declared, by angelical beings. An age wiser than ours will probably believe him.

Most readers will realise with a shock that Blake was a contemporary of Wordsworth, Byron, Shelley and Keats: but at the time of his death he was not considered to be the poetic equal of Kirke White or Thomas Haynes Bayley.

71   Song

How sweet I roam'd from field to field
And tasted all the summer's pride,
Till I the Prince of Love beheld
Who in the sunny beams did glide!

He show'd me lilies for my hair,
And blushing roses for my brow;
He led me through his gardens fair
Where all his golden pleasures grow.

With sweet May dews my wings were wet,
And Phœbus fir'd my vocal rage;
He caught me in his silken net,
And shut me in his golden cage.

He loves to sit and hear me sing,
Then, laughing, sports and plays with me;
Then stretches out my golden wing,
And mocks my loss of liberty.

72   'I heard an Angel singing'

I heard an Angel singing
When the day was springing:
'Mercy, Pity, Peace
Is the world's release'.

Thus he sang all day
Over the new-mown hay,
Till the sun went down,
And haycocks looked brown.

I heard a Devil curse
Over the heath and the furze;
'Mercy could be no more
If there was nobody poor,

'And Pity no more could be,
If all were as happy as we'.
At his curse the sun went down,
And the heavens gave a frown.

(Down pour'd the heavy rain
Over the new reap'd grain;
And Misery's increase
Is Mercy, Pity, Peace.)

73   Blake's Testament

To see a World in a grain of sand,
And a Heaven in a wild flower,
Hold Infinity in the palm of your hand,
And Eternity in an hour.

A robin redbreast in a cage
Puts all Heaven in a rage.
A dove-house fill'd with doves and pigeons
Shudders Hell thro' all its regions.
A dog starv'd at his master's gate
Predicts the ruin of the State.
A horse misus'd upon the road
Calls to Heaven for human blood.
Each outcry of the hunted hare
A fibre from the brain does tear.
A skylark wounded in the wing,
A cherubim does cease to sing.
The game-cock clipt and arm'd for fight
Does the rising sun affright.
Every wolf's and lion's howl
Raises from Hell a Human soul.
The wild deer, wandering here and there,
Keeps the Human soul from care.
The lamb misus'd breeds public strife,
And yet forgives the butcher's knife.
He who shall hurt the little wren
Shall never be belov'd by men.
He who the ox to wrath has mov'd
Shall never be by woman lov'd.
The wanton boy that kills the fly
Shall feel the spider's enmity.
He who torments the chafer's sprite
Weaves a bower in endless night.
The caterpillar on the leaf
Repeats to thee thy mother's grief.
Kill not the moth nor butterfly,
For the Last Judgement draweth nigh.

He who shall train the horse to war
Shall never pass the polar bar.
The beggar's dog and widow's cat,
Feed them, and thou wilt grow fat.

The bat that flits at close of eve
Has left the brain that won't believe.
The owl that calls upon the night
Speaks the unbeliever's fright.
The gnat that sings his summer's song
Poison gets from Slander's tongue.
The poison of the snake and newt
Is the sweat of Envy's foot.
The poison of the honey-bee
Is the artist's jealousy.
A truth that's told with bad intent
Beats all the lies you can invent.

Joy and woe are woven fine,
A clothing for the soul divine;
Under every grief and pine
Runs a joy with silken twine.
It is right it should be so;
Man was made for joy and woe;
And when this we rightly know,
Thro' the world we safely go.

The babe is more than swaddling-bands;
Throughout all these human lands
Tools were made, and born were hands,
Every farmer understands.
Every tear from every eye
Becomes a babe in Eternity;
This is caught by Females bright,
And return'd to its own delight.
The bleat, the bark, bellow, and roar
Are waves that beat on Heaven's shore,
The babe that weeps the rod beneath
Writes revenge in realms of death.

He who mocks the infant's faith
Shall be mock'd in Age and Death.
He who shall teach the child to doubt
The rotting grave shall ne'er get out.
He who respects the infant's faith
Triumphs over Hell and Death.
The child's toys and the old man's reasons
Are the fruits of the two seasons.
The questioner, who sits so sly,
Shall never know how to reply.
He who replies to words of Doubt
Doth put the light of knowledge out.
A riddle, or the cricket's cry,
Is to Doubt a fit reply.
The emmet's inch and eagle's mile
Make lame Philosophy to smile.
He who doubts from what he sees
Will ne'er believe, do what you please.
If the sun and moon should doubt,
They'd immediately go out.

The prince's robes and beggar's rags
Are toadstools on the miser's bags.
The beggar's rags, fluttering in air,
Does to rags the heavens tear.
The poor man's farthing is worth more
Than all the gold on Afric's shore.
One mite wrung from the labourer's hands
Shall buy and sell the miser's lands;
Or, if protected from on high,
Does that whole nation sell and buy.
The soldier, arm'd with sword and gun,
Palsied strikes the summer's sun.
The strongest poison ever known
Came from Cæsar's laurel crown.
Nought can deform the human race
Like to the armour's iron brace.
When gold and gems adorn the plough
To peaceful arts shall Envy bow.

To be in a passion you good may do,
But no good if a passion is in you.
The whore and gambler, by the state
Licensed, build that nation's fate.
The harlot's cry from street to street
Shall weave Old England's winding-sheet.
The winner's shout, the loser's curse,
Dance before dead England's hearse.

Every night and every morn
Some to misery are born.
Every morn and every night
Some are born to sweet delight.
Some are born to sweet delight,
Some are born to endless night.
We are led to believe a lie
When we see with, not thro', the eye,
Which was born in a night, to perish in a night,
When the soul slept in beams of light.
God appears, and God is Light,
To those poor souls who dwell in Night;
But does a Human Form display
To those who dwell in realms of Day.

PART FIVE

Part Five

THE FIRST GREAT cycle of English poetry was now finished. It had died away in the wintry verse of the unenthusiastic eighteenth century: for William Blake is obviously a genius who had almost no kinship with his age. Reason had conquered romance, and the trees stood bare. But just as the Age of Reason caused its best inhabitants to realise that slavery was an abomination, and to attempt prison reform, so was a new age of poetry working steadily within the dark soil of that century. We have seen it beginning in Cowper, though he had not the strength of mind to rise out of his period. Few men have, very few: and Cowper may at any moment call a breeze 'the zephyr'. Then, too, came the French Revolution, that terrific upheaval of the subconscious mind. A French nobleman who survived it, said in late life—and with convincing sobriety—that life, he believed, could never have been more civilised or more exquisitely desirable than it was for an aristocrat in France just before the Revolution.

When our historians know more about spiritual forces and the manner in which they strike across the familiar world, we may perceive how the surging upward of the Common Man was another symptom of that change of soul which we can now so easily perceive in the poetry of the new age. An orthodox interpreter of the times would say, as we quite well know, that the French Revolution 'produced' Burns, Wordsworth and Shelley; but 'if we see *through*, not *with*, the eye', we shall discern that a force from the after-death 'world' was once more modifying the conditions of this material planet, and precipitated both the new poetry and the new social ideal.

Now, therefore, we are again to watch a Springtime in English verse. It could not be more aptly indicated than by the work of Scotland's National Poet. Robert Burns, who in our calendar succeeds to the place of Chaucer, characteristically announced that

> 'The rank is but the guinea-stamp:
> The man's the man for a' that!'

a fine, ringing, memorable phrase, and the best slogan of the democrat.

152

Burns was so natural a singer, and I use the word 'singer' because half his output is made up of lyrics to be sung, that he could scribble a pleasant enough string of verses on any subject at any time: but occasionally the wild tragic wind of deep poetry went sorrowing through his brain. A later poet, W. B. Yeats, drew the attention of poetry-lovers to those two lines which, once read, can never be forgotten. . . . .

> 'The pale moon is setting beyond the white wave,
> And time is setting wi' me, O'.

It is impossible to discover why the word 'white' is here so evocative.

That Chaucer, the first poet of Springtime, and Burns, his successor, should both have written about the daisy is, presumably, a fluke of literature.

Robert Burns: 1759–1796

Burns was the son of a farmer, a good but unfortunate man. The poet was born in a cottage about two miles from Ayr. At fifteen he was already overworked as a farm-hand. After the death of their father, Burns and his brother farmed one hundred and eighteen acres at Mossgiel. Subsequently he held a small Government post as an exciseman, but almost lost it by reason of his sympathy with the French revolutionaries. He could at any moment make a song about anything or anyone, as though gay and sad tunes were ever running in his brain, or make love to a lassie, or make short work of a whisky bottle. Coming back from a carouse with the local gentry, he fell asleep by the roadside. Rheumatic fever followed, and he died at Dumfries.

Sir Walter Scott says: 'His person was robust, his manners rustic, not clownish. . . . His countenance was more massive than it looks in any of the portraits. There was a strong expression of shrewdness in his lineaments; the eye alone indicated the poetic character and temperament. It was large and of a dark cast, and literally glowed when he spoke with feeling or interest. I never saw such another eye in a human head. His conversation expressed perfect self-confidence, without the least intrusive forwardness'.

Almost the earliest of those who fully recognised his genius was William Pitt. Professional critics may then have plucked up heart.

74 To a Mountain Daisy

On Turning One Down with the Plough in April, 1786

Wee, modest, crimson-tippèd flower,
Thou's met me in an evil hour;
For I maun crush amang the stoure
                Thy slender stem:
To spare thee now is past my power,
                Thou bonny gem.

Alas! it's no thy neibor sweet,
The bonny lark, companion meet,
Bending thee 'mang the dewy weet,
                Wi' speckled breast,
When upward springing, blithe, to greet
                The purpling east.

Cauld blew the bitter-biting north
Upon thy early, humble, birth;
Yet cheerfully thou glinted forth
                Amid the storm,
Scarce rear'd above the parent earth
                Thy tender form.

The flaunting flowers our gardens yield,
High sheltering woods and wa's maun shield;
But thou, beneath the random bield
                O' clod or stane,
Adorns the histie stibble-field,
                Unseen, alane.

There, in thy scanty mantle clad,
Thy snawie bosom sun-ward spread,
Thou lifts thy unassuming head
                In humble guise;
But now the *share* uptears thy bed,
                And low thou lies

Such is the fate of artless maid,
Sweet floweret of the rural shade!
By love's simplicity betray'd,
               And guileless trust,
Till she, like thee, all soil'd, is laid
               Low i' the dust.

Such is the fate of simple bard,
On life's rough ocean luckless starr'd!
Unskilful he to note the card
               Of prudent lore,
Till billows rage, and gales blow hard,
               And whelm him o'er!

Such fate to suffering worth is given,
Who long with wants and woes has striven,
By human pride or cunning driven
               To misery's brink,
Till, wrench'd of every stay but Heaven,
               He, ruin'd, sink!

Even thou who mourn'st the Daisy's fate,
That fate is thine—no distant date;
Stern Ruin's ploughshare drives, elate,
               Full on thy bloom,
Till, crush'd beneath the furrow's weight,
               Shall be thy doom!

75   Ae Fond Kiss

Ae fond kiss, and then we sever;
Ae fareweel, alas, for ever!
Deep in heart-wrung tears I'll pledge thee,
Warring sighs and groans I'll wage thee.

Who shall say that Fortune grieves him,
While the star of hope she leaves him?
Me, nae cheerfu' twinkle lights me;
Dark despair around benights me.

I'll ne'er blame my partial fancy,
Naething could resist my Nancy;
But to see her was to love her;
Love but her, and love for ever.

Had we never loved sae kindly,
Had we never loved sae blindly,
Never met—or never parted,
We had ne'er been broken-hearted.

Fare thee weel, thou first and fairest!
Fare thee weel, thou best and dearest!
Thine be ilka joy and treasure,
Peace, Enjoyment, Love, and Pleasure!

Ae fond kiss, and then we sever;
Ae fareweel, alas! for ever!
Deep in heart-wrung tears I'll pledge thee,
Warring sighs and groans I'll wage thee!

76   Green Grow the Rashes, O!

Green grow the rashes, O!
Green grow the rashes, O!
The sweetest hours that e'er I spend,
Are spent amang the lasses, O!

There's nought but care on every han',
  In every hour that passes, O;
What signifies the life o' man,
  An 'twere na for the lasses, O?

The warl'ly race may riches chase,
  And riches still may fly them, O;
And though at last they catch them fast,
  Their hearts can ne'er enjoy them, O.

But gie me a canny 1 hour at een,
  My arms about my dearie, O,
And warl'ly cares, and warl'ly men,
  May a' gae tapsalteerie,2 O.

1 Canny, lucky.   2 Tapsalteerie, topsy-turvy.

For you sae douce,[1] ye sneer at this,
  Ye're nought but senseless asses, O;
The wisest man the warl' e'er saw
  He dearly loved the lasses, O.

Auld Nature swears the lovely dears
  Her noblest work she classes, O;
Her 'prentice hand she tried on man,
  And then she made the lasses, O.

William Wordsworth: 1770–1850

One of many poets who studied at St. John's College, Cambridge. Predestined to be our nature-poet in chief, he was appropriately born at Cockermouth, Cumberland, the son of a local attorney. He travelled in France at a time when the Revolution was at its peak, or just past it; and the wild enthusiasm for an impossible freedom so captured his mind that he said of this period:

'Bliss was it in that dawn to be alive,
  And to be young was very heaven. . . .'

In early middle life he became so oppressively righteous and so unassailably respectable that most readers were thankful when a scholar discovered that Wordsworth had had an affair with a French girl named Annette. He hushed it up.

In 1799, prematurely solemn and middle-aged, he settled with his delightful sister Dorothy at Grasmere, in the Lake District. In 1802 he married Mary Hutchinson. Forty-one years later he succeeded Southey as poet-laureate, having throughout this long stretch of time continued to pour out 'effusions' in verse, all of which he regarded with equal respect. Wordsworth is one of the countless poets who, finely inspired in their earlier years, contract a habit of versifying which they are not strong enough to discontinue.

1 Douce, grave.

The publication of *Lyrical Ballads* (in 1798 and in collaboration with Coleridge) is a lighthouse in our literary history. Wordsworth, vitalised by the best part of the French revolutionary spirit, shook himself clear of the eighteenth century and deliberately set about to show that poetry need not be 'elevated' or peruked, and can be made out of the simplest themes expressed in the simplest language. He did not escape the opposite of the high-falutin', and wrote a larger number of ludicrous lines than ever came from any other important poet. Had he taken himself even a little less solemnly, he could not have begun a sonnet with the invocation—

'Spade! with which Wilkinson hath tilled his soil',

or have referred to 'The Street which from Oxford hath borrowed its name', or have addressed a stuffed parrot as

'O bird of the saloon'!

Wordsworth takes himself so solemnly that it is difficult to be patient with him: but, although to us he may seem to sentimentalise Nature, and to ignore her ferocity, he could sometimes achieve a 'sublimity' which is for ever beyond the range of the humorous man. He had the qualities of his defects.

77   From *The Prelude*

From early days,
Beginning not long after that first time
In which, a Babe, by intercourse of touch
I held mute dialogues with my Mother's heart,
I have endeavoured to display the means
Whereby this infant sensibility,
Great birthright of our being, was in me
Augmented and sustained. Yet is a path
More difficult before me; and I fear
That in its broken windings we shall need
The chamois' sinews, and the eagle's wing:

For now a trouble came into my mind
From unknown causes. I was left alone
Seeking the visible world, nor knowing why,
The props of my affections were removed,
And yet the building stood, as if sustained
By its own spirit! All that I beheld
Was dear, and hence to finer influxes
The mind lay open to a more exact
And close communion. Many are our joys
In youth, but oh! what happiness to live
When every hour brings palpable access
Of knowledge, when all knowledge is delight,
And sorrow is not there! The seasons came,
And every season wheresoe'er I moved
Unfolded transitory qualities,
Which, but for this most watchful power of love,
Had been neglected; left a register
Of permanent relations, else unknown.
Hence life, and change, and beauty, solitude
More active ever than 'best society'—
Society made sweet as solitude
By silent inobtrusive sympathies,
And gentle agitations of the mind
From manifold distinctions, difference
Perceived in things, where, to the unwatchful eye,
No difference is, and hence, from the same source,
Sublimer joy; for I would walk alone,
Under the quiet stars, and at that time
Have felt whate'er there is of power in sound
To breathe an elevated mood, by form
Of image unprofaned; and I would stand,
If the night blackened with a coming storm,
Beneath some rock, listening to notes that are
The ghostly language of the ancient earth,
Or make their dim abode in distant winds.
Thence did I drink the visionary power;
And deem not profitless those fleeting moods
Of shadowy exultation: not for this

That they are kindred to our purer mind
And intellectual life; but that the soul,
Remembering how she felt, but what she felt
Remembering not, retains an obscure sense
Of possible sublimity, whereto
With growing faculties she doth aspire,
With faculties still growing, feeling still
That whatsoever point they gain, they yet
Have something to pursue.

78   Inside of King's College Chapel, Cambridge

Tax not the royal Saint with vain expense,
With ill-matched aims the Architect who planned—
Albeit labouring for a scanty band
Of white robed Scholars only—this immense
And glorious Work of fine intelligence!
Give all thou canst; high Heaven rejects the lore
Of nicely-calculated less or more;
So deemed the man who fashioned for the sense
These lofty pillars, spread that branching roof
Self-poised, and scooped into ten thousand cells,
Where light and shade repose, where music dwells
Lingering—and wandering on, as loth to die;
Like thoughts whose very sweetness yieldeth proof
That they were born for immortality.

The English mind had become sadly puritan and utilitarian when a great poet's first thought as he walked into the glory of King's Chapel was that business men might consider its beauty to be a wanton extravagance of funds.

In the lines which come next, Wordsworth shows how even a confession of slight inebriety can be made without loss of self-esteem.

79   From *The Prelude*

Beside the pleasant Mill of Trompington
I laughed with Chaucer in the hawthorn shade;
Heard him, while birds were warbling, tell his tales
Of amorous passion. And that gentle Bard,
Chosen by the Muses for their Page of State—
Sweet Spenser, moving through his clouded heaven
With the moon's beauty and the moon's soft pace,
I called him Brother, Englishman, and Friend!
Yea, our blind Poet, who in his later day,
Stood almost single; uttering odious truth—
Darkness before, and danger's voice behind,
Soul awful—if the earth has ever lodged
An awful soul—I seemed to see him here
Familiarly, and in his scholar's dress
Bounding before me, yet a stripling youth—
A boy, no better, with his rosy cheeks
Angelical, keen eye, courageous look,
And conscious step of purity and pride.
Among the band of my compeers was one
Whom chance had stationed in the very room
Honoured by Milton's name. O temperate Bard!
Be it confest that, for the first time, seated
Within thy innocent lodge and oratory,
One of a festive circle, I poured out
Libations, to thy memory drank, till pride
And gratitude grew dizzy in a brain
Never excited by the fumes of wine
Before that hour, or since. Then, forth I ran
From the assembly; through a length of streets,
Ran, ostrich-like, to reach our chapel door
In not a desperate or opprobrious time,
Albeit long after the importunate bell
Had stopped, with wearisome Cassandra voice
No longer haunting the dark winter night.

It is in a poem such as this sonnet on Venice that we see Wordsworth as a poet of the first magnitude, and this is partly because he has forgotten himself in his fine, funereal theme.

161

80   On the Extinction of the Venetian Republic

Once did She hold the gorgeous east in fee;
And was the safeguard of the west: the worth
Of Venice did not fall below her birth.
Venice, the eldest Child of Liberty,
She was a maiden City, bright and free;
No guile seduced, no force could violate;
And, when she took unto herself a Mate,
She must espouse the everlasting Sea.
And what if she had seen those glories fade,
Those titles vanish, and that strength decay;
Yet shall some tribute of regret be paid
When her long life hath reached its final day;
Men are we, and must grieve when even the Shade
Of that which once was great, is passed away.

1802.

Here again is the poet in a mood which eclipsed his egoism: and in a poem which is little known.

81   To The Men of Kent

October, 1803

Vanguard of Liberty, ye men of Kent,
Ye children of a Soil that doth advance
Her haughty brow against the coast of France,
Now is the time to prove your hardiment!
To France be words of invitation sent!
They from their fields can see the countenance
Of your fierce war, may ken the glittering lance
And hear you shouting forth your brave intent.
Left single, in bold parley, ye, of yore,
Did from the Norman win a gallant wreath;
Confirmed the charters that were yours before;—
No parleying now! In Britain is one breath;
We all are with you now from shore to shore;—
Ye men of Kent, 'tis victory or death!

And here are two of the 'crown jewels'.

82   Composed upon Westminster Bridge, Sept. 3, 1802

Written on the roof of a coach, on my way to France

Earth has not anything to show more fair:
Dull would he be of soul who could pass by
A sight so touching in its majesty:
This City now doth, like a garment, wear
The beauty of the morning; silent, bare,
Ships, towers, domes, theatres, and temples lie
Open unto the fields, and to the sky;
All bright and glittering in the smokeless air.
Never did sun more beautifully steep
In his first splendour, valley, rock, or hill;
Ne'er saw I, never felt, a calm so deep!
The river glideth at his own sweet will:
Dear God! the very houses seem asleep;
And all that mighty heart is lying still!

83   Calais, August 1802

Is it a reed that's shaken by the wind,
Or what is it that ye go forth to see?
Lords, lawyers, statesmen, squires of low degree,
Men known, and men unknown, sick, lame, and blind,
Post forward all, like creatures of one kind,
With first-fruit offerings crowd to bend the knee
In France, before the new-born Majesty.
'Tis ever thus. Ye men of prostrate mind,
A seemly reverence may be paid to power;
But that's a loyal virtue, never sown
In haste, nor springing with a transient shower:
When truth, when sense, when liberty were flown,
What hardship had it been to wait an hour?
Shame on you, feeble Heads, to slavery prone!

The last of our Wordsworth poems is of peculiar interest, seeing that the poet once remarked that he had written no love poetry because his 'passions were too strong'. Shakespeare was not so careful.

84   A Lover's Dark Fancy

Strange fits of passion have I known:
And I will dare to tell,
But in the Lover's ear alone,
What once to me befell.

When she I loved looked every day
Fresh as a rose in June,
I to her cottage bent my way,
Beneath an evening-moon.

Upon the moon I fixed my eye,
All over the wide lea;
With quickening pace my horse drew nigh
Those paths so dear to me.

And now we reached the orchard-plot;
And, as we climbed the hill,
The sinking moon to Lucy's cot
Came near, and nearer still.

In one of those sweet dreams I slept,
Kind Nature's gentlest boon!
And all the while my eyes I kept
On the descending moon.

My horse moved on: hoof after hoof
He raised, and never stopped:
When down behind the cottage roof,
At once, the bright moon dropped.

What fond and wayward thoughts will slide
Into a Lover's head!
'O mercy'! to myself I cried,
'If Lucy should be dead'!

Robert Southey: 1774–1843

Robert Southey must always be of some interest because he wrote
rhymeless epics which held the young Shelley spellbound, and because,

when he abandoned the principles of the French Revolution, he became
the chief target for Byron's invective.

Southey, to his credit, was expelled from Westminster School
because he protested against flogging. He then proceeded, in 1792, to
Balliol College, Oxford. He was married twice. The rest of his long
life is an honourable record of extraordinary industry. There have been
few writers who worked equally hard. He wrote what is still an absorb-
ing *Life of Nelson*: and among his voluminous works we poetry lovers
must remember his *Life*, and edition, of Cowper. In 1813 the laureate-
ship was offered to Sir Walter Scott. He refused it, and Southey stepped
into the purple.

Living mostly at Keswick, Southey became known as one of 'the
Lake Poets', a group which easily survived the contempt of the lingering eighteenth-century minds.

This poem by Southey shows at least that he could transcend the
mode of his period: and that is always a notable achievement.

85   The Widow

Sapphics

Cold was the night wind, drifting fast the snow fell,
Wide were the downs and shelterless and naked,
When a poor Wanderer struggled on her journey,
   Weary and way-sore.

Drear were the downs, more dreary her reflections;
Cold was the night-wind, colder was her bosom:
She had no home, the world was all before her,
   She had no shelter.

Fast o'er the heath a chariot rattled by her,
'Pity me'! feebly cried the lonely wanderer;
'Pity me, strangers! lest with cold and hunger
   Here I should perish.

'Once I had friends,—though now by all forsaken!
Once I had parents,—they are now in Heaven!
I had a home once—I had once a husband—
   Pity me, strangers!

'I had a home once—I had once a husband—
I am a widow, poor and broken-hearted'!
Loud blew the wind, unheard was her complaining,
    On drove the chariot.

Then on the snow she laid her down to rest her;
She heard a horseman, 'Pity me'! she groan'd out;
Loud was the wind, unheard was her complaining,
    On went the horseman.

Worn out with anguish, toil and cold and hunger,
Down sunk the Wanderer, sleep had seized her senses;
There did the traveller find her in the morning;
    God had released her.

    Bristol, 1795.

Walter Savage Landor: 1775–1864

Here was another violent poet. Something of his temperament is shown in the report that once when he was living in Italy, Landor threw his cook out of the window and, as the man fell, cried remorsefully, 'Oh, my poor violets'! 'Savage', however, was merely his mother's maiden name. Leigh Hunt likened him to 'a stormy mountain pine which should produce lilies'; and Swinburne considered that he stood 'midway between Byron and Shelley—about as far above the former as below the latter'. There is, however, no resemblance among the three poets.

He was educated at Rugby and at Trinity College, Oxford. He 'saw some fighting as a volunteer in Spain'—that is, against Napoleon. At various times he lived at Bath, Bristol, Wells, Como, Pisa, Florence,—and at Florence he died.

Robert Browning said of him 'Whatever he may profess, the thing he really loves is a pretty girl to talk nonsense with'. He transformed his Welsh mistresses, whose names were Jones and Jane, into Ione and Ianthe.

Still, few cameos can be so perfectly cut as the following nutshell-pastoral. . . .

86   Alciphron and Leucippe

An ancient chestnut's blossoms threw
Their heavy odour over two:
Leucippe, it is said, was one,
The other then was Alciphron.
'Come, come! why should we stand beneath
This hollow tree's unwholesome breath',
Said Alciphron, 'here's not a blade
Of grass or moss, and scanty shade.
Come; it is just the hour to rove
In the lone dingle shepherds love,
There, straight and tall, the hazel twig
Divides the crooked rock-held fig,
O'er the blue pebbles where the rill
In winter runs, and may run still.
Come then, while fresh and calm the air,
And while the shepherds are not there'.

Leucippe

But I would rather go when they
Sit round about and sing and play.
Then why so hurry me? for you
Like play and song and shepherds too.

Alciphron

I like the shepherds very well,
And song and play, as you can tell.
But there is play I sadly fear,
And song I would not have you hear.

Leucippe

What can it be? what can it be?

Alciphron

To you may none of them repeat
The play that you have played with me,
The song that made your bosom beat.

Leucippe

Don't keep your arm about my waist.

Alciphron

Might not you stumble?

Leucippe

Well then, do.
But why are we in all this haste?

Alciphron

To sing.

Leucippe

Alas! and not play too?

87   The Little Dainty Poet

Pleasant it is to wink and sniff the fumes
The little dainty poet blows for us,
Kneeling in his soft cushion at the hearth,
And patted on the head by passing maids.
Who would discourage him? who bid him off?
Invidious or morose! Enough, to say
(Perhaps too much unless 'tis mildly said)
That slender twigs send forth the fiercest flame,
Not without noise, but ashes soon succeed,
While the broad chump leans back against the stones,
Strong with internal fire, sedately breathed,
And heats the chamber round from morn till night.

Edward Thomas observed of this poem: 'Landor is, however, no overwhelming authority, and he probably wants us to believe that he is the honest "broad chump"—in vain'.

88   Milton

Will mortals never know each other's station
Without the herald? O abomination!
Milton, even Milton, rankt with living men!
Over the highest Alps of mind he marches,
And far below him spring the baseless arches
Of Iris, colouring dimly lake and fen.

89 Age

Death, tho' I see him not, is near
And grudges me my eightieth year.
Now, I would give him all these last
For one that fifty have run past.
Ah! he strikes all things, all alike,
But bargains: those he will not strike.

Thomas Campbell: 1777–1844

It is strange that a Scotish poet, born in Glasgow, should have inflated the patriotic British trumpet which had been blown to such rousing purpose, long ago, by Michael Drayton. Campbell first achieved success with a didactic poem of eighteenth-century flavour, *The Pleasures of Hope*, which 'owed much to the fact that it dealt with topics near to men's hearts, with the French Revolution, the partition of Poland, and with negro slavery' (*Enc. Brit.*). When the Russians captured Warsaw in 1831, he said 'Poland preys on my heart night and day': and he helped to found an 'Association of Friends of Poland'.

He 'took an active share in the foundation of the University of London', and was thrice elected rector of Glasgow University. His wife died in 1828. One of his sons perished in infancy, the other became insane. He himself died in Boulogne, and his body was buried in Westminster Abbey.

It is useless to seek for some undetected masterpiece in Campbell's poetry. When he was not writing, better than any one else, what we may call national poems, he was merely a remnant of the later eighteenth century. *The Battle* may be hackneyed, but it is magnificently wrought and will repay the minutest examination. And here at long last is a companion-piece to Drayton's *Agincourt*.

90 The Battle of the Baltic

Of Nelson and the North
Sing the glorious day's renown,
When to battle fierce came forth
All the might of Denmark's crown,

And her arms along the deep proudly shone;
By each gun the lighted brand
In a bold determined hand,
And the Prince of all the land
Led them on.

Like leviathans afloat
Lay their bulwarks on the brine,
While the sign of battle flew
On the lofty British line:
It was ten of April morn by the chime:
As they drifted on their path
There was silence deep as death,
And the boldest held his breath
For a time.

But the might of England flush'd
To anticipate the scene;
And her van the fleeter rush'd
O'er the deadly space between:
'Hearts of oak'! our captains cried, when each gun
From its adamantine lips
Spread a death-shade round the ships,
Like the hurricane eclipse
Of the sun.

Again! again! again!
And the havoc did not slack,
Till a feeble cheer the Dane
To our cheering sent us back;—
Their shots along the deep slowly boom:—
Then ceased—and all is wail,
As they strike the shatter'd sail,
Or in conflagration pale
Light the gloom.

Out spoke the victor then
As he hail'd them o'er the wave:
'Ye are brothers! ye are men!
And we conquer but to save:—

So peace instead of death let us bring;
But yield, proud foe, thy fleet,
With the crews, at England's feet,
And make submission meet
To our King'. . . .

Now joy, old England, raise!
For the tidings of thy might,
By the festal cities' blaze,
Whilst the wine-cup shines in light!
And yet amidst that joy and uproar,
Let us think of them that sleep
Full many a fathom deep,
By thy wild and stormy steep,
Elsinore!

Leigh Hunt: 1784–1856

In the literary world, as a writer may slowly discover, there are skilful, unpretentious and likeable men not one of whom ever becomes the Most Popular Boy in the School. Why these particular writers are overlooked or vilified we shall never understand. Leigh Hunt must have been one of the kindliest and most intelligent of men, and a writer not lacking in energy or sense-of-beauty, and yet throughout his long life he was baited by the forgotten animalculæ of journalism. Even toward the end of that gentle life he suffered caricature at the hands of Dickens, who should never be pardoned for his hypocrisy in doing the vile deed and in then disclaiming it.

Hunt, moreover, has the finest of all records as a literary critic. In 1820 he was championing those unpopular upstarts, Shelley and Keats. In 1850 he had only to read Rossetti's *juvenilia* to acclaim immediately the rise of a new poet. These facts alone should establish him as a very rare mind.

He was a Christ's Hospital boy. In 1811 he was prosecuted unsuccessfully for protesting against flogging in the army. In 1813 he was imprisoned for two years because he had referred (in print) to the Prince Regent as 'a fat Adonis of fifty'.

He introduced Shelley to Keats and was present, with Byron, at the burning of Shelley's drowned body on the shore of Italy.

There is no more beautiful example than this of a life dedicated to art, music, literature and the cause of humanity. He was buried at Kensal Rise; but it is impossible that a personality so attractive and a writer so delightful should not soon sail splendidly into an appreciation which, in his lifetime, he only half-tasted. In his earlier years the prejudice against him was political. He challenged Privilege. In our time the political prejudice blows from the opposite quarter.

This grasshopper sonnet was written one evening in friendly competition with Keats, whose own sonnet begins 'The poetry of earth is never dead. . . .'

91   To the Grasshopper and the Cricket

(First published in 'The Examiner', September 21, 1817; reprinted 1818, 1832, 1844–60)

> Green little vaulter in the sunny grass,
>   Catching your heart up at the feel of June,
>   Sole voice that's heard amidst the lazy noon,
> While ev'n the bees lag at the summoning brass;—
> And you, warm little housekeeper, who class
>   With those who think the candles come too soon,
>   Loving the fire, and with your tricksome tune
> Nick the glad silent moments as they pass;—
>
> Oh sweet and tiny cousins, that belong,
>   One to the fields, the other to the hearth,
> Both have your sunshine; both, though small, are strong
>   At your clear hearts; and both were sent on earth
> To sing in thoughtful ears this natural song—
>   In doors and out,—summer and winter,—Mirth.

* * *

The astonishing brilliance of the following translation can be assessed only by those who are already word-perfect in the original. It is difficult to believe that Hunt's version could ever be even equalled: though we have to overlook the now-comic word 'female'.

92 Paulo and Francesca

('Inferno', Canto V, 70–142)

Scarce had I learnt the names of all that press
Of knights and dames, than I beheld a sight
Nigh reft my wits for very tenderness.

'O guide'! I said, 'fain would I, if I might,
Have speech with yonder pair, that hand in hand
Seem borne before the dreadful wind so light'.

'Wait', said my guide, 'until thou seest their band
Sweep round. Then beg them, by that love, to stay;
And they will come, and hover where we stand'.

Anon the whirlwind flung them round that way;
And then I cried, 'Oh, if I ask nought ill,
Poor weary souls, have speech with me, I pray'.

As doves, that leave some bevy circling still,
Set firm their open wings, and through the air
Sweep homewards, wafted by their pure good will;

So broke from Dido's flock that gentle pair,
Cleaving, to where we stood, the air malign;
Such strength to bring them had a loving prayer.

The female spoke. 'O living soul benign',
She said, 'thus, in this lost air, visiting
Us, who with blood stained the sweet earth divine;

'Had we a friend in heaven's eternal King,
We would beseech him keep thy conscience clear,
Since to our anguish thou dost pity bring.

'Of what it pleaseth thee to speak and hear,
To that we also, till this lull be o'er
That falleth now, will speak and will give ear.

'The place where I was born is on the shore,
Where Po brings all his rivers to depart
In peace, and fuse them with the ocean floor.

'Love, that soon kindleth in a gentle heart,
Seized him thou look'st on for the form and face,
Whose end still haunts me like a rankling dart.

'Love, which by love will be denied no grace,
Gave me a transport in my turn so true,
That lo! 'tis with me, even in this place.

'Love brought us to one grave. The hand that slew,
Is doomed to mourn us in the pit of Cain'.
Such were the words that told me of those two.

Downcast I stood, looking so full of pain
To think how hard and sad a case it was,
That my guide asked what held me in that vein.

His voice aroused me: and I said, 'Alas!
All their sweet thoughts then, all the steps that led
To love, but brought them to this dolorous pass'.

Then turning my sad eyes to theirs, I said,
'Francesca, see—these human cheeks are wet—
Truer and sadder tears were never shed.

'But tell me. At the time when sighs were sweet,
What made thee strive no longer?—hurried thee
To the last step where bliss and sorrow meet'?

'There is no greater sorrow', answered she,
'And this thy teacher here knoweth full well,
Than calling to mind joy in misery.

'But since thy wish be great to hear us tell
How we lost all but love, tell it I will,
As well as tears will let me. It befell,

'One day, we read how Lancelot gazed his fill
At her he loved, and what his lady said.
We were alone, thinking of nothing ill.

'Oft were our eyes suspended as we read,
And in our cheeks the colour went and came;
Yet one sole passage struck resistance dead.

'Twas where the lover, moth-like in his flame,
Drawn by her sweet smile, kissed it. O then, he
Whose lot and mine are now for aye the same,

'All in a tremble, on the mouth kissed *me*.
The book did all. Our hearts within us burned
Through that alone. That day no more read we',

While thus one spoke, the other spirit mourned
With wail so woful, that at his remorse
I felt as though I should have died. I turned
Stone-stiff; and to the ground, fell like a corse.

George Gordon (Lord) Byron: 1788–1824

The Dictionary of National Biography states roundly that the poet was the 'son of a profligate' and of 'an hysterical Scotch heiress'. He was educated at Aberdeen grammar school and afterwards, having succeeded to the title in 1798, at Harrow and at Trinity College, Cambridge. He married Isabella Milbanke in 1815 but, a year later, was accused by her of insanity and was by her deserted. The real cause of this break-up was his 'immoral' relations with his half-sister.

His literary success came early and was of the fairy-story type, the sudden wide success of which all beginners dream. It was, indeed, of Byron that 'he woke to find himself famous' was first said. Pursued by creditors and by amorous women he took up the pose of being the Great Man Misunderstood and, as has been unkindly observed, trailed over much of Europe the 'pageant of his bleeding heart'. There was much of the star-actor in him, and something of the poet: much of the cad, and a little of the hero. As all the world knows, he joined the Greeks in their military struggle for independence and died, of marsh-fever, at Missolonghi.

As a literary influence he remained potent in England until his contemporaries had died. In 1824, Tennyson, as a lad of fifteen, went about all one day murmuring 'Byron is dead, Byron is dead'. His influence in Europe, even in Russia, lasted much longer. Moreover, a critic so sound as Matthew Arnold confidently predicted that by 1900 people would perceive that the greatest English poets of the past century were Byron and Wordsworth. By 1900, however, Blake, Keats, Shelley, Tennyson, Browning, Rossetti, Swinburne and Arnold himself stood far higher than Byron in critical assessment. His huge reputation was of the kind which depends mysteriously upon personality. With the disappearance of the personality which inspires it, such a reputation suddenly or gradually collapses, never again to coagulate.

His vast success on the Continent demonstrates that it is second-rate verse which can best be translated.

First, the romantic Byron. . . .

93   So, We'll go no more a-roving

So, we'll go no more a-roving
    So late into the night,
Though the heart be still as loving,
    And the moon be still as bright.

For the sword outwears its sheath,
    And the soul wears out the breast,
And the heart must pause to breathe,
    And love itself have rest.

Though the night was made for loving,
    And the day returns too soon,
Yet we'll go no more a-roving
    By the light of the moon.

                                    1817.

Then, the hearty good fellow. . . .

94   To Thomas Moore

My boat is on the shore,
    And my bark is on the sea;
But before I go, Tom Moore,
    Here's a double health to thee!

Here's a sigh to those who love me,
  And a smile to those who hate;
And, whatever sky's above me,
  Here's a heart for every fate.

Though the ocean roar around me,
  Yet it still shall bear me on;
Though a desert should surround me,
  It hath springs that may be won.

Were't the last drop in the well,
  As I gasp'd upon the brink,
Ere my fainting spirit fell,
  'Tis to thee that I would drink.

With that water, as this wine,
  The libation I would pour
Should be—peace with thine and mine,
  And a health to thee, Tom Moore.

July, 1817.

Lastly, the true Byron: worldly, cynical, smart, brilliant—everything, in a word, which precludes the genuine poetic emotion. His essays in serious poetry ring false because he was not simple enough to be a poet. His rhetoric, however, could still entrance, in early years, so late a poet as Harold Monro.

95   From *Don Juan*

(Canto the Thirteenth)

I now mean to be serious;—it is time,
  Since laughter now-a-days is deem'd too serious;
A jest at Vice by Virtue's call'd a crime,
  And critically held as deleterious:
Besides, the sad's a source of the sublime,
  Although when long a little apt to weary us;
And therefore shall my lay soar high and solemn,
As an old temple dwindled to a column.

The Lady Adeline Amundeville
    ('Tis an old Norman name, and to be found
In pedigrees, by those who wander still
    Along the last fields of that Gothic ground)
Was high-born, wealthy by her father's will,
    And beauteous, even where beauties most abound,
In Britain—which of course true patriots find
The goodliest soil of body and of mind.

I'll not gainsay them; it is not my cue;
    I'll leave them to their taste, no doubt the best:
An eye's an eye, and whether black or blue,
    Is no great matter, so 't is in request;
'Tis nonsense to dispute about a hue—
    The kindest may be taken as a test.
The fair sex should be always fair; and no man
Till thirty, should perceive there's a plain woman.

And after that serene and somewhat dull
    Epoch, that awkward corner turn'd for days
More quiet, when our moon's no more at full,
    We may presume to criticise or praise;
Because indifference begins to lull
    Our passions, and we walk in wisdom's ways;
Also because the figure and the face
Hint, that 'tis time to give the younger place.

I know that some would fain postpone this era,
    Reluctant as all placemen to resign
Their post; but theirs is merely a chimera,
    For they have pass'd life's equinoctial line:
But then they have their claret and Madeira
    To irrigate the dryness of decline;
And county meetings, and the parliament,
And debt, and what not, for their solace sent.

And is there not religion, and reform,
    Peace, war, the taxes, and what's called the 'Nation'?
The struggle to be pilots in a storm?
    The landed and the monied speculation?

The joys of mutual hate to keep them warm,
  Instead of love, that mere hallucination?
Now hatred is by far the longest pleasure;
Men love in haste, but they detest at leisure.

Rough Johnson, the great moralist, profess'd,
  Right honestly, 'he liked an honest hater'!—
The only truth that yet has been confest
  Within these latest thousand years or later.
Perhaps the fine old fellow spoke in jest:—
  For my part, I am but a mere spectator,
And gaze where'er the palace or the hovel is,
Much in the mode of Goethe's Mephistopheles;

But neither love nor hate in much excess;
  Though 't was not once so. If I sneer sometimes,
It is because I cannot well do less,
  And now and then it also suits my rhymes.
I should be very willing to redress
  Men's wrongs, and rather check than punish crimes,
Had not Cervantes, in that too true tale
Of Quixote, shown how all such efforts fail.

Of all tales 't is the saddest—and more sad,
  Because it makes us smile: his hero's right,
And still pursues the right;—to curb the bad
  His only object, and 'gainst odds to fight
His guerdon: 't is his virtue makes him mad!
  But his adventures form a sorry sight;—
A sorrier still is the great moral taught
By that real epic unto all who have thought.

Redressing injury, revenging wrong,
  To aid the damsel and destroy the caitiff
Opposing singly the united strong,
  From foreign yoke to free the helpless native:—
Alas! must noblest views, like an old song
  Be for mere fancy's sport a theme creative,
A jest, a riddle, Fame through thin and thick sought!
And Socrates himself but Wisdom's Quixote!

> Cervantes smiled Spain's chivalry away;
>   A single laugh demolish'd the right arm
> Of his own country;—seldom since that day
>   Has Spain had heroes. While Romance could charm,
> The world gave ground before her bright array;
>   And therefore have his volumes done such harm,
> That all their glory, as a composition,
> Was dearly purchased by his land's perdition. . . .

Percy Bysshe Shelley: 1792–1822

One of the aristocratic poets, although he swiftly became what we should now call a 'communist'. At Eton he was tormented, and was known as 'mad Shelley'. He was expelled from Oxford for writing a pamphlet, now worth much fine gold, with the title 'The Necessity of Atheism'. A monument in University College, Oxford, strangely records his fruitless contact with the University.

He was a child of the age, of the French Revolution, of the supposition that all men were perfectible and, if free, would become perfect. He first married Harriet Westbrook, who could not keep up with him; who succumbed (it seems) to one of his friends who was an 'ordinary decent chap', as Mr. Priestley would say; and, failing again, she committed suicide. The Victorians held Shelley responsible for this unhappy event, and accordingly tempered their delight in the new music and the other-world aspiration which characterised his poetry. The poet, after Harriet's death, married the daughter of two Persons of Importance in Their Own Time,—William Godwin, a Frenchified philosopher, and Mary Wollstonecraft, a pioneer of Womens' Rights.

He was drowned in a storm off Spezzia, in Italy, and when his body was recovered from the sea, they found in one of his coat-pockets a copy of Æschylus. Byron and Leigh Hunt witnessed the cremation of his body on the sea-shore. Trelawney, another witness, took care lest Byron should snatch the skull from the pyre, perhaps to use it as an inkpot. The heart, it is reported, would not catch fire.

Shelley has for some time been out of favour. Since his opinions were as red as possible, it must be the admixture of poetry in his nature to which the men of the moment object. Be that as it may, Shelley made words more translucent than any former poet had done; and in many ways his art is comparable with Turner's. If poetry could benefit by illustration, then Turner ought certainly to 'illustrate' Shelley. There is a quite new music or verbal melody in this work: something not achieved by any earlier poet except, perhaps, Coleridge.

96   From *Prometheus Unbound*

Asia

My soul is an enchanted boat,
    Which, like a sleeping swan, doth float
Upon the silver waves of thy sweet singing;
    And thine doth like an angel sit
    Beside a helm conducting it,
Whilst all the winds with melody are ringing,
    It seems to float ever, for ever,
    Upon that many-winding river,
    Between mountains, woods, abysses,
    A paradise of wildernesses!
Till, like one in slumber bound,
Borne to the ocean, I float down, around,
Into a sea profound, of ever-spreading sound:

    Meanwhile thy spirit lifts its pinions
    In music's most serene dominions;
Catching the winds that fan that happy heaven.
    And we sail on, away, afar,
    Without a course, without a star,
But, by the instinct of sweet music driven;
    Till through Elysian garden islets
    By thee, most beautiful of pilots,
    Where never mortal pinnace glided,
    The boat of my desire is guided:
Realms where the air we breathe is love,
Which in the winds and on the waves doth move,
Harmonising this earth with what we feel above.

We have pass'd Age's icy caves,
And Manhood's dark and tossing waves,
And Youth's smooth ocean, smiling to betray:
Beyond the glassy gulphs we flee
Of shadow-peopled Infancy,
Through Death and Birth, to a diviner day;
A paradise of vaulted bowers,
Lit by downward-gazing flowers,
And watery paths that wind between
Wildernesses calm and green,
Peopled by shapes too bright to see,
And rest, having beheld; somewhat like thee;
Which walk upon the sea, and chaunt melodiously!

97 To Jane: 'The Keen Stars were Twinkling'

The keen stars were twinkling,
And the fair moon was rising among them,
Dear Jane!
The guitar was tinkling,
But the notes were not sweet till you sung them
Again.

As the moon's soft splendour
O'er the faint cold starlight of heaven
Is thrown,
So your voice most tender
To the strings without soul had then given
Its own.

The stars will awaken,
Though the moon sleep a full hour later,
To-night;
No leaf will be shaken
Whilst the dews of your melody scatter
Delight.

Though the sound overpowers,
Sing again, with your dear voice revealing
    A tone
Of some world far from ours,
Where music and moonlight and feeling
    Are one.

98   Love's Philosophy

The Fountains mingle with the River
    And the Rivers with the Ocean,
The winds of Heaven mix for ever
    With a sweet emotion;
Nothing in the world is single;
    All things by a law divine
In one spirit meet and mingle.
    Why not I with thine?—

See the mountains kiss high Heaven
    And the waves clasp one another;
No sister-flower would be forgiven
    If it disdained its brother,
And the sunlight clasps the earth
    And the moonbeams kiss the sea:
What is all this sweet work worth
    If thou kiss not me?

99   From *Prometheus Unbound*

The Moon

As in the soft and sweet eclipse,
When soul meets soul on lovers' lips,
High hearts are calm, and brightest eyes are dull;
    So when thy shadow falls on me,
    Then am I mute and still, by thee
Covered; of thy love, Orb most beautiful,
    Full, oh, too full!

Thou art speeding round the sun
Brightest world of many a one;
Green and azure sphere which shinest
With a light which is divinest
Among all the lamps of Heaven
To whom life and light is given;
I, thy crystal paramour
Borne beside thee by a power
Like a polar Paradise,
Magnet-like of lovers' eyes;
I, a most enamoured maiden
Whose weak brain is overladen
With the pleasure of her love,
Maniac-like around thee move
Gazing, an insatiate bride,
On thy form from every side
Like a Mænad, round the cup
Which Agave lifted up
In the weird Cadmæn forest.
Brother, wheresoe'er thou soarest
I must hurry, whirl and follow
Through the heavens wide and hollow,
Sheltered by the warm embrace
Of thy soul from hungry space,
Drinking from thy sense and sight
Beauty, majesty, and might,
As a lover or chameleon
Grows like what it looks upon,
As a violet's gentle eye
Gazes on the azure sky
Until its hue grows like what it beholds,
As a gray and watery mist
Glows like solid amethyst
Athwart the western mountain it enfolds,
When the sunset sleeps
Upon its snow.

Even so lately as forty years ago there was a small and current volume of verses called *Poetical Remains of Kirke White, Shelley and Keats*. Kirke White, who died at the age of twenty-one, was regarded for some time as the best poet of the three. He was, in reality, writing in the manner of the Day Before Yesterday, and in consequence has long since dropped out of the running. John Clare, on the other hand, has recently been revived, not without justification.

John Clare: 1793–1864

Clare, like Burns, was of the working class, and he too was partly inspired to write verse by reading the poetry of James Thomson. He was the son of a Northamptonshire labourer, and was born at Helpstone, Peterborough. As a child he tended sheep and geese. A few years later he acquired at a night-school the rudiments of education. Subsequently he became a pot-boy, a gardener, a militiaman, a lime-burner and a camper with the raggle-taggle gipsies-O.

When his verses brought fame, he took to drink and soon reduced himself to destitution. In 1837 he was placed in a private asylum; and in 1864 he died in the lunatic asylum at Northampton. His work, as coming from a farm labourer, excited the insecure interest and thoughtless praise which, in our own time, were given to W. H. Davies because he had really and truly been a tramp: but the reader will probably find something of the charm of an old brown-ink engraving in the following extract from one of Clare's descriptive poems.

100   Recollections after an Evening Walk

Just as the even-bell rang, we set out
To wander the fields and the meadows about;
And the first thing we mark'd that was lovely to view,
Was the sun hung on nothing, just bidding adieu:
He seem'd like a ball of pure gold in the west,
In a cloud like a mountain blue, dropping to rest;
The skies all around him were ting'd with his rays,
And the trees at a distance seem'd all on a blaze,

Till, lower and lower, he sank from our sight,
And the blue mist came creeping with silence and night.
The woodman then ceas'd with his hatchet to hack,
And bent away home with his kid on his back;
The mower too lapt up his scythe from our sight,
And put on his jacket, and bid us good-night;
The thresher once lumping, we heard him no more,
He left his barn-dust, and had shut up his door;
The shepherd had told all his sheep in his pen,
And humming his song, sought his cottage agen:
But the sweetest of all seeming music to me,
Were the songs of the clumsy brown-beetle and bee;
The one was seen hast'ning away to his hive,
The other was just from his sleeping alive,—
'Gainst our hats he kept knocking as if he'd no eyes,
And when batter'd down he was puzzled to rise.
The little gay moth too was lovely to view,
A-dancing with lily-white wings in the dew;
He whisk'd o'er the water-pudge flirting and airy,
And perch'd on the down-headed grass like a fairy.
And then came the snail from his shell peeping out,
As fearful and cautious as thieves on the rout;
The sly jumping frog too had ventur'd to tramp,
And the glow-worm had just 'gun to light up his lamp;
To sip of the dew the worm peep'd from his den,
But dreading our footsteps soon vanish'd agen;
And numbers of creatures appear'd in our sight,
That live in the silence and sweetness of night,
Climbing up the tall grasses or scaling the bough,
But these were all nameless, unnotic'd till now.
And then we wound round 'neath the brook's willow row,
And look'd at the clouds that kept passing below;
The moon's image too, in the brook we could see't,
As if 'twas the other world under our feet;
And we listen'd well pleas'd at the guggles and groans
The water made passing the pebbles and stones.
And then we turn'd up by the rut-rifted lane,
And sought for our cot and the village again:

For night gather'd round, and shut all from the eye,
And a black sultry cloud crept all over the sky;
The dew on the bush, soon as touch'd it would drop,
And the grass 'neath our feet was as wet as a mop:
And, as to the town we approach'd very fast,
The bat even popp'd in our face as he past;
And the crickets sang loud as we went by the house,
And by the barn-side we saw many a mouse
Quirking round for the kernels that, litter'd about,
Were shook from the straw which the thresher hurl'd out.
And then we came up to our cottage once more,
And shut out the night-dew, and lock'd up the door:
The dog bark'd a welcome, well-pleas'd at our sight,
And the owl o'er our cot flew, and whoop'd a 'good-night'.

Clare's jigging couplets are a good example of a metre which does not suit the subject. It was, in fact, a metre which had already been employed in the writing of facetious and gossiping 'rhymed epistles'.

John Keats: 1795–1821

To those who cannot believe that Shakespeare of Stratford wrote his own plays, we can always advance the story of Keats who was the son of a livery stableman in Moorfields, London. Burns, it was true, was a ploughman, and James Hogg was rightly called 'The Ettrick Shepherd', but their work is always simple, not elaborate, and apparently not drawn from a rich intellect. Keats, although much influenced by Spenser, Milton and Dryden, is certainly a Shakespearean type of poet.

At first Keats proposed to become a surgeon, and he did in fact work as a dresser at Guy's Hospital. After a short time he decided to try his fortune as a writer—indeed, as a poet, poetry being at this time remarkably saleable—but he soon had to rely for support upon two or three friends. His three published books were scornfully reviewed, chiefly because he was associated with Leigh Hunt and therefore with Liberalism.

He contracted tuberculosis, and in hope of benefit from the climate, sailed for Italy in September 1820. His condition was aggravated by a seemingly hopeless but devouring passion for Miss Fanny Brawne; and in February 1821 he died at Rome. Both in their philosophical and their literary interest his lively unselfconscious letters, fortunately preserved by their recipients, are as remarkable as even his poems are. That is to say, they are in the front rank.

Remember that Keats, 'a jealous honourer' of Spenser, follows his earliest master by—nearly always—meaning the syllable 'ed' at the end of a verb to be sounded as a separate syllable. Otherwise, he writes 'wither'd', and so on.

101   La Belle Dame Sans Merci

O, what can ail thee, knight-at-arms,
   Alone and palely loitering:
The sedge is wither'd from the lake,
   And no birds sing.

O, what can ail thee, knight-at-arms,
   So haggard and so woe-begone?
The squirrel's granary is full,
   And the harvest's done.

I see a lilly on thy brow.
   With anguish moist and fever dew;
And on thy cheek a fading rose
   Fast withereth too.

'I met a lady in the meads
   Full beautiful, a faery's child;
Her hair was long, her foot was light,
   And her eyes were wild.

I made a garland for her head,
   And bracelets too, and fragrant zone;
She look'd at me as she did love,
   And made sweet moan.

I set her on my pacing steed,
   And nothing else saw all day long;
For sideways would she lean, and sing
   A faery's song.

She found me roots of relish sweet,
  And honey wild, and manna dew;
And sure in language strange she said,
  I love thee true.

She took me to her elfin grot,
  And there she gaz'd and sigh'd full sore,
And there I shut her wild wild eyes
  With kisses four.

And there she lulléd me asleep,
  And there I dream'd, ah woe betide,
The latest dream I ever dream'd
  On the cold hill side.

I saw pale kings, and princes too,
  Pale warriors, death-pale were they all;
They cry'd—'La belle Dame sans merci
  Hath thee in thrall'!

I saw their starv'd lips in the gloam
  With horrid warning gapéd wide,
And I awoke, and found me here
  On the cold hill side.

And this is why I sojourn here
  Alone and palely loitering,
Though the sedge is wither'd from the lake,
  And no birds sing'.

102   Sonnet

To Sleep

O soft embalmer of the still midnight,
  Shutting, with careful fingers and benign,
Our gloom-pleas'd eyes, embower'd from the light,
  Enshaded in forgetfulness divine:
O soothest Sleep! if so it please thee, close
  In midst of this thine hymn my willing eyes,
Or wait the 'Amen', ere thy poppy throws
  Around my bed its lulling charities.

Then save me, or the passéd day will shine
Upon my pillow, breeding many woes,—
Save me from curious Conscience, that still hoards
Its strength for darkness, burrowing like a mole;
Turn the key deftly in the oiléd wards,
And seal the hushéd Casket of my Soul.

Although Conscience hoarding its strength until in darkness it can most effectively trouble us is, undoubtedly, a little far-fetched and a phrase dictated by the need of rhyme, the image is at least ingenious and almost justifies itself.

103   To Autumn

Season of mists and mellow fruitfulness,
Close bosom-friend of the maturing sun:
Conspiring with him how to load and bless
With fruit the vines that round the thatch-eves run;
To bend with apples the moss'd cottage-trees,
And fill all fruit with ripeness to the core:
To swell the gourd, and plump the hazel shells
With a sweet kernel; to set budding more,
And still more, later flowers for the bees,
Until they think warm days will never cease,
For Summer has o'er-brimm'd their clammy cells.

Who hath not seen thee oft amid thy store?
Sometimes whoever seeks abroad may find
Thee sitting careless on a granary floor,
Thy hair soft-lifted by the winnowing wind;
Or on a half-reap'd furrow sound asleep,
Drows'd with the fume of poppies, while thy hook
Spares the next swath and all its twinéd flowers:
And sometimes like a gleaner thou dost keep
Steady thy laden head across a brook:
Or by a cyder-press, with patient look,
Thou watchest the last oozings hours by hours.

Where are the songs of Spring? Ay, where are they?
Think not of them, thou hast thy music too,—
While barréd clouds bloom the soft-dying day,
And touch the stubble-plains with rosy hue;

Then in a wailful choir the small gnats mourn
Among the river sallows, borne aloft
Or sinking as the light wind lives or dies;
And full-grown lambs loud bleat from hilly bourn;
Hedge-crickets sing; and now with treble soft
The red-breast whistles from a garden-croft;
And gathering swallows twitter in the skies.

In Stanza two (lines 2 and 3) there is an ugly example of what is called *enjambement*,—find/Thee. The ugliness comes from the fact that 'find thee' are words which go intimately together and that they are artificially split by the emphasis given to 'find' as the end-word of a line. In other words, the second line would naturally end with 'find thee', but to read it so is to ruin the rhyme-pattern. It is for the same reason (that the two words are essentially one word) that a split infinitive is a flaw in style.

To introduce John Keats (or Junkets, as Leigh Hunt nicknamed him) without giving the slightest sample of his humour and high spirits is to misrepresent a writer who might have manifested in due time a Shakespearian width of genius. Here, therefore, are some playful verses in the manner of Spenser, the point about them being, of course, that his friend Brown was in all respects the opposite of Keats's description. These verses were part of a long gossipping letter, but so skilled are they and so amusing that they do no discredit to Keats as a serious poet.

104   Spenserian Stanzas on Charles Brown

He is to weet a melancholy carle:
Thin in the waist, with bushy head of hair,
As hath the seeded thistle when in parle
It holds the Zephyr, ere it sendeth fair
Its light balloons into the summer air;
Therto his beard had not begun to bloom,
No brush had touch'd his chin or razor sheer;
No care had touch'd his cheek with mortal doom,
But new he was and bright as scarf from Persian loom.

Ne caréd he for wine, or half-and-half,
Ne caréd he for fish or flesh or fowl,

And sauces held he worthless as the chaff;
He sdeigned the swine-head at the wassail-bowl;
Ne with lewd ribbalds sat he cheek by jowl;
Ne with sly Lemans in the scorner's chair;
But after water-brooks this Pilgrim's soul
Panted, and all his food was woodland air
Though he would oft-times feast on gilliflowers rare.

The slang of cities in no wise he knew,
Tipping the wink to him was heathen Greek;
He sipp'd no olden Tom or ruin blue,
Or nantz or cherry-brandy, drank full meek
By many a damsel hoarse and rouge of cheek;
Nor did he know each agéd watchman's beat,
Nor in obscuréd purlieus would he seek
For curléd Jewesses, with ankles neat,
Who as they walk abroad make tinkling with their feet.

105 Sonnet

'BRIGHT STAR': SECOND VERSION

Written in Severn's copy of Shakespeare's Poems, September 30, 1820

Bright star, would I were stedfast as thou art—
    Not in lone splendour hung aloft the night
And watching, with eternal lids apart,
    Like nature's patient, sleepless Eremite,
The moving waters at their priestlike task
    Of pure ablution round earth's human shores,
Or gazing on the new soft-fallen mask
    Of snow upon the mountains and the moors—
No—yet still stedfast, still unchangeable,
    Pillow'd upon my fair love's ripening breast,
To feel for ever its soft fall and swell,
    Awake for ever in a sweet unrest,
Still, still to hear her tender-taken breath,
And so live ever—or else swoon to death.

This deep-felt, rich-toned poem makes a lovely reverberation on a
later page of this book, as the reader will find with interest when he
comes to the poems of Thomas Hardy.

PART SIX

Part Six

THE EMOTIONAL SHOCK of the French Revolution abruptly wiped out the eighteenth century; and after the kaleidoscopic effects of Napoleon, the old century exerted no further influence upon men's lives and thoughts. We can perceive how sudden was the change if we reflect that, despite the date of her birth (1775), Jane Austen impresses everybody as being a nineteenth-century author. It is true that over-massive prose persisted here and there for perhaps three decades, but Hazlitt was winning; and there is nothing left of the eighteenth century in any of the varied poets who represent this Second Summer of English Poetry. It is a long and magnificent summer. It stretches almost exactly across the eighty-one years of Queen Victoria's life,—from 1819 to 1900.

The major event in English history between the battle of Waterloo (1815) and the outbreak of the Second Boer War (1899) was not the industrialisation of the country, for that had been in dismal progress for at least two generations; nor was it the passing of the Reform Bill in 1832, although to privileged persons it seemed like the down-

194

fall of England; nor the rapid spread of railways; nor the economic success of Free Trade; nor the imperialisation of India: no, the major event of this great, energetic, thronged, ever-changing epoch was the impact of scientific thinking, as exemplified by Darwin, upon the naïf belief in 'revealed religion' which had satisfied Milton, Nelson and Wordsworth. There is no limiting the radiation of a great spiritual event, an event, that is, which alters man's opinion of himself and of his place in the universe: and the world-wide tragedies of the present century show clearly what is one result of deciding that the spiritual world is a fable.

Naturally enough, the new perceptions had a hard struggle against the inborn inertia of most men: but decade by decade the scientific view of existence gained ground because it had within it so much incontestable truth. Meanwhile, however, right up to the end of the nineteenth century the majority of English (and American) folk accepted, though with diminishing conviction, the evangelical type of Christianity which Wesley had disseminated throughout our land. This involved a strong sense of sin: and avoidance of sin led to an almost universal cult of respectability; but so lofty an ideal, involving so many forms of abstinence, inevitably produced the notorious hypocrisy of the Victorians. Since few persons are natural saints, the rest of humanity could maintain the façade of saintliness only by disacknowledging a number of its deeds. Even the prurient attitude toward sex-pleasure was not so vile as the refusal of many pious persons to consider the un-Christian source of their comfortable incomes.

Of the eighteen poets in this section two were Roman Catholics (Patmore and Hopkins), five were almost orthodox Christians of other creeds (Barnes, Longfellow, Browning, Christina Rossetti and Stevenson), one (Blunt) was a Mahommedan, three were mystics (Emerson, Tennyson and Whitman), five were sceptics (Fitzgerald, Meredith, Arnold, Morris and Swinburne), while Gabriel Rossetti had at least some belief in spiritualism, and as for Lord Lytton I do not know enough to classify him. The point of this tabulation is that the religious issue was so vital during the nineteenth century that it is possible to segregate its writers within various camps of thought.

The age is the Age of Tennyson. Not since Pope had any English poet influenced so many writers over so long a period; and once again did a large part of the literary world feel that poetry had achieved perfection. Not only was Tennyson a poetic genius of the first order, he was also, as the ensuing examples of his work will show, an artificer with a skill in words which none but Milton had equalled. Moreover, in Tennyson we find more definitely than in any other poet an expression of the intellectual disturbance caused by the advance of science. This was indeed an age of great poetry. It is probable that when posterity makes a final assessment of the Victorian harvest, men will say that the two greatest among all these poets were Alfred Tennyson and Walt Whitman.

We should note that at this time a poet who aimed at the highest kind of reputation was solely a poet, and wrote either very little prose or none at all. We should also note how strongly American poets, now that their mighty civilisation was taking clear form, contribute to the poetry written in our language.

Let us begin—chronologically—with

William Barnes: 1801–1886

He was the son of a farmer who farmed in the Vale of Blackmoor. In 1818 (when so many major poets were alive) he entered the office of a Dorchester solicitor. We hear next that he is executing woodcuts. Somewhat late in life, but following the poetic tradition, he went to St. John's College, Cambridge. In the end he became a clergyman, and for his last twenty-four years was rector of Came. He wrote books about that dialect of Dorset which he used with so much charm in his poems: and so hotly did he loathe all words of Latin origin that he strove to find 'Saxon' words for every object. Thus, an omnibus was to him a 'folkwain'. The rural life which these two poems describe is probably that of about a hundred years ago when, in the West of England, railways were still rarities and when personality had not been obliterated by the newspaper and the cinema.

106 Harvest Hwome

THE VU'ST PEART. THE SUPPER

Since we wer striplèns, naïghbour John,
The good wold merry times be gone:
But we do like to think upon
    What we've a-zeed an' done.
When I wer up a hardish lad,
At harvest hwome the work-vo'k had
Sich suppers, they wer jumpèn mad
    Wi' feästen an' wi' fun.

At uncle's, I do mind, woone year,
I zeed a vill o' hearty cheer;
Fat beef an' pudden, eäle an' beer,
    Vor ev'ry workman's crop;
An' after they'd a-gie'd God thanks,
They all zot down, in two long ranks,
Along a teäble-bwoard o' planks,
    Wi' uncle at the top.

An' there, in platters, big and brown,
Wer red fat beäcon, an' a roun'
O' beef wi' gravy that would drown
    A little rwoastèn pig;
Wi' beäns an' teäties vull a zack,
An' cabbage that would meäke a stack,
An' puddèns brown, a-speckled black
    Wi' figs, so big's my wig.

An' uncle, wi' his elbows out,
Did carve, an' meäke the gravy spout;
An' aunt did gi'e the mugs about
    A-frothèn to the brim.
Pleätes werden then ov e'then ware;
They ate off pewter, that would bear
A knock; or wooden trenchers, square,
    Wi' zalt-holes at the rim.

An' zoo they munch'd their hearty cheer,
An' dipp'd their beards in frothy-beer,
An' laugh'd, an' jok'd—they couldden hear
   What woone another zaid.
An' all o'm drink'd, wi' woone accword,
The wold vo'k's health: an' beät the bwoard,
An' swung their eärms about, an' roar'd,
   Enough to crack woone's head.

107   Harvest Hwome

SECOND PEART. WHAT THEY DID AFTER SUPPER

Zoo after supper wer a-done,
They clear'd the teäbles, an' begun
To have a little bit o' fun,
   As long as they mid stop.
The wold woones took their pipes to smoke,
An' tell their teäles, an' laugh an' joke,
A-lookèn at the younger vo'k,
   That got up vor a hop.

Woone screäp'd away, wi' merry grin,
A fiddle stuck below his chin;
An' woone o'm took the rollèn pin,
   An' beät the fryèn pan.
An' tothers, dancèn to the soun',
Went in an' out, an' droo an' roun',
An' kick'd, an' beät the tuèn down,
   A-laughèn, maid an' man.

An' then a maïd, all up tip-tooe,
Vell down; an' woone o'm wi' his shoe
Slit down her pocket-hole in two,
   Vrom top a-most to bottom.
An' when they had a-danc'd enough,
They got a-playèn blindman's buff,
An' sard the maïdens pretty rough,
   When woonce they had a-got em.

An' zome did drink, an' laugh, an' roar,
An' lots o' teäles they had in store,
O' things that happen'd years avore
   To them, or vo'k they know'd.
An' zome did joke, an' zome did zing,
An' meäke the girt wold kitchen ring;
Till uncle's cock, wi' flappèn wing,
   Stratch'd out his neck an' crow'd.

Ralph Waldo Emerson: 1803–1882

The famous American essayist, whose pungent short-sentenced prose
was new in his day and perhaps was characteristically American, issued
into outer things (as the Irish poet Æ would have said) in Boston,
Massachusetts. He came of puritan preaching stock, but fortunately discovered in himself a vein of clear fine mysticism which caused him to
outsoar mere puritanism and ethics. Indeed, he is among the earliest
of great writers to respond to the works of Swedenborg and Jacob
Boehme, and to the deep philosophy of the Upanishads and the Vedanta.
He is the noblest of the small group of American writers who have been
called Transcendentalists; and if the universe is a vision which is seen
with least falseness by the mystic, Emerson's diamond-clear essays will
again and again excite new enthusiasm.

He spent the evening of his life serenely at Concord, and it was in
Sleepy Hollow, a cemetery in a grove near the village of Concord, that
his body was buried.

Terminus is written in an idiom remarkably like that of his prose at
its best, and it is probably too ejaculatory to come into the sphere of
pure poetry: but Emerson has at least recorded a poetic emotion of
old age which had not hitherto been expressed by any one.

108   Terminus

It is time to be old,
To take in sail:—
The god of bounds,
Who sets to seas a shore,

Came to me in his fatal rounds,
And said—'No more!
No farther shoot
Thy broad ambitious branches, and thy root.
Fancy departs: no more invent;
Contract thy firmament
To compass of a tent.
There's not enough for this and that,
Make thy option which of two;
Economise the failing river,
Not the less revere the Giver,
Leave the many and hold the few.
Timely wise accept the terms,
Soften the fall with wary foot;
A little while
Still plan and smile,
And,—fault of novel germs,—
Mature the unfallen fruit.
Curse, if thou wilt, thy sires,
Bad husbands of their fires,
Who, when they gave thee breath,
Failed to bequeath
The needful sinew stark as once,
The Baresark marrow to thy bones,
But left a legacy of ebbing veins,
Inconstant heat and nerveless reins,—
Amid the Muses, left thee deaf and dumb,
Amid the gladiators, halt and numb'.

As the bird trims her to the gale,
I trim myself to the storm of time,
I man the rudder, reef the sail,
Obey the voice at eve obeyed at prime:
'Lowly faithful, banish fear,
Right onward drive unharmed:
The port, well worth the cruise, is near,
And every wave is charmed'.

1867.

109 Suum Cuique

The rain has spoiled the farmer's day;
Shall sorrow put my books away?
Thereby are two days lost.
Nature shall mind her own affairs,
I will attend my proper cares,
In rain, or sun, or frost.

1841.

Henry Wadsworth Longfellow: 1807–1882

Born at Portland, Maine, he travelled extensively in Europe, learning languages; married in 1831; and, having become Professor of Belles-Lettres and Modern Languages at Harvard University, he lived a quiet high-souled scholarly life, and toward the end of it, collected numerous academic honours. Poe vigorously—and it must be said, effectively—accused him of plagiarism: and even his Red Indian epic, *Hiawatha*, owes much to the Finnish epic, *Kalevala*: much, but not everything, for in the best portions of *Hiawatha*, Longfellow somehow succeeds in evoking the very smell of the mould and the air in 'the forest primeval'. He was too conscious that 'life is real, life is earnest' to please readers who do not read for moral stimulus, but during the last fifty years he has been absurdly ignored or despised. A moderate familiarity with his work should make any one realise that Longfellow was a man of genuinely poetic mind. Charles Kingsley said that Longfellow's was 'the most beautiful face he had ever seen',—a verdict which late-life photographs render easily understandable.

In order to counteract, if possible, the prejudice of readers who think Longfellow's verse to be so simple as not to merit examination, let us first savour a well-rendered winter landscape expressed in a rare and attractive metre.

110 The Golden Mile-stone

Leafless are the trees; their purple branches
Spread themselves abroad, like reefs of coral,
Rising silent
In the Red Sea of the Winter sunset.

From the hundred chimneys of the village,
Like the Afreet in the Arabian story,
  Smoky columns
Tower aloft into the air of amber.

At the window winks the flickering fire-light;
Here and there the lamps of evening glimmer,
  Social watch-fires
Answering one another through the darkness.

On the hearth the lighted logs are glowing,
And like Ariel in the cloven pine-tree
  For its freedom
Groans and sighs the air imprisoned in them.

By the fireside there are old men seated,
Seeing ruined cities in the ashes,
  Asking sadly
Of the Past what it can ne'er restore them.

By the fireside there are youthful dreamers,
Building castles fair, with stately stairways,
  Asking blindly
Of the Future what it cannot give them.

By the fireside tragedies are acted
In whose scenes appear two actors only,
  Wife and husband,
And above them God the sole spectator.

By the fireside there are peace and comfort,
Wives and children, with fair, thoughtful faces,
  Waiting, watching
For a well-known footstep in the passage.

Each man's chimney is his Golden Mile-stone;
Is the central point, from which he measures
  Every distance
Through the gateways of the world around him.

In his farthest wanderings still he sees it;
Hears the talking flame, the answering night-wind,
  As he heard them
When he sat with those who were, but are not.

Happy he whom neither wealth nor fashion,
Nor the march of the encroaching city,
   Drives an exile
From the hearth of his ancestral homestead.

We may build more splendid habitations,
Fill our rooms with paintings and with sculptures,
   But we cannot
Buy with gold the old associations!

111 Song (from the Spanish)

If thou art sleeping, maiden,
 Awake, and open thy door,
'Tis the break of day, and we must away,
 O'er meadow, and mount, and moor.

Wait not to find thy slippers,
 But come with thy naked feet;
We shall have to pass through the dewy grass,
 And waters wide and fleet.

And then there is Longfellow at his most popular, perhaps at his most hackneyed, for I do not know whether the *Blacksmith* is still as familiar as it was at the turn of the century. It is only possible to despise the simple emotions and the simple phrasing of this old poem if we have become too clever for the world of poetry. What is amiss with the poem? It is hackneyed; it is simple; it records a feeling that might well up in a man if he overheard the mother's voice within the daughter's; and the poet sees a moral lesson in the manly life which he has been describing: but a poem becomes hackneyed because it has touched many hearts; Homer is, for the most part, a simple, direct poet; there is no reason why a poet should ignore an emotion which might be aroused within any man; and, lastly, there is no intellectual disgrace in trying to increase by reflection and admiration the fortitude with which we must be ready to face the sorrow of life. When poets are afraid of being simple, they are in danger of altogether divorcing themselves from the springs of poetry.

112 The Village Blacksmith

Under a spreading chestnut tree
  The village smithy stands;
The smith, a mighty man is he,
  With large and sinewy hands;
And the muscles of his brawny arms
  Are strong as iron bands.

His hair is crisp, and black, and long,
  His face is like the tan;
His brow is wet with honest sweat,
  He earns whate'er he can,
And looks the whole world in the face,
  For he owes not any man.

Week in, week out, from morn till night,
  You can hear his bellows blow;
You can hear him swing his heavy sledge,
  With measured beat and slow,
Like a sexton ringing the village bell,
  When the evening sun is low.

And children coming home from school
  Look in at the open door:
They love to see the flaming forge,
  And hear the bellows roar,
And catch the burning sparks that fly
  Like chaff from a threshing floor.

He goes on Sunday to the church,
  And sits among his boys;
He hears the parson pray and preach,
  He hears his daughter's voice,
Singing in the village choir,
  And makes his heart rejoice.

It sounds to him like her mother's voice,
  Singing in Paradise!
He needs must think of her once more,
  How in the grave she lies;
And with his hard, rough hand he wipes
  A tear out of his eyes.

Toiling,—rejoicing,—sorrowing,
  Onward through life he goes;
Each morning sees some task begin,
  Each evening sees it close;
Something attempted, something done,
  Has earned a night's repose.

Thanks, thanks to thee, my worthy friend,
  For the lesson thou hast taught!
Thus at the flaming forge of life
  Our fortunes must be wrought:
Thus on its sounding anvil shaped
  Each burning deed and thought!

* * *

We must turn now to another American, but a wild genius, an un-respectable bohemian.

Edgar Allan Poe: 1809–1849

Born at Boston, Massachusetts. His father was a lawyer, his mother an English actress; and in view of his turgid imagination it is tempting to conceive that Mrs. Poe was one who would tear a passion to tatters. The legal strain shows clearly in *The Philosophy of Composition*, a brilliant essay in which Poe pretends to reveal a purely rational and calculating system behind the making of his most famous piece,—*The Raven*.

As a young man he developed a passion for gambling and drink. He enlisted, and for two years served in the American Army. From 1835 onwards he worked as contributor or editor on many magazines and newspapers in the States: and it was during this period that he guaranteed to solve within twenty-four hours any cryptogram in any of several languages.

His success came early, first with his unapproached tales of horror, and then with *The Raven*, for which he received only ten dollars. In 1835 he married his cousin Virginia Clemm, who was then fourteen. She died in 1847, and the poet, who drank spirits raw, never again took any care of himself.

He had the high honour of being translated by Baudelaire.

This first poem is a lustrous example of poetic precocity. Poe wrote it when he was thirteen: and there is no evidence that he subsequently retouched an original. The lyric is, in fact, just one of those premature and fleeting manifestations of the soul to which I referred in an early portion of this book.

113   To Helen

Helen, thy beauty is to me
  Like those Nicean barks of yore
That gently, o'er a perfumed sea,
  The weary way-worn wanderer bore
  To his own native shore.

On desperate seas long wont to roam,
  Thy hyacinth hair, thy classic face,
Thy Naiad airs have brought me home
  To the glory that was Greece,
And the grandeur that was Rome.

Lo! in yon brilliant window niche
  How statue-like I see thee stand,
  The agate lamp within thy hand!
Ah, Psyche, from the regions which
  Are holy-land.

* * *

When Swinburne wrote of Poe as 'the American mocking-bird whose songs were all too few', he must have been thinking of Poe's delight in almost exactly repeating a melodious line. This characteristic of his style is used in *The Raven* and again in *Ulalume*. He stated that in *Ulalume* he set out to use only sad or eerie vowels and words: but in the rich, liquid quality of the third and fourth stanzas he has, very wisely, varied the sound scheme. On the other hand, there can be nowhere any assemblage of lines comparable in gloominess of tone with the twenty-three lines which end the poem.

114 Ulalume

The skies they were ashen and sober;
   The leaves they were crisped and sere—
   The leaves they were withering and sere;
It was night in the lonesome October
   Of my most immemorial year;
It was hard by the dim lake of Auber,
   In the misty mid region of Weir—
It was down by the dank tarn of Auber,
   In the ghoul-haunted woodland of Weir.

Here once, through an alley Titanic
   Of cypress, I roamed with my Soul—
   Of cypress, with Psyche, my Soul.
Those were days when my heart was volcanic
   As the scoriac rivers that roll—
   As the lavas that restlessly roll
Their sulphurous currents down Yaanek
   In the ultimate climes of the pole—
That groan as they roll down Mount Yaanek
   In the realms of the boreal pole.

Our talk had been serious and sober,
   But our thoughts they were palsied and sere—
   Our memories were treacherous and sere—
For we knew not the month was October,
   And we marked not the night of the year—
   (Ah, night of all nights in the year!)
We noted not the dim lake of Auber—
   (Though once we had journeyed down here)—
Remembered not the dank tarn of Auber,
   Nor the ghoul-haunted woodland of Weir.

And now, as the night was senescent
   And star-dials pointed to morn—
   As the star-dials hinted of morn—
At the end of our path a liquescent
   And nebulous lustre was born,

Out of which a miraculous crescent
   Arose with a duplicate horn—
Astarte's bediamonded crescent
   Distinct with its duplicate horn.

And I said—'She is warmer than Dian:
   She rolls through an ether of sighs—
   She revels in a region of sighs:
She has seen that the tears are not dry on
   These cheeks, where the worm never dies,
And has come past the stars of the Lion
   To point us the path to the skies—
   To the Lethean peace of the skies—
Come up, in despite of the Lion,
   To shine on us with her bright eyes—
Come up through the lair of the Lion,
   With love in her luminous eyes'.

But Psyche, uplifting her finger,
   Said—'Sadly this star I mistrust—
   Her pallor I strangely mistrust:—
Oh, hasten!—oh, let us not linger!
   Oh, fly!—let us fly!—for we must'.
In terror she spoke, letting sink her
   Wings till they trailed in the dust—
In agony sobbed, letting sink her
   Plumes till they trailed in the dust—
   Till they sorrowfully trailed in the dust.

I replied—'This is nothing but dreaming:
   Let us on by this tremulous light!
   Let us bathe in this crystalline light!
Its Sybilic splendor is beaming
   With Hope and in Beauty to-night:—
   See!—it flickers up the sky through the night!
Ah, we safely may trust to its gleaming,
   And be sure it will lead us aright—
We safely may trust to a gleaming,
   That cannot but guide us aright,
   Since it flickers up to Heaven through the night'.

Thus I pacified Psyche and kissed her,
  And tempted her out of her gloom—
  And conquered her scruples and gloom;
And we passed to the end of the vista,
  But were stopped by the door of a tomb—
  By the door of a legended tomb;
And I said—'What is written, sweet sister,
  On the door of this legended tomb'?
  She replied—'Ulalume—Ulalume—
  'Tis the vault of thy lost Ulalume!'

Then my heart it grew ashen and sober
  As the leaves that were crisped and sere—
  As the leaves that were withering and sere,
And I cried—'It was surely October
  On *this* very night of last year
  That I journeyed—I journeyed down here—
  That I brought a dread burden down here—
  On this night of all nights in the year,
  Ah! what demon has tempted me here?
Well I know, now, this dim lake of Auber—
  This misty mid region of Weir—
Well I know, now, this dark tarn of Auber,
  This ghoul-haunted woodland of Weir'.

* * *

The force of Poe's personality as a writer is the more astonishing in
view of the mediocre intellectual life of the United States in his time.
And now—like Jove to an assembly on Olympus—comes the master-
poet of the whole period. . . .

Alfred (Lord) Tennyson: 1809–1892

His father was rector of Somersby, Lincolnshire. He matriculated at
Trinity College, Cambridge, where he became a good classics-reader.
His early work failed, and after the 1832 volume he waited ten years
before again publishing. The 1842 volume, which contained (as we
should expect) much of his finest work, was an instantaneous success:
and thenceforward he made a Royal Progress through the Victorian

century. In 1850, when Wordsworth died, he became Poet Laureate and filled the post more magnificently than any of his predecessors or, indeed, than any one in the future is likely to do. The longest poem in this anthology is one of many proofs that he wrote well when a theme was thrust upon him: innumerable poems, including most of the once-renowned *Idylls of the King*, show how his genius flagged when he had first to hunt for a subject.

When his long rambling elegy, *In Memoriam*, appeared anonymously, one well-known critic opined that it must be the work of an officer's widow. As Winston Churchill, breaking into his mother-tongue, might say—'Some widow'!

He refused a knighthood and a baronetcy, but in 1884 became the first poet to receive a peerage. He died, with a volume of Shakespeare in his hands, and was buried in Westminster Abbey.

Tennyson was not only one of the greatest of English poets, and as fine a word-artist as any among them, being equalled only by Milton, but, marvellous to record, his career was nevertheless a crescendo of triumph from the age of thirty-three. In 1903 I stayed as a lad in a Norfolk rectory. The rector's wife told me (and I all ears, as you can imagine) that in the late 'eighties she had boarded a P. and O. liner which was about to steam for Australia. There was the usual hubbub of a hundred departures: but suddenly everybody stopped talking, and a dead silence fell upon the ship. 'Lord Tennyson', said the rector's wife, 'had come on board to say farewell to his son Hallam'. No later poet has made a similar impression upon Great Britain.

It was not only pretentious poetasters and straw-brained journalists who, soon after the beginning of our century, made themselves ridiculous by belittling Tennyson. So good a writer as George Moore attempted to puncture his prestige by observing pettishly 'There is too much rectory lawn in Tennyson'. No doubt Moore had in mind the over-smooth surface of *The Princess* and of nearly all the somnolent *Idylls of the King*; but if he had spoken aloud the tremendous music of the following address to Virgil, he might have realised, with Mr. and Mrs. Ramsbotham, that you cannot with impunity prod an apparently sleeping lion.

115 To Virgil

(Written at the request of the Mantuans for the Nineteenth Centenary of Virgil's Death)

Roman Virgil, thou that singest
  Ilion's lofty temples robed in fire,
Ilion falling, Rome arising,
  wars, and filial faith, and Dido's pyre;

Landscape-lover, lord of language
  more than he that sang the Works and Days,
All the chosen coin of fancy
  flashing out from many a golden phrase;

Thou that singest wheat and woodland,
  tilth and vineyard, hive and horse and herd;
All the charm of all the Muses
  often flowering in a lonely word;

Poet of the happy Tityrus
  piping underneath his beechen bowers;
Poet of the poet-satyr
  whom the laughing shepherd bound with flowers;

Chanter of the Pollio, glorying
  in the blissful years again to be,
Summers of the snakeless meadow,
  unlaborious earth and oarless sea;

Thou that seest Universal
  Nature moved by Universal Mind;
Thou majestic in thy sadness
  at the doubtful doom of human kind;

Light among the vanish'd ages;
  star that gildest yet this phantom shore;
Golden branch amid the shadows,
  kings and realms that pass to rise no more;

Now thy Forum roars no longer,
  fallen every purple Cæsar's dome—
Tho' thine ocean-roll of rhythm,
  sound for ever of Imperial Rome—

Now the Rome of slaves hath perish'd,
   and the Rome of freemen holds her place,
I, from out the Northern Island
   sunder'd once from all the human race,

I salute thee, Mantovano,
   I that loved thee since my day began,
Wielder of the stateliest measure
   ever moulded by the lips of man.

Here again is a noble tribute from one great poet to another: and
here, too, a lyric magnificent not in sound alone but in its imagery.

116   Milton

(Alcaics)

O mighty-mouth'd inventor of harmonies,
O skill'd to sing of Time or Eternity,
   God-gifted organ-voice of England,
      Milton, a name to resound for ages;
Whose Titan angels, Gabriel, Abdiel,
Starr'd from Jehovah's gorgeous armouries,
   Tower, as the deep-domed empyrëan
      Rings to the roar of an angel onset—
Me rather all that bowery loneliness,
The brooks of Eden mazily murmuring,
   And bloom profuse and cedar arches
      Charm, as a wanderer out in ocean,
Where some refulgent sunset of India
Streams o'er a rich ambrosial ocean isle,
   And crimson-hued the stately palm-woods
      Whisper in odorous heights of even.

Tennyson was perhaps unique in achieving some of his mightiest
triumphs when a subject came to him from the world of affairs. So it
was that the *Virgil* poem was born: so, too, that this Bach-like national
elegy came forth in response to a public event. The verbal virtuosity of
this poem should remain for ever a matter for the utmost admiration
to any poetry lover who is not enslaved by the mode of his own period.

117   Ode on the death of the Duke of Wellington

Bury the Great Duke
    With an empire's lamentation,
Let us bury the Great Duke
    To the noise of the mourning of a mighty nation,
Mourning when their leaders fall,
Warriors carry the warrior's pall,
And sorrow darkens hamlet and hall.

Where shall we lay the man whom we deplore?
Here, in streaming London's central roar.
Let the sound of those he wrought for,
And the feet of those he fought for,
Echo round his bones for evermore.

Lead out the pageant: sad and slow,
As fits an universal woe,
Let the long long procession go,
And let the sorrowing crowd about it grow,
And let the mournful martial music blow;
The last great Englishman is low.

Mourn, for to us he seems the last,
Remembering all his greatness in the past.
No more in soldier fashion will he greet
With lifted hand the gazer in the street.
O friends, our chief state-oracle is mute:
Mourn for the man of long-enduring blood,
The statesman-warrior, moderate, resolute,
Whole in himself, a common good.
Mourn for the man of amplest influence,
Yet clearest of ambitious crime,
Our greatest yet with least pretence,
Great in council and great in war,
Foremost captain of his time,
Rich in saving common-sense,
And, as the greatest only are,
In his simplicity sublime.

O good gray head which all men knew,
O voice from which their omens all men drew,
O iron nerve to true occasion true,
O fall'n at length that tower of strength
Which stood four-square to all the winds that blew!
Such was he whom we deplore.
The long self-sacrifice of life is o'er.
The great World-victor's victor will be seen no more.

All is over and done:
Render thanks to the Giver,
England, for thy son.
Let the bell be toll'd.
Render thanks to the Giver,
And render him to the mould.
Under the cross of gold
That shines over city and river,
There he shall rest for ever
Among the wise and the bold.
Let the bell be toll'd:
And a reverent people behold
The towering car, the sable steeds:
Bright let it be with its blazon'd deeds,
Dark in its funeral fold.
Let the bell be toll'd:
And a deeper knell in the heart be knoll'd;
And the sound of the sorrowing anthem roll'd
Thro' the dome of the golden cross;
And the volleying cannon thunder his loss;
He knew their voices of old.
For many a time in many a clime
His captain's ear has heard them boom
Bellowing victory, bellowing doom:
When he with those deep voices wrought,
Guarding realms and kings from shame;
With those deep voices our dead captain taught
The tyrant, and asserts his claim
In that dread sound to the great name,
Which he has worn so pure of blame,

In praise and in dispraise the same,
A man of well-attemper'd frame.
O civic muse, to such a name,
To such a name for ages long,
To such a name,
Preserve a broad approach of fame,
And ever-echoing avenues of song.

Who is he that cometh, like an honour'd guest,
With banner and with music, with soldier and with priest,
With a nation weeping, and breaking on my rest?
Mighty Seaman, this is he
Was great by land as thou by sea.
Thine island loves thee well, thou famous man,
The greatest sailor since our world began.
Now, to the roll of muffled drums,
To thee the greatest soldier comes;
For this is he
Was great by land as thou by sea;
His foes were thine; he kept us free;
O give him welcome, this is he
Worthy of our gorgeous rites,
And worthy to be laid by thee;
For this is England's greatest son,
He that gain'd a hundred fights,
Nor ever lost an English gun;
This is he that far away
Against the myriads of Assaye
Clash'd with his fiery few and won;
And underneath another sun,
Warring on a later day,
Round affrighted Lisbon drew
The treble works, the vast designs
Of his labour'd rampart-lines,
Where he greatly stood at bay,
Whence he issued forth anew,
And ever great and greater grew,
Beating from the wasted vines

P

Back to France her banded swarms,
Back to France with countless blows,
Till o'er the hills her eagles flew
Beyond the Pyrenean pines,
Follow'd up in valley and glen
With blare of bugle, clamour of men,
Roll of cannon and clash of arms,
And England pouring on her foes.
Such a war had such a close.
Again their ravening eagle rose
In anger, wheel'd on Europe-shadowing wings,
And barking for the thrones of kings;
Till one that sought but Duty's iron crown
On that loud sabbath shook the spoiler down;
A day of onsets of despair!
Dash'd on every rocky square
Their surging charges foam'd themselves away;
Last, the Prussian trumpet blew;
Thro' the long-tormented air
Heaven flash'd a sudden jubilant ray,
And down we swept and charged and overthrew.
So great a soldier taught us there,
What long-enduring hearts could do
In that world-earthquake, Waterloo!
Mighty Seaman, tender and true,
And pure as he from taint of craven guile.
O saviour of the silver-coasted isle,
O shaker of the Baltic and the Nile,
If aught of things that here befall
Touch a spirit among things divine,
If love of country move thee there at all,
Be glad, because his bones are laid by thine!
And thro' the centuries let a people's voice
In full acclaim,
A people's voice,
The proof and echo of all human fame,
A people's voice, when they rejoice
At civic revel and pomp and game,

Attest their great commander's claim
With honour, honour, honour, honour to him,
Eternal honour to his name.

A people's voice! we are a people yet.
Tho' all men else their nobler dreams forget,
Confused by brainless mobs and lawless Powers;
Thank Him who isled us here, and roughly set
His Briton in blown seas and storming showers,
We have a voice, with which to pay the debt
Of boundless love and reverence and regret
To those great men who fought, and kept it ours.
And keep it ours, O God, from brute control;
O Statesmen, guard us, guard the eye, the soul
Of Europe, keep our noble England whole,
And save the one true seed of freedom sown
Betwixt a people and their ancient throne,
That sober freedom out of which there springs
Our loyal passion for our temperate kings;
For, saving that, ye help to save mankind
Till public wrong be crumbled into dust,
And drill the raw world for the march of mind,
Till crowds at length be sane and crowns be just.
But wink no more in slothful overtrust.
Remember him who led your hosts;
He bad you guard the sacred coasts.
Your cannons moulder on the seaward wall;
His voice is silent in your council-hall
For ever; and whatever tempests lour
For ever silent; even if they broke
In thunder, silent; yet remember all
He spoke among you, and the Man who spoke;
Who never sold the truth to serve the hour,
Nor palter'd with Eternal God for power;
Who let the turbid streams of rumour flow
Thro' either babbling world of high and low;
Whose life was work, whose language rife
With rugged maxims hewn from life;
Who never spoke against a foe;

Whose eighty winters freeze with one rebuke
All great self-seekers trampling on the right:
Truth-teller was our England's Alfred named;
Truth-lover was our English Duke;
Whatever record leap to light
He never shall be shamed.

Lo, the leader in these glorious wars
Now to glorious burial slowly borne,
Follow'd by the brave of other lands,
He, on whom from both her open hands
Lavish Honour shower'd all her stars,
And affluent Fortune emptied all her horn.
Yea, let all good things await
Him who cares not to be great,
But as he saves or serves the state.
Not once or twice in our rough island-story,
The path of duty was the way to glory:
He that walks it, only thirsting
For the right, and learns to deaden
Love of self, before his journey closes,
He shall find the stubborn thistle bursting
Into glossy purples, which outredden
All voluptuous garden-roses.
Not once or twice in our fair island-story,
The path of duty was the way to glory:
He, that ever following her commands,
On with toil of heart and knees and hands,
Thro' the long gorge to the far light has won
His path upward, and prevail'd,
Shall find the toppling crags of Duty scaled
Are close upon the shining table-lands
To which our God Himself is moon and sun.
Such was he: his work is done.
But while the races of mankind endure,
Let his great example stand
Colossal, seen of every land,
And keep the soldier firm, the statesman pure:
Till in all lands and thro' all human story

The path of duty be the way to glory:
And let the land whose hearths he saved from shame
For many and many an age proclaim
At civic revel and pomp and game,
And when the long-illumined cities flame,
Their ever-loyal iron leader's fame,
With honour, honour, honour, honour to him,
Eternal honour to his name.

Peace, his triumph will be sung
By some yet unmoulded tongue
Far on in summers that we shall not see:
Peace, it is a day of pain
For one about whose patriarchal knee
Late the little children clung:
O peace, it is a day of pain
For one, upon whose hand and heart and brain
Once the weight and fate of Europe hung.
Ours the pain, his the gain!
More than is of man's degree
Must be with us, watching here
At this, our great solemnity.
Whom we see not we revere;
We revere, and we refrain
From talk of battles loud and vain,
And brawling memories all too free
For such a wise humility
As befits a solemn fane:
We revere, and while we hear
The tides of Music's golden sea
Setting toward eternity,
Uplifted high in heart and hope are we,
Until we doubt not that for one so true
There must be other nobler work to do
Than when he fought at Waterloo,
And Victor he must ever be.
For tho' the Giant Ages heave the hill
And break the shore, and evermore
Make and break, and work their will;

Tho' world on world in myriad myriads roll
Round us, each with different powers,
And other forms of life than ours,
What know we greater than the soul?
On God and Godlike man we build our trust.
Hush, the Dead March wails in the people's ears:
The dark crowd moves, and there are sobs and tears:
The black earth yawns: the mortal disappears;
Ashes to ashes, dust to dust;
He is gone who seem'd so great.—
Gone; but nothing can bereave him
Of the force he made his own
Being here, and we believe him
Something far advanced in State,
And that he wears a truer crown
Than any wreath that man can weave him.
Speak no more of his renown,
Lay your earthly fancies down,
And in the vast cathedral leave him.
God accept him, Christ receive him.

It seems strange that parodists should not have been able to keep
away from a poem of such profound grief as

118 'Break, break, break . . .'

Break, break, break,
 On thy cold gray stones, O Sea!
And I would that my tongue could utter
 The thoughts that arise in me.

O well for the fisherman's boy,
 That he shouts with his sister at play!
O well for the sailor lad,
 That he sings in his boat on the bay!

And the stately ships go on
 To their haven under the hill;
But O for the touch of a vanish'd hand,
 And the sound of a voice that is still!

> Break, break, break,
> At the foot of thy crags, O Sea!
> But the tender grace of a day that is dead
> Will never come back to me.

Tennyson said of *Tears* that few people realise that it is a lyric in blank verse. There could be no stronger witness to its marvellous music. Something of its unmatched sorrowful beauty is caused by the unexpected bringing together of the words 'happy' and 'autumn'. A careful judge might give as his opinion that this is the most beautiful poem in the English language.

119   Tears, idle tears

> Tears, idle tears, I know not what they mean,
> Tears from the depth of some divine despair
> Rise in the heart, and gather to the eyes,
> In looking on the happy Autumn-fields,
> And thinking of the days that are no more.
>
> Fresh as the first beam glittering on a sail,
> That brings our friends up from the underworld,
> Sad as the last which reddens over one
> That sinks with all we love below the verge;
> So sad, so fresh, the days that are no more.
>
> Ah, sad and strange as in dark summer dawns
> The earliest pipe of half-awaken'd birds
> To dying ears, when unto dying eyes
> The casement slowly grows a glimmering square;
> So sad, so strange, the days that are no more.
>
> Dear as remember'd kisses after death,
> And sweet as those by hopeless fancy feign'd
> On lips that are for others; deep as love,
> Deep as first love, and wild with all regret;
> O Death in Life, the days that are no more.

The age was so bursting with genius that here, directly after five superb masterpieces, come fragments of another. Persian poetry lacks organic structure, and indeed it is usually likened to a string of pearls. We ruin nothing, therefore, if we extract some of the finest of Fitzgerald's jewels. This poem is certainly a result of the Scientific Awakening which occurred in the nineteenth century. Its popularity with men who knew no other verse was astonishing and must have been due to the exquisitely sad cadence of the stanza, the sound as of an autumn wind, the poet's acceptance of 'annihilation' as the end of consciousness, and the attractive recklessness with which he seeks comfort or oblivion in 'the grape'.

Edward Fitzgerald: 1809–1883

A lifelong friend of Tennyson, whom he met when they were students at Trinity College, Cambridge. Fitzgerald, who seems to have had no desire for marriage, lived a secluded and crotchetty life. His too tentative versions of plays by the great Spanish dramatist, Calderon, are still of deep interest: but he slowly made his present renown by tackling and paraphrasing *The Rubá‘iyát of Omar Khayyám*. This book appeared in 1859. It was, naturally, ignored. It sank into the 'tuppeny' book-box where D. G. Rossetti found it, and realised its kaleidoscopic splendour. Swinburne, having borrowed it, produced, almost in a twinkling, his long poem in the same metre, *Laus Veneris*, but the Swinburne poem has none of Fitzgerald's 'cello notes.

In later life Fitzgerald took to sailing a small craft, aided by a young boatman, and he named the craft 'Meum and Tuum'. He was a vegetarian.

Tennyson dedicated a late book to him and wrote a graceful poem in which he says that

'none can say
That Lenten fare makes Lenten thought,
Who reads your golden Eastern lay,
Than which I know no version done
In English more divinely well. . . .'

In 1905, when I 'sailed' in a German steamer to Australia, Tennyson's deathless work was overclouded, but even the ship's doctor had Fitzgerald's Persian poem by his bunk-side. The real Omar may have been a mystic, not a sad sybarite. There is, for example, this little-known stanza (not used by Fitzgerald):

> The heart that love and charity do leaven,
> Whether to mosque or church its praise be given—
> His name that's written in the Book of Love,
> What fears he Hell, what care hath he for Heaven?

120   Stanzas from *The Ruba'iyát of Omar Khayyam*

> I sometimes think that never blows so red
> The Rose as where some buried Cæsar bled;
> That every Hyacinth the Garden wears
> Dropt in its Lap from some once lovely Head.

> And this delightful Herb whose tender Green
> Fledges the River's Lip on which we lean—
> Ah, lean upon it lightly! for who knows
> From what once lovely Lip it springs unseen!

> Ah, my Beloved, fill the Cup that clears
> TO-DAY of past Regrets and future Fears—
> *To-morrow?*—Why, To-morrow I may be
> Myself with Yesterday's Sev'n Thousand Years.

> Lo, some we loved, the loveliest and best
> That Time and Fate of all their Vintage prest,
> Have drunk their Cup a Round or two before,
> And one by one crept silently to Rest.

> And we that now make merry in the Room
> They left, and Summer dresses in new bloom,
> Ourselves must we beneath the Couch of Earth
> Descend, ourselves to make a Couch—for whom?

> Ah, make the most of what we yet may spend,
> Before we too into the Dust descend;
> Dust into Dust, and under Dust to lie,
> Sans Wine, sans Song, sans Singer, and—sans End!

Indeed the Idols I have loved so long
Have done my Credit in Men's Eye much wrong:
    Have drown'd my Honour in a shallow Cup,
And sold my Reputation for a Song.

Indeed, indeed, Repentance oft before
I swore—but was I sober when I swore?
    And then and then came Spring, and Rose-in-hand
My threadbare Penitence apieces tore.

And much as Wine has played the Infidel,
And robb'd me of Robe of Honour—well,
    I often wonder what the Vintners buy
One half so precious as the Goods they sell.

Alas, that Spring should vanish with the Rose!
That Youth's sweet-scented manuscript should close!
    The Nightingale that in the Branches sang,
Ah, whence, and whither flown again, who knows!

Ah Love! could thou and I with Fate conspire
To grasp this sorry Scheme of Things entire,
    Would we not shatter it to bits—and then
Re-mould it nearer to the Heart's Desire!

Ah, Moon of my Delight who know'st no wane,
The Moon of Heav'n is rising once again:
    How oft hereafter rising shall she look
Through this same Garden after me—in vain!

And when Thyself with shining Foot shall pass
Among the Guests Star-scatter'd on the Grass,
    And in thy joyous Errand reach the Spot
Where I made one—turn down an empty Glass!

Robert Browning: 1812–1889

Tennyson said of Browning, who more than any other man stood as
his rival, that 'he has plenty of music in him but he cannot get it out'.
It is certainly strange that Browning, who was a reasonably accomplished musician, should have written such a line as

        'no ambiguous dabchick hatched to strut',

whereas Tennyson did not care for music and Swinburne had no ear for it at all. And yet though he does nothing to aid or allure the reader, Browning does by sheer energy of imagination and warmth of heart frequently arouse enthusiasm. Like Tennyson, he wrote hardly any prose: a fact which gives point to the criticism made by W. B. Yeats concerning a prose passage that 'it is the only prose treatise which Browning did not write in verse'. His contemporary popularity was largely due to qualities not essentially poetic,—his optimism, his liberalism, his championship of Christianity.

Browning's father was a clerk in the Bank of England, but he disliked the post and was unique among parents in actually wishing that his son might prove to be a poet. In early years the poet 'wrote settings for a number of songs' which, if they survive, ought to be floated on to the air.

It was as if by a miracle of his own robust health that Browning revived the moribund poetess, Elizabeth Barrett, whom he eloped with and married. Poe, rather unexpectedly, set an immensely high value on her poetic work.

Perhaps Browning cannot much delight a man's feeling for style, but his vivid sense of the past may entertain us if we are spellbound on-lookers of the centuries: and just now and then the sheer poetry of his nature creates a living lyric which, willy-nilly, has a music of its own. Much in his style can be attributed to the fact that his maternal grandfather was German.

He was buried in Westminster Abbey. Swinburne wrote a fine threnody for him: and from early days he had won the valuable admiration of D. G. Rossetti. . . .

Here is a nugget of pure gold in the general roughcast of Browning's versification. . . .

121 Meeting at Night

The grey sea and the long black land;
And the yellow half-moon large and low;
And the startled little waves that leap
In fiery ringlets from their sleep,
As I gain the cove with pushing prow,
And quench its speed i' the slushy sand.

Then a mile of warm sea-scented beach;
Three fields to cross till a farm appears;
A tap at the pane, the quick sharp scratch
And blue spurt of a lighted match,
And a voice less loud, thro' its joys and fears,
Than the two hearts beating each to each!

The reader should now prepare to decide whether he believes that good 'sense' unaccompanied by magically evocative 'sound' really justifies the use of verse.

122   The Bishop Orders His Tomb at Saint Praxed's Church

Rome, 15—

Vanity, saith the preacher, vanity!
Draw round my bed: is Anselm keeping back?
Nephews—sons mine . . . ah God, I know not! Well—
She, men would have to be your mother once,
Old Gandolf envied me, so fair she was!
What's done is done, and she is dead beside,
Dead long ago, and I am Bishop since,
And as she died so must we die ourselves,
And thence ye may perceive the world's a dream.
Life, how and what is it? As here I lie
In this state-chamber, dying by degrees,
Hours and long hours in the dead night, I ask
'Do I live, am I dead'? Peace, peace seems all.
Saint Praxed's ever was the church for peace:
And so, about this tomb of mine. I fought
With tooth and nail to save my niche, ye know:
—Old Gandolf cozened me, despite my care;
Shrewd was that snatch from out the corner South
He graced his carrion with, God curse the same!
Yet still my niche is not so cramped but thence
One sees the pulpit o' the epistle-side,
And somewhat of the choir, those silent seats,

And up into the aery dome where live
The angels, and a sunbeam's sure to lurk:
And I shall fill my slab of basalt there,
And 'neath my tabernacle take my rest,
With those nine columns round me, two and two,
The odd one at my feet where Anselm stands:
Peach-blossom marble all, the rare, the ripe
As fresh-poured red wine of a mighty pulse.
—Old Gandolf with his paltry onion-stone,
Put me where I may look at him! True peach,
Rosy and flawless: how I earned the prize!
Draw close: that conflagration of my church
—What then? So much was saved if aught were missed!
My sons, ye would not be my death? Go dig
The white-grape vineyard where the oil-press stood,
Drop water gently till the surface sink,
And if ye find . . . Ah God, I know not, I! . . .
Bedded in store of rotten fig-leaves soft,
And corded up in a tight olive-frail,
Some lump, ah God, of *lapis lazuli*,
Big as a Jew's head cut off at the nape,
Blue as a vein o'er the Madonna's breast . . .
Sons, all have I bequeathed you, villas, all,
That brave Frascati villa with its bath,
So, let the blue lump poise between my knees,
Like God the Father's globe on both his hands
Ye worship in the Jesu Church so gay,
For Gandolf shall not choose but see and burst!
Swift as a weaver's shuttle fleet our years:
Man goeth to the grave, and where is he?
Did I say basalt for my slab, sons? Black—
'Twas ever antique-black I meant! How else
Shall ye contrast my frieze to come beneath?
The bas-relief in bronze ye promised me,
Those Pans and Nymphs ye wot of, and perchance
Some tripod, thyrsus, with a vase or so,
The Saviour at his sermon on the mount,
Saint Praxed in a glory, and one Pan

Ready to twitch the Nymph's last garment off,
And Moses with the tables . . . but I know
Ye mark me not! What do they whisper thee,
Child of my bowels, Anselm? Ah, ye hope
To revel down my villas while I gasp
Bricked o'er with beggar's mouldy travertine
Which Gandolf from his tomb-top chuckles at!
Nay, boys, ye love me—all of jasper, then!
'Tis jasper ye stand pledged to, lest I grieve.
My bath must needs be left behind, alas!
One block, pure green as a pistachio-nut,
There's plenty jasper somewhere in the world—
And have I not Saint Praxed's ear to pray
Horses for ye, and brown Greek manuscripts,
And mistresses with great smooth marbly limbs?
—That's if ye carve my epitaph aright,
Choice Latin, picked phrase, Tully's every word,
No gaudy ware like Gandolf's second line—
Tully, my masters? Ulpian serves his need!
And then how I shall lie through centuries,
And hear the blessed mutter of the mass,
And see God made and eaten all day long,
And feel the steady candle-flame, and taste
Good strong thick stupefying incense-smoke!
For as I lie here, hours of the dead night,
Dying in state and by such slow degrees,
I fold my arms as if they clasped a crook,
And stretch my feet forth straight as stone can point,
And let the bedclothes, for a mortcloth, drop
Into great laps and folds of sculptor's-work:
And as yon tapers dwindle, and strange thoughts
Grow, with a certain humming in my ears,
About the life before I lived this life,
And this life too, popes, cardinals and priests,
Saint Praxed at his sermon on the mount,
Your tall pale mother with her talking eyes,
And new-found agate urns as fresh as day,
And marble's language, Latin pure, discreet,

—Aha, ELUCESCEBAT quoth our friend?
No Tully, said I, Ulpian at the best!
Evil and brief hath been my pilgrimage.
All *lapis*, all, sons! Else I give the Pope
My villas! Will ye ever eat my heart?
Ever your eyes were as a lizard's quick,
They glitter like your mother's for my soul,
Or ye would heighten my impoverished frieze,
Piece out its starved design, and fill my vase
With grapes, and add a vizor and a Term,
And to the tripod ye would tie a lynx
That in his struggle throws the thyrsus down,
To comfort me on my entablature
Whereon I am to lie till I must ask
'Do I live, am I dead'? There, leave me, there!
For ye have stabbed me with ingratitude
To death—ye wish it—God, ye wish it! Stone—
Gritstone, a-crumble! Clammy squares which sweat
As if the corpse they keep were oozing through—
And no more *lapis* to delight the world!
Well go! I bless ye. Fewer tapers there,
But in a row: and, going, turn your backs
—Ay, like departing altar-ministrants,
And leave me in my church, the church for peace,
That I may watch at leisure if he leers—
Old Gandolf, at me, from his onion-stone,
As still he envied me, so fair she was!

Walt Whitman: 1819–1892

This immense personality was provided with a robust body by a father of English stock who was a 'farmer and carpenter' and by a mother who was descended from Dutch sailors. He was born on Long Island, New York.

He worked successively as an errand boy in a lawyer's office, a printer's devil, a country school-teacher, editor of various unimportant news sheets, and builder and seller of small houses in Brooklyn. During the American Civil War he acted as a volunteer nurse in the army of the

Northern States. He was unmarried: but it was rumoured in the nineteen-twenties that eight living American poets were his sons. In 1873 he was invalided for life by a paralytic stroke.

Whitman was a natural democrat, a man who liked ordinary folk. He is also one of the few great poets who obviously were extraverts. The sexual frankness of his earlier poems aroused the customary storm. This frankness, together with a wide-winged poetic emotion, which often causes his long rhythms to soar like kestrels, inspired Swinburne to address to him an enthusiastic but mediocre poem. Swinburne afterwards changed his attitude, and sprayed Whitman with vitriolic invective.

Whitman is a rhapsodist: and for two thousand years the civilised world had been too self-conscious to produce one. Here, to begin with, is a magnificent rhapsody, the strong emotional words and cadences pouring vehemently from an uninhibited, child-wondering mind. Note the powerful rhythmic pulse of this free-verse innovator.

123   Death

Come lovely and soothing death,
Undulate round the world, serenely arriving, arriving,
In the day, in the night, to all, to each,
Sooner or later delicate death.

Prais'd be the fathomless universe,
For life and joy, and for objects and knowledge curious,
And for love, sweet love—but praise! praise! praise!
For the sure-enwinding arms of cool-enfolding death.

Dark mother always gliding near with soft feet,
Have none chanted for thee a chant of fullest welcome?
Then I chant it for thee, I glorify thee above all,
I bring thee a song that when thou must indeed come, come unfalteringly.

Approach, strong deliveress,
When it is so, when thou hast taken them I joyously sing the dead,
Lost in the loving floating ocean of thee,
Laved in the flood of thy bliss O death.

From me to thee glad serenades,
Dances for thee I propose saluting thee, adornments and feastings for
    thee,
And the sights of the open landscape and the high-spread sky are fitting,
And life and the fields, and the huge and thoughtful night.

The night in silence under many a star,
The ocean shore and the husky whispering wave whose voice I know,
And the soul turning to thee O vast and well-veil'd death,
And the body gratefully nestling close to thee.

Over the tree-tops I float thee a song,
Over the rising and sinking waves, over the myriad fields and the
    prairies wide,
Over the dense-pack'd cities all and the teeming wharves and ways,
I float this carol with joy, with joy to thee O death.

*   *   *

Whitman uses rhyme and a fairly steady metre with some awkward-
ness or, as he would have put it, gaucherie: but this fine snapshot of an
agéd slave-woman might have lost something if it had not the Repeated
Rhythm of the heart-beat. A 'guidon' was a small flag carried by the
leader or guide of a cavalry or artillery regiment in the United States
army.

124   Ethiopia Saluting the Colors

Who are you dusky woman, so ancient hardly human,
With your woolly-white and turban'd head, and bare bony feet?
Why rising by the roadside here, do you the colors greet?

('Tis while our army lines Carolina's sands and pines,
Forth from thy hovel door thou, Ethiopia, com'st to me,
As under doughty Sherman I march toward the sea.)

Me master years a hundred since from my parents sunder'd,
A little child, they caught me as the savage beast is caught,
Then hither me across the sea the cruel slaver brought.

Q

No further does she say, but lingering all the day,
Her high-borne turban'd head she wags, and rolls her darkling eye,
And courtsies to the regiments, the guidons moving by.

What is it fateful woman, so blear, hardly human?
Why wag your head with turban bound, yellow, red and green?
Are the things so strange and marvelous you see or have seen?

* * *

And at this point the reader should finally make up his mind whether
he looks to poetry for the cold cleverness of inexperience or for a
vibration of those emotions which are universally human.

125　As Toilsome I Wander'd Virginia's Woods

As toilsome I wander'd Virginia's woods,
To the music of rustling leaves kick'd by my feet, (for 'twas autumn,)
I mark'd at the foot of a tree the grave of a soldier;
Mortally wounded he and buried on the retreat, (easily all could I
　understand,)
The halt of a mid-day hour, when up! no time to lose—yet this sign left,
On a tablet scrawl'd and nail'd on the tree by the grave,
Bold, cautious, true, and my loving comrade.

Long, long I muse, then on my way go wandering,
Many a changeful season to follow, and many a scene of life,
Yet at times through changeful season and scene, abrupt, alone, or in
　the crowded street,
Comes before me the unknown soldier's grave, comes the inscription
　rude in Virginia's woods,
Bold, cautious, true, and my loving comrade.

* * *

This is one of the *Leaves of Grass* which outraged the United States.
Anti-puritanism could go no further. Even now it is a red-rag poem for
all those who have not yet learned that the sex of the body is perhaps
the most formative of the soul's conditions.

126 A Woman Waits for Me

A woman waits for me, she contains all, nothing is lacking,
Yet all were lacking if sex were lacking, or if the moisture of the right
    man were lacking.

Sex contains all, bodies, souls,
Means, proofs, purities, delicacies, results, promulgations,
Songs, commands, health, pride, the maternal mystery, the seminal
    milk,
All hopes, benefactions, bestowals, all the passions, loves, beauties,
    delights of the earth,
All the governments, judges, gods, follow'd persons of the earth,
These are contain'd in sex as parts of itself and justifications of itself.

Without shame the man I like knows and avows the deliciousness of
    his sex,
Without shame the woman I like knows and avows hers.

Now I will dismiss myself from impassive women,
I will go stay with her who waits for me, and with those women that
    are warm-blooded and sufficient for me,
I see that they understand me and do not deny me,
I see that they are worthy of me, I will be the robust husband of those
    women.

They are not one jot less than I am,
They are tann'd in the face by shining suns and blowing winds,
Their flesh has the old divine suppleness and strength, ·
They know how to swim, row, ride, wrestle, shoot, run, strike, retreat,
    advance, resist, defend themselves,
They are ultimate in their own right—they are calm, clear, well
    possess'd of themselves.

I draw you close to me, you women,
I cannot let you go, I would do you good,
I am for you, and you are for me, not only for our own sake, but for
    others' sakes,
Envelop'd in you sleep greater heroes and bards,
They refuse to awake at the touch of any man but me.

It is I, you women, I make my way,
I am stern, acrid, large, undissuadable, but I love you,
I do not hurt you any more than is necessary for you,
I pour the stuff to start sons and daughters fit for these States,   press
    with slow rude muscle,
I brace myself effectually, I listen to no entreaties,
I dare not withdraw till I deposit what has so long accumulated within
    me.

Through you I drain the pent-up rivers of myself,
In you I wrap a thousand onward years,
On you I graft the grafts of the best-beloved of me and America,
The drops I distil upon you shall grow fierce and athletic girls, new
    artists, musicians, and singers,
The babes I beget upon you are to beget babes in their turn,
I shall demand perfect men and women out of my love-spendings,
I shall expect them to interpenetrate with others, as I and you inter-
    penetrate now,
I shall count on the fruits of the gushing showers of them, as I count on
    the fruits of the gushing showers I give now,
I shall look for loving crops from the birth, life, death, immortality,
    I plant so lovingly now.

Matthew Arnold: 1822–1888

Son of Dr. Arnold, the headmaster of Rugby School, who may almost be said to be responsible for the Old School Tie. Matthew Arnold was educated at Winchester and at Balliol College, Oxford.

During most of his adult life he worked as an Inspector of Schools, but neither this routine-task nor his academic background was sufficient to smother the strong poetic quality of his mind. His sense of form is high above the English average.

In his own day he was less famous as a poet than as a literary critic, a Darwinian agnostic, and a champion of culture. 'He adopted from Swift' (we are told) 'the phrase "Sweetness and Light" to explain his literary and social creed'. He used these words in the sense of reason-ableness and intelligence.

Few men so extremely educated have avoided poetic sterilisation.

The first line of this first poem has the ring of Sophocles' most famous, most handsome, and most inspiring 'chorus'. Even the rhymeless measure is somewhat akin to that of the chorus by Sophocles.

127   The Future

A wanderer is man from his birth.
He was born in a ship
On the breast of the river of Time;
Brimming with wonder and joy
He spreads out his arms to the light,
Rivets his gaze on the banks of the stream.

As what he sees is, so have his thoughts been.
Whether he wakes,
Where the snowy mountainous pass,
Echoing the screams of the eagles,
Hems in its gorges the bed
Of the new-born clear-flowing stream;
Whether he first sees light
Where the river in gleaming rings
Sluggishly winds through the plain;
Whether in sound of the swallowing sea—
As is the world on the banks,
So is the mind of the man.

Vainly does each, as he glides,
Fable and dream
Of the lands which the river of Time
Had left ere he woke on its breast,
Or shall reach when his eyes have been closed.
Only the tract where he sails
He wots of; only the thoughts,
Raised by the objects he passes, are his.

Who can see the green earth any more
As she was by the sources of Time?
Who imagines her fields as they lay
In the sunshine, unworn by the plough?

Who thinks as they thought,
The tribes who then roam'd on her breast,
Her vigorous, primitive sons?

What girl
Now reads in her bosom as clear
As Rebekah read, when she sate
At eve by the palm-shaded well?
Who guards in her breast
As deep, as pellucid a spring
Of feeling, as tranquil, as sure?

What bard,
At the height of his vision, can deem
Of God, of the world, of the soul,
With a plainness as near,
As flashing as Moses felt
When he lay in the night by his flock
On the starlit Arabian waste?
Can rise and obey
The beck of the Spirit like him?

This tract which the river of Time
Now flows through with us, is the plain.
Gone is the calm of its earlier shore.
Border'd by cities and hoarse
With a thousand cries is its stream.
And we on its breast, our minds
Are confused as the cries which we hear,
Changing and shot as the sights which we see.

And we say that repose has fled
For ever the course of the river of Time.
That cities will crowd to its edge
In a blacker, incessanter line;
That the din will be more on its banks,
Denser the trade on its stream,
Flatter the plain where it flows,
Fiercer the sun overhead;

That never will those on its breast
See an ennobling sight,
Drink of the feeling of quiet again.

But what was before us we know not,
And we know not what shall succeed.

Haply, the river of Time—
As it grows, as the towns on its marge
Fling their wavering lights
On a wider, statelier stream—
May acquire, if not the calm
Of its early mountainous shore,
Yet a solemn peace of its own.

And the width of the waters, the hush
Of the grey expanse where he floats,
Freshening its current and spotted with foam
As it draws to the Ocean, may strike
Peace to the soul of the man on its breast—
As the pale waste widens around him,
As the banks fade dimmer away,
As the stars come out, and the night-wind
Brings up the stream
Murmurs and scents of the infinite sea.

Here again, in the third section of the poem, we meet with the
sorrow of the nineteenth-century intelligent man who felt that Darwin
had shattered religion and abolished the soul.

128 Dover Beach

The sea is calm to-night.
The tide is full, the moon lies fair
Upon the straits;—on the French coast the light
Gleams and is gone; the cliffs of England stand,
Glimmering and vast, out in the tranquil bay,
Come to the window, sweet is the night-air!
Only, from the long line of spray

Where the sea meets the moon-blanch'd land,
Listen! you hear the grating roar
Of pebbles which the waves draw back, and fling,
At their return, up the high strand,
Begin, and cease, and then again begin,
With tremulous cadence slow, and bring
The eternal note of sadness in.

Sophocles long ago
Heard it on the Aegaean, and it brought
Into his mind the turbid ebb and flow
Of human misery; we
Find also in the sound a thought,
Hearing it by this distant northern sea.

The Sea of Faith
Was once, too, at the full, and round earth's shore
Lay like the folds of a bright girdle furl'd.
But now I only hear
Its melancholy, long, withdrawing roar,
Retreating, to the breath
Of the night-wind, down the vast edges drear
And naked shingles of the world.

Ah, love, let us be true
To one another! for the world, which seems
To lie before us like a land of dreams,
So various, so beautiful, so new,
Hath really neither joy, nor love, nor light,
Nor certitude, nor peace, nor help for pain;
And we are here as on a darkling plain
Swept with confused alarms of struggle and flight,
Where ignorant armies clash by night.

* * *

Arnold is followed, in birth-date, by a personality of 'El Greco'
type: fastidious, aristocratic, perfect guillotine-fodder, and a Roman
Catholic who had so far waked up from the heavy dream of physical
life as to know that sex-union need not be blindly animal.

Coventry Patmore : •1823–1896

His father was an author, now forgotten. It is surprising to find that Coventry Patmore contributed to *The Germ*, the famous though short-lived magazine created by the 'Pre-Raphaelites' in their first enthusiasm.

His earliest successful work is also perhaps his worst. *The Angel in the House* was a brave attempt to transmute the trivialities of daily life and the commonplaces of marriage into the key of poetry, but the result was often a bathos which only Wordsworth might seriously have rivalled. Here, in fact, is one of the few poets whose latest work is also his best. In the Odes, whether mystical, political or domestic, we are exquisitely surprised, over and over again, by the perfect choice of an unexpected word and by emotionally apt variations of rhythm. Patmore is probably the most underrated of all considerable English poets. The reason may be that in his mind he mingled sex and mysticism, a blend which is said to be particularly offensive to the English temperament.

He was received into the Catholic Church in 1864.

Scientific upstarts, confident that they can tell us what Light is, would profit if they ever brought themselves to ponder this defiant poem. . . .

129   The Two Deserts

> Not greatly moved with awe am I
> To learn that we may spy
> Five thousand firmaments beyond our own.
> The best that's known
> Of the heavenly bodies does them credit small.
> View'd close, the Moon's fair ball
> Is of ill objects worst,
> A corpse in Night's highway, naked, fire-scarr'd, accurst;
> And now they tell
> That the Sun is plainly seen to boil and burst
> Too horribly for hell.
> So, judging from these two,
> As we must do,

The Universe, outside our living Earth,
Was all conceiv'd in the Creator's mirth,
Forecasting at the time Man's spirit deep,
To make dirt cheap.
Put by the Telescope!
Better without it man may see,
Stretch'd awful in the hush'd midnight,
The ghost of his eternity.
Give me the nobler glass that swells to the eye
The things which near us lie,
Till Science rapturously hails,
In the minutest water-drop,
A torment of innumerable tails.
These at the least do live.
But rather give
A mind not much to pry
Beyond our royal-fair estate
Betwixt these deserts blank of small and great.
Wonder and beauty our own courtiers are,
Pressing to catch our gaze,
And out of obvious ways
Ne'er wandering far.

130   Magna est Veritas

Here, in this little Bay,
Full of tumultuous life and great repose,
Where, twice a day,
The purposeless, glad ocean comes and goes,
Under high cliffs, and far from the huge town,
I sit me down.
For want of me the world's course will not fail:
When all its work is done, the lie shall rot;
The truth is great, and shall prevail,
When none cares whether it prevail or not.

Dante Gabriel Rossetti: 1828–1882

His birth bestowed glamour on Charlotte Street, Portland Place, London. His father was an Italian liberal and also a commentator on Dante.

D. G. Rossetti, painter and poet, was so completely an artist that on one occasion he remarked 'What do I care if the sun goes round the earth or the earth round the sun'? His precocity was astounding. Impatient of art-schooling, he asked Madox Brown to accept him as a pupil; and in 1849 he exhibited the familiar picture (which includes a portrait of his poet-sister) 'The Girlhood of Mary, Virgin'. Already his general direction—truth to nature, and minute workmanship—was evident. Even earlier, at the age of eighteen, the 'marvellous boy' wrote the first version of his most famous poem *The Blessed Damozel*: and his almost miraculous verse-translations of early Italian poetry were written by 1849 or very soon after.

His life was darkened by the suicide of Elizabeth Siddal (a milliner's assistant), who, after years of procrastination, had become his wife. He placed the manuscript book of his poems in the coffin, half hiding it within her bright auburn hair. Years afterwards, in 1869, the book was disinterred by lantern light. Rossetti was not present.

In later life Rossetti (whom even the small-souled Whistler termed 'a king of men') became a chloral-addict and a recluse. He had, says one who knew him well, 'a rare and most winning personality which attracted towards itself, as if by an unconscious magnetism, the love of all his friends, the love, indeed, of all who knew him'. It is not too much to say that something of that magnetism persists even now; and is likely to persist.

131   Catch: On a Wet Day

(From the Italian of Franco Sacchetti)

As I walked thinking through a little grove,
  Some girls that gather'd flowers came passing me,
  Saying, 'Look here! look there'! delightedly.
'Oh here it is'! 'What's that'? 'A lily, love'.

'And there are violets'!
'Further for roses! Oh the lovely pets—
The darling beauties! Oh the nasty thorn!
Look here, my hand's all torn'!
'What's that that jumps'? 'Oh don't! it's a grass-hopper'!
'Come run, come run,
Here's bluebells'! 'Oh what fun'!
'Not that way! Stop her'!
'Yes, this way'! 'Pluck them, then'!
'Oh, I've found mushrooms! Oh, look here'! 'Oh, I'm
Quite sure that further on we'll get wild thyme'.

'Oh we shall stay too long, it's going to rain!
There's lightning, oh there's thunder!'
'Oh shan't we hear the vesper-bell, I wonder'?
'Why, it's not nones, you silly little thing;
And don't you hear the nightingales that sing
Fly away, O die away'?
'I feel so funny! Hush'!
'Why, where? what is it then'? 'Ah! in that bush'!
So every girl here knocks it, shakes and shocks it,
Till with the stir they make
Out skurries a great snake.
'O Lord! O me! Alack! Ah me! alack!'
They scream, and then all run and scream again,
And then in heavy drops down comes the rain.

Each running at the other in a fright,
Each trying to get before the other, and crying
And flying, stumbling, tumbling, wrong or right;
One sets her knee
There where her foot should be;
One has her hands and dress
All smother'd up with mud in a fine mess;
And one gets trampled on by two or three.
What's gather'd is let fall
About the woods and not pick'd up at all.
The wreaths of flowers are scatter'd on the ground;
And still as screaming hustling without rest

They run this way and that and round and round,
She thinks herself in luck who runs the best.

I stood quite still to have a perfect view,
And never noticed till I got wet through.

132 · A Virgin declares her Beauties

(From the Italian of Francesco da Barberino)

Do not conceive that I shall here recount
All my own beauty: yet I promise you
That you, by what I tell, shall understand
All that befits and that is well to know.

My bosom, which is very softly made,
Of a white even colour without stain,
Bears two fair apples, fragrant, sweetly-savour'd,
Gather'd together from the Tree of Life
The which is in the midst of Paradise.
And these no person ever yet has touch'd;
For out of nurse's and of mother's hands
I was, when God in secret gave them me.
These ere I yield I must know well to whom;
And for that I would not be robb'd of them,
I speak not all the virtue that they have;
Yet thus far speaking:—blessed were the man
Who once should touch them, were it but a little;—
See them I say not, for that might not be.

My girdle, clipping pleasure round about,
Over my clear dress even unto my knees
Hangs down with sweet precision tenderly;
And under it Virginity abides.
Faithful and simple and of plain belief
She is, with her fair garland bright like gold;
And very fearful if she overhears
Speech of herself; the wherefore ye perceive
That I speak soft lest she be made ashamed.

Lo! this is she who hath for company
The son of God and Mother of the Son;
Lo! this is she who sits with many in heaven;
Lo! this is she with whom are few on earth.

* * *

After these peerless translations, or translations equalled only by
Fitzgerald, the reader should confront the direct personality of this
'king of men', who seems to have been equally poised between spirit
and sense. The last line almost vitalises the over-elaborate manufacture
of the other thirteen.

133   Supreme Surrender

To all the spirits of Love that wander by
    Along his love-sown harvest-field of sleep
    My lady lies apparent; and the deep
Calls to the deep; and no man sees but I.
The bliss so long afar, at length so nigh,
    Rests there attained. Methinks proud Love must weep
    When Fate's control doth from his harvest reap
The sacred hour for which the years did sigh.

First touched, the hand now warm around my neck
    Taught memory long to mock desire: and lo!
    Across my breast the abandoned hair doth flow,
Where one shorn tress long stirred the longing ache:
    And next the heart that trembled for its sake
    Lies the queen-heart in sovereign overthrow.

George Meredith: 1828–1909

Meredith claimed to have both Welsh and Irish blood in him. He was
born at Portsmouth, where his father was 'a naval outfitter' or, as some
would say, a tailor. From the age of three to the age of sixteen the poet
lived in Germany. In 1849 he married a daughter of the novelist Thomas

Love Peacock. She was then a widow and was eight years older than Meredith. This marriage was unhappy, and in 1864 he married again—with seemingly better results. He acted for many years as 'reader' to the firm of Chapman and Hall. During most of his lifetime his work was almost entirely ignored, but when he had passed sixty years the Intellectuals regarded him with so much admiration that, despite the inhuman coldness of his mind, some of them wished to set him up on an equality with Shakespeare. This critical grotesquerie transpires even in the academic pages of the *Encyclopædia Britannica*. The critic would not have believed that by 1940 Meredith, as a novelist, would be ignored: but his championship of intellect, as being the faculty which enables us to see that life is comical, prevented him from recognising that life is basically tragic. He was, like Bernard Shaw, too clever for immortality.

In his poems of *Modern Love*, through the hot-house of Victorian society Meredith swept like a high wind that blows open the glass door. Here are just a few of them: bitter, real, torn from anguish, appallingly unrespectable and passionate cries.

134

She issues radiant from her dressing-room,
Like one prepared to scale an upper sphere:
—By stirring up a lower, much I fear!
How deftly that oiled barber lays his bloom!
That long-shanked dapper Cupid with frisked curls,
Can make known women torturingly fair;
The gold-eyed serpent dwelling in rich hair,
Awakes beneath his magic whisks and twirls.
His art can take the eyes from out my head,
Until I see with eyes of other men;
While deeper knowledge crouches in its den,
And sends a spark up:—is it true we are wed?
Yea! filthiness of body is most vile,
But faithlessness of heart I do hold worse.
The former, it were not so great a curse
To read on the steel-mirror of her smile.

135

He felt the wild beast in him betweenwhiles
So masterfully rude, that he would grieve
To see the helpless delicate thing receive
His guardianship through certain dark defiles.
Had he not teeth to rend, and hunger too?
But still he spared her. Once: 'Have you no fear'?
He said: 't was dusk; she in his grasp, none near.
She laughed: 'No, surely; am I not with you'?
And uttering that soft starry 'you', she leaned
Her gentle body near him, looking up;
And from her eyes, as from a poison-cup,
He drank until the flittering eyelids screened.
Devilish malignant witch! and oh, young beam
Of heaven's circle-glory! Here thy shape
To squeeze like an intoxicating grape—
I might, and yet thou goest safe, supreme.

136

I think she sleeps: it must be sleep, when low
Hangs that abandoned arm toward the floor;
The face turned with it. Now make fast the door.
Sleep on: it is your husband, not your foe.
The Poet's black stage-lion of wronged love,
Frights not our modern dames:—well if he did!
Now will I pour new light upon that lid,
Full-sloping like the breasts beneath. 'Sweet dove,
Your sleep is pure. Nay, pardon: I disturb.
I do not? good'! Her waking infant-stare
Grows woman to the burden my hands bear:
Her own handwriting to me when no curb
Was left on Passion's tongue. She trembles through;
A woman's tremble—the whole instrument:—
I show another letter lately sent.
The words are very like: the name is new.

137

At dinner, she is hostess, I am host.
Went the feast ever cheerfuller? She keeps
The Topic over intellectual deeps
In buoyancy afloat. They see no ghost.
With sparkling surface-eyes we ply the ball:
It is in truth a most contagious game:
HIDING THE SKELETON, shall be its name.
Such play as this, the devils might appal!
But here's the greater wonder; in that we
Enamoured of an acting nought can tire,
Each other, like true hypocrites, admire;
Warm-lighted looks, Love's ephemeride,
Shoot gaily o'er the dishes and the wine,
We waken envy of our happy lot.
Fast, sweet, and golden, shows the marriage-knot.
Dear guests, you now have seen Love's corpse-light shine.

138

You like not that French novel? Tell me why.
You think it quite unnatural. Let us see.
The actors are, it seems, the usual three :
Husband, and wife, and lover. She—but fie !
In England we'll not hear of it. Edmond,
The lover, her devout chagrin doth share;
Blanc-mange and absinthe are his penitent fare,
Till his pale aspect makes her over-fond:
So, to preclude fresh sin, he tries rosbif.
Meantime the husband is no more abused:
Auguste forgives her ere the tear is used.
Then hangeth all on one tremendous IF:—
If she will choose between them. She does choose;
And takes her husband, like a proper wife.
Unnatural? My dear, these things are life:
And life, some think, is worthy of the Muse.

Along the garden terrace, under which
A purple valley (lighted at its edge
By smoky torch-flame on the long cloud-ledge
Whereunder dropped the chariot), glimmers rich,
A quiet company we pace, and wait
The dinner-bell in præ-digestive calm.
So sweet up violet banks the Southern balm
Breathes round, we care not if the bell be late:
Though here and there grey seniors question Time
In irritable coughings. With slow foot
The low rosed moon, the face of Music mute,
Begins among her silent bars to climb.
As in and out, in silvery dusk, we thread,
I hear the laugh of Madam, and discern
My Lady's heel before me at each turn.
Our tragedy, is it alive or dead?

* * *

After so vehement an expression of marital anguish, let us turn to a vestal poetess: though it may have been merely the Victorian ideal of woman which, disastrously, kept her among the Vestals. If a woman takes up a pen, we hope for a letter which no man-friend could write. If a woman writes novels or verses we hope to find a quality unattainable by a man-poet. Christina Rossetti sometimes achieved poetry of the distaff side: and here are three poems which a man could not have penned.

Christina Rossetti: 1830–1894

A younger sister of D. G. Rossetti. She was born in London. Edmund Gosse admirably wrote 'hers was a cloistered spirit, timid, nun-like, bowed down by suffering (Grave's Disease) and humility; her character was so retiring as to be almost invisible'; and also 'the union of fixed religious faith (High Anglican) with a hold upon physical beauty and the richer parts of nature has been pointed to as the most original feature of her poetry'. She and her brothers, at least in their early days, wrote many bouts-rimés verses in competition (verses written to a given set of rhymes), and nearly all her work suffers from an Italian fluency which is, of course, invaluable in 'bouts-rimés'.

She sat for her portrait to Rossetti, Millais, Holman Hunt and Madox Brown. Swinburne profoundly honoured and admired her, and late in life he dedicated to her *A Century of Roundels*.

140   Portraits

An easy lazy length of limb,
   Dark eyes and features from the South,
A short-legged meditative pipe
   Set in a supercilious mouth:[1]
Ink and a pen and papers laid
   Down on a table for the night,
Beside a semi-dozing man [2]
   Who wakes to go to bed by light.

*   *   *   *   *

A pair of brothers brotherly,
   Unlike and yet how much the same
In heart and high-toned intellect,
   In face and bearing, hope and aim:
Friends of the selfsame treasured friends
   And of one home the dear delight,
Beloved of many a loving heart,
   And cherished both in mine,—Good-night.

9 May 1853.

* * *

Poems of joy are not numerous; and the reason probably is that by expressing an emotion we partly get rid of it. Here, however, is a brilliantly successful joy-poem.

[1] William Michael Rossetti.   [2] Dante Gabriel Rossetti.

141   A Birthday

My heart is like a singing bird
    Whose nest is in a watered shoot:
My heart is like an apple-tree
    Whose boughs are bent with thickset fruit;
My heart is like a rainbow shell
    That paddles in a halcyon sea;
My heart is gladder than all these
    Because my love is come to me.

Raise me a dais of silk and down;
    Hang it with vair and purple dyes;
Carve it in doves and pomegranates,
    And peacocks with a hundred eyes;
Work it in gold and silver grapes,
    In leaves and silver fleur-de-lys;
Because the birthday of my life
    Is come, my love is come to me.

18 November 1857.

* * *

The following sonnet is so well known that perhaps it ought not to appear once more; but it appears because it is a rare and lovely specimen of strictly feminine poetry.

142   Remember

Remember me when I am gone away,
    Gone far away into the silent land;
    When you can no more hold me by the hand,
Nor I half turn to go yet turning stay.
Remember me when no more day by day
    You tell me of our future that you plann'd:
    Only remember me; you understand
It will be late to counsel then or pray.

CHRISTINA ROSSETTI

> Yet if you should forget me for a while
>> And afterwards remember, do not grieve:
> For if the darkness and corruption leave
>> A vestige of the thoughts that once I had,
> Better by far you should forget and smile
>> Than that you should remember and be sad.

Edward Bulwer (Lord) Lytton: 1831–1891

He was the first Earl of Lytton, his father having been Baron Lytton—the renowned and hard-working novelist. The Earl was educated at Harrow and Bonn. He acted in the diplomatic service at The Hague, Vienna, Belgrade, Copenhagen, Athens, Lisbon, Madrid and Paris. From 1876 to 1880 he was Viceroy of India. He wrote (verse and prose) under the name of 'Owen Meredith'.

The following extraordinary poem vividly demonstrates the dire effects of sex-repression as advocated and admired by the lopsided Victorians. Lytton did not fuse his bitter material into high poetry, but we can at least recognise that these fierce verses were torn out of a man's anguish.

143   Twins

> There are two women; one I love, and one
>> I hate. None knows, nor guesses that I know,
> The difference, visible to me alone,
>> Between the two.

> The world believes the one I hate to be
>> The one I love. So little knows it either!
> And tho' one house holds both, you never see
>> The two together.

> The woman that I hate is circumspect,
>> In all her intimacies pure of taint,
> In all her conduct carefully correct,
>> A social saint!

> The woman that I love has other ways,
>> Is passionate, spontaneous, quick, intense;
> No social code her wild warm will obeys,
>> Nor moral sense.

She whom I hate is studiously devout,
    And a good Christian, sure of her salvation;
Nor ever thinks, feels, speaks, or acts without
      Deliberation.

She whom I love is neither saint nor sinner,
    But a wild creature unashamed of truth
To the glad animal life that glows within her,
      And her hot youth.

One has no heart, the other has no head:
    One is all prudence, and all pulse the other;
Yet both when babes on the same milk were fed
      By the same mother.

Each by the other is despised and shunn'd:
    Each to the other is a startling stranger:
Each for the other stores a secret fund
      Of nameless danger!

And all the difference there is between
    These women, comprehensive tho' it be,
By nobody in all the world is seen
      Except by me.

But sometimes, when the night is lone and late,
    And done the pious day's puritanic task,
Panting for breath, the woman that I hate
      Shakes off her mask.

Unbuckles her immaculate girdle, lets
    Her spotless vesture in disorder'd layers
Fall at her feet, and sinfully forgets
      To say her prayers.

Then, from that hated woman's robe set free,
    In all her fearless fervours manifold
The woman that I love leaps forth to me,
      Naked and bold!

William Morris: 1834–1896

Born at Walthamstow. His father was a successful discount-broker. Morris went to Marlborough School and to Exeter College, Oxford, where at first, strangely enough, he studied with a view to taking Holy Orders. He then became an architect's pupil, the change probably being due to the general effect of Darwin's revelation.

Meanwhile, he had begun to write poetry—of which his earliest work, as represented in this book, is the best. 'If that's poetry', he exclaimed, with surprise, 'it's easy'. By degrees Morris, whose energy was inexhaustible, applied himself to the reformation of house furniture, wall-papers and domestic architecture. He also engaged in weaving, designing stained glass, missal-painting and ultimately in printing. His influence was widespread and, despite his mannerisms as a designer, wholly good.

Late in life he became a socialist, and is said to have ruined his health by speech-making in the open air of winter. His socialism was, of course, a scandalous development at the time, but as socialism became the crusade of the Intellectuals, about the turn of the century, his courageous championship of the doctrine may have increased his reputation even beyond his great deserts.

His later verse was too facile and diffuse.

144 The Eve of Crecy

Gold on her head, and gold on her feet,
And gold where the hems of her kirtle meet,
And a golden girdle round my sweet;
    Ah! qu'elle est belle La Marguerite.

Margaret's maids are fair to see,
Freshly dress'd and pleasantly;
Margaret's hair falls down to her knee;
    Ah! qu'elle est belle La Marguerite.

If I were rich I would kiss her feet;
I would kiss the place where the gold hems meet,
And the golden girdle round my sweet:
    Ah! qu'elle est belle La Marguerite.

Ah me! I have never touch'd her hand;
When the arriere-ban goes through the land,
Six basnets under my pennon stand;
    Ah! qu'elle est belle La Marguerite.

And many an one grins under his hood;
Sir Lambert du Bois, with all his men good,
Has neither food nor firewood;
    Ah! qu'elle est belle La Marguerite.

If I were rich I would kiss her feet,
And the golden girdle of my sweet,
And thereabouts where the gold hems meet;
    Ah! qu'elle est belle La Marguerite.

Yet even now it is good to think,
While my few poor varlets grumble and drink,
In my desolate hall, where the fires sink,
    Ah! qu'elle est belle La Marguerite.

Of Margaret sitting glorious there,
In glory of gold and glory of hair,
And glory of glorious face most fair;
    Ah! qu'elle est belle La Marguerite.

Likewise to-night I make good cheer,
Because this battle draweth near;
For what have I to lose or fear?
    Ah! qu'elle est belle La Marguerite.

For, look you, my horse is good to prance
A right fair measure in this war-dance,
Before the eyes of Philip of France;
    Ah! qu'elle est belle La Marguerite.

And sometimes it may hap, perdie,
While my new towers stand up three and three,
And my hall gets painted fair to see,
    Ah! qu'elle est belle La Marguerite,

That folks may say: Times change, by the rood,
For Lambert, banneret of the wood,
Has heaps of food and firewood;
    Ah! qu'elle est belle La Marguerite.

And wonderful eyes, too, under the hood
Of a damsel of right noble blood.
St. Ives, for Lambert of the Wood!
Ah! qu'elle est belle La Marguerite.

* * *

The student should pause to wonder at the young poet's outrageous confidence in using so often within so small a space of sound the word 'glory', and at his undeniable success. Here is an example of genius breaking a good rule.

It was near-nonsense, like the haunting refrain of this wholly irrational poem, which enraged the realistic Tolstoy when he was writing 'What is Art'? but we now know, surely, that two and two make five in heaven, and that poetry may lie exactly half-way between worldly sense and heavenly nonsense.

145   The Tune of Seven Towers

No one goes there now;
　For what is left to fetch away
From the desolate battlements all arow,
　And the lead roof heavy and grey?
Therefore, said fair Yoland of the flowers,
This is the tune of Seven Towers.

No one walks there now;
　Except in the white moonlight
The white ghosts walk in a row;
　If one could see it, an awful sight.
Listen! said fair Yoland of the flowers,
This is the tune of Seven Towers.

But none can see them now,
　Though they sit by the side of the moat,
For half in the water, there in a row,
　Long hair in the wind afloat.
Therefore, said fair Yoland of the flowers,
This is the tune of Seven Towers.

If any will go to it now,
    He must go to it all alone,
Its gates will not open to any row
    Of glittering spears: will *you* go alone?
Listen! said fair Yoland of the flowers,
This is the tune of Seven Towers.

By my love go there now,
    To fetch me my coif away,
My coif and my kirtle, with pearls arow,
    Oliver, go to-day!
Therefore, said fair Yoland of the flowers,
This is the tune of Seven Towers.

I am unhappy now,
    I cannot tell you why;
If you go, the priests and I in a row
    Will pray that you may not die.
Listen! said fair Yoland of the flowers,
This is the tune of Seven Towers.

If you will go for me now,
    I will kiss your mouth at last;
                (She sayeth inwardly.)
    (The graves stand grey in a row.)
        Oliver, hold me fast!
Therefore, said fair Yoland of the flowers,
This is the tune of Seven Towers.

Algernon Charles Swinburne: 1837–1909

An aristocrat who, partly out of admiration for Shelley, became a perfervid republican, Swinburne, born in London, was the son of an admiral and of an earl's daughter. He went to Eton and to Balliol College, Oxford; but, despite his fine classical knowledge, he left without taking a degree. There has been no literary scandal in England to equal that which followed the publication in 1866 of his (First) *Poems and Ballads*. Even Rossetti, no prude, observed '*Poeta nascitur* but *non fit* for publication'. So new and so haunting, however, were the metres and the almost miraculous word-music achieved by the young poet that undergraduates, it is said, used for a generation to declaim the wild anti-moral stanzas of *Dolores* and *Laus Veneris*. Swinburne is the first of our poets completely to master the swift-running (anapæstic or dactyllic) metres, although Shelley had achieved considerable success in the management of them.

Swinburne's intemperance produced a serious breakdown. He was taken in hand by a literary lawyer named Theodore Watts-Dunton who, for the longer part of his life, kept him under strict surveillance. As a young man he was almost drowned, being, in fact, picked up in the nick of time by Guy de Maupassant in a passing yacht. Too much swimming caused Swinburne to become practically stone deaf.

He was buried at Bonchurch, in the Isle of Wight.

146   In the Orchard

(*Provencal Burden*)

Leave go my hands, let me catch breath and see;
Let the dew-fall drench either side of me;
   Clear apple-leaves are soft upon that moon
Seen sidelong like a blossom in the tree;
   Ah God, ah God, that day should be so soon.

The grass is thick and cool, it lets us lie.
Kissed upon either cheek and either eye,
   I turn to thee as some green afternoon
Turns toward sunset, and is loth to die;
   Ah God, ah God, that day should be so soon.

Lie closer, lean your face upon my side,
Feel where the dew fell that has hardly dried,
   Hear how the blood beats that went nigh to swoon;
The pleasure lives there when the sense has died;
   Ah God, ah God, that day should be so soon.

O my fair lord, I charge you leave me this:
Is it not sweeter than a foolish kiss?
   Nay take it then, my flower, my first in June,
My rose, so like a tender mouth it is:
   Ah God, ah God, that day should be so soon.

Love, till dawn sunder night from day with fire,
Dividing my delight and my desire,
  The crescent life and love the plenilune,
Love me though dusk begin and dark retire;
  Ah God, ah God, that day should be so soon.

Ah, my heart fails, my blood draws back; I know,
When life runs over, life is near to go;
  And with the slain of love love's ways are strewn,
And with their blood, if love will have it so;
  Ah God, ah God, that day should be so soon.

Ah, do thy will now; slay me if thou wilt;
There is no building now the walls are built,
  No quarrying now the corner-stone is hewn,
No drinking now the vine's whole blood is spilt;
  Ah God, ah God, that day should be so soon.

Nay, slay me now; nay, for I will be slain;
Pluck thy red pleasure from the teeth of pain,
  Break down thy vine ere yet grape-gatherers prune,
Slay me ere day can slay desire again;
  Ah God, ah God, that day should be so soon.

Yea, with thy sweet lips, with thy sweet sword; yea
Take life and all, for I will die, I say;
  Love, I gave love, is life a better boon?
For sweet night's sake I will not live till day;
  Ah God, ah God, that day should be so soon.

Nay, I will sleep then only; nay, but go.
Ah sweet, too sweet to me, my sweet, I know
  Love, sleep, and death go to the sweet same tune;
Hold my hair fast, and kiss me through it so.
  Ah God, ah God, that day should be so soon.

* * *

In this next piece a poetry student may find the ultimate perfection
of verse-craft.

147 The Roundel

A roundel is wrought as a ring or a starbright sphere,
With craft of delight and with cunning of sound unsought,
That the heart of the hearer may smile if to pleasure his ear
    A roundel is wrought.

Its jewel of music is carven of all or of aught—
Love, laughter, or mourning—remembrance of rapture or fear—
That fancy may fashion to hang in the ear of thought.

As a bird's quick song runs round, and the hearts in us hear
Pause answer to pause, and again the same strain caught,
So moves the device whence, round as a pearl or tear
    A roundel is wrought.

*   *   *

And here, half-forgotten in our own time, is a poem of passion and
longing which might well stand as the song of all those who can love
without reservation. We should note the emphatic heart-beat in this
metre.

148 Oblation

Ask nothing more of me, sweet;
    All I can give you I give;
    Heart of my heart, were it more,
More should be laid at your feet:
    Love that should help you to live,—
    Song that should spur you to soar.

All things were nothing to give,
    Once to have sense of you more,—
    Touch you and taste of you, sweet,
Think you and breathe you, and live
    Swept of your wings as they soar,
    Trodden by chance of your feet.

I, who have love and no more,
  Bring you but love of you, sweet.
    He that hath more, let him give;
  He that hath wings, let him soar:
    Mine is the heart at your feet
      Here, that must love you to live.

Wilfred Scawen Blunt: 1840–1922

A wealthy eccentric, he bred Arab steeds, became for some time a
Mahommedan, formed a small aristocratic literary group from among
his friends, and spent a vast amount of energy in opposing the various
British governments of his long life.

Blunt's verse, like Meredith's love poems, introduced a note of
reality—of persons who had to eat, sleep, wear clothes,—which in its
own day was new. For some fifty years a poet had been supposed to have
no corporeal personality, and his 'lady' or 'love' to have, like the queen,
'no legs'. Tennyson and Browning and Queen Victoria were responsible
for this enervating assumption. It is difficult in our own day to realise
the *bravado* of writing such a line, in the 'eighties, as

    'You wore a little *fichu* trimmed with lace'.

Blunt's contemporaries would have regarded it as unpoetical because
it was definite.

149 Juliet

I see you, Juliet, still, with your straw hat
Loaded with vines, and with your dear pale face,
On which those thirty years so lightly sat,
And the white outline of your muslin dress.
You wore a little *fichu* trimmed with lace
And crossed in front, as was the fashion then,
Bound at your waist with a broad band or sash,
All white and fresh and virginally plain.
There was a sound of shouting far away
Down in the valley, as they called to us,

And you, with hands clasped seeming still to pray
Patience of fate, stood listening to me thus
With heaving bosom. There a rose lay curled.
It was the reddest rose in all the world.

150   Roumeli Hissar

A Sonnet

The empire of the East, grown dull to fear
By long companionship with angry fate,
In silent anguish saw her doom appear
In this dark fortress built upon the strait,
And Sultan Mahmoud standing at her gate,
For she must perish. Hissar many a year
Struck terror into all who gazed thereat,
Till in his turn the Turk had learned to wear
The purple and fine linen of the State,
And fell in impotence. These walls to-day,
With Judas tree and lilac overgrown,
Move all men's hearts. For close on barbarous power
Tread lust and indolence, and then decay
Till we forgive.—The very German boor,
Who in his day of fortune moves our scorn,
Purged of his slough, in after ages may
Invite the tears of nations yet unborn.

Gerard Manley Hopkins: 1844–1889

A Jesuit priest, Hopkins drove a lone furrow in the 'eighties: experimenting brilliantly with the possibilities of a poetry which should burst all the confines of grammar and syntax. His work might never have appeared were it not that Robert Bridges, after becoming Poet Laureate, sponsored the publication of his poems. Their 'sprung rhythm' and their general jettisoning of rules, delighted the inter-war versemen. Nevertheless, were it not for his intense Christian mysticism, Hopkins's work might be a mere curiosity in our literature.

151   The Starlight Night

Look at the stars! look, look up at the skies!
  O look at all the fire-folk sitting in the air!
  The bright boroughs, the circle-citadels there!
Down in dim woods the diamond delves! the elves'-eyes!
The grey lawns cold where gold, where quickgold lies!
  Wind-beat whitebeam! airy abeles set on a flare!
  Flake-doves sent floating forth at a farmyard scare!—
Ah well! it is all a purchase, all is a prize.

Buy then! bid then!—What?—Prayer, patience, alms, vows,
Look, look: a May-mess, like on orchard boughs!
  Look! March-bloom, like on mealed-with-yellow sallows!
These are indeed the barn; withindoors house
The shocks. This piece-bright paling shuts the spouse
  Christ home, Christ and his mother and all his hallows.

152   The Windhover: To Christ Our Lord

I caught this morning morning's minion, kingdom of daylight's dauphin,
  Dapple-dawn-drawn Falcon, in his riding
Of the rolling level underneath him steady air, and striding
High there, how he rung upon the rein of a wimpling wing
In his ecstasy! then off, off forth on swing,
  As a skate's heel sweeps smooth on a bow-bend: the hurl and gliding
Rebuffed the big wind. My heart in hiding
Stirred for a bird,—the achieve of, the mastery of the thing!

Brute beauty and valour and act, oh, air, pride, plume, here
  Buckle! AND the fire that breaks from thee then, a billion
Times told lovelier, more dangerous, O my chevalier!

 No wonder of it: sheer plod makes plough down sillion
Shine, and blue-bleak embers, ah my dear,
  Fall, gall themselves, and gash gold-vermilion.

Robert Louis Stevenson: 1850–1894

Born in Edinburgh. His father was a civil engineer, and 'R. L. S.' progressed far enough in the same direction as to read a specialist paper about improvement in lighthouses. However, he soon caught the tide of literature, probably speaking mere truth when he said, subsequently, that his talent was almost entirely the fruit of enthusiastic industry.

Success came early,—with *Treasure Island*.

In youth Stevenson was, they say, decidedly sportive, but as years multiplied, the Scottish moralist within him gained the field. Always delicate (from the age of six), he developed tuberculosis and spent the end of his life for the sake of health in Samoa. The natives loved him and gave him the name of Tusitala,—story-teller.

Stevenson's elegant ingratiating prose has been ponderously attacked in recent years, when elegance had become suspect, but, as an air-pilot said to the present writer, 'Style always returns—in time'. As a poet, Stevenson is almost grotesquely underrated: if indeed he is still read.

153   After reading *Antony and Cleopatra*

As when the hunt by holt and field
Drives on with horn and strife,
Hunger of hopeless things pursues
Our spirits throughout life.

The sea's roar fills us aching full
Of objectless desire—
The sea's roar, and the white moon-shine,
And the reddening of the fire.

Who talks to me of reason now?
It would be more delight
To have died in Cleopatra's arms
Than be alive to-night.

154   Since years ago for evermore

Since years ago for evermore
My cedar ship I drew to shore;
And to the road and riverbed
And the green, nodding reeds, I said
Mine ignorant and last farewell:
Now with content at home I dwell,
And now divide my sluggish life
Betwixt my verses and my wife:
In vain: for when the lamp is lit
And by the laughing fire I sit,
Still with the tattered atlas spread
Interminable roads I tread.

PART SEVEN

Part Seven

WE MUST REALISE that, once again, the monarch of England, at this time a Queen, had sealed the moral character of the age: and, as Queen Victoria grew older, her son became more sportive, and, by degrees, the influence of the King-to-be affected British society, from Mayfair to Maida Vale; so that, in the upshot, it was inevitable that young intelligent men—men interested, I mean, in the arts,—should rebel, and over-rebel, against the moral blinkers of the Victorian ideal.

Here, then,—in this Second Autumn of England Verse—we meet with 'decadence' (or Accepted Autumn) together with an over-emphatic manliness. The manliest of all these poets was Rudyard Kipling; but he so often wrote to a hurdy-gurdy tune in his brain and so often used a metre inappropriate to his theme, and sometimes, as in *The Brushwood Boy*, indulged in poeticalness which delights only confirmed boarding-housers that, except for *Lest We Forget* and his fine brief lyric about the First German War, he cannot reasonably be rated among the versemen who had due respect for their instrument.

Henley and Davidson—and Stevenson, too,—were manly voices: and yet most of the poets of this after-Tennyson era were indubitably over-ripe. They were, in the true sense, refined. They were literary sieves, and coarse matter would not go through their mesh. The 'nineties was a brief period of intense art-worship. Young men strove hard to attain 'style': and by style they meant a use of words so fastidious that, quite ignoring 'the ordinary decent chap', it should delight the palate of the most exacting reader. If my own reader is 'exacting', let him try on his palate the delicious *Memory* by Arthur Symons.

In 1895 Oscar Wilde, the most entertaining talker in Europe and probably in the whole world, crashed to infamy when he was suddenly convicted of oblique desires. This event had wide effects. In Great Britain the vast majority, which was made up of Puritans, rejoiced that a disconcertingly witty man, and a man who had said that 'all art is useless', should have been tarred and feathered. Wilde's disgrace made

266

'art' suspect. The British public rushed toward Kipling: and within a few years there came a movement for hiking (it was then called 'camping') and 'the wide open spaces'. Any delicacy of perception looked much like sin and elegance was confused with affectation.

The importance of this brief period is that the Cavalier once more challenged the Puritan: and that only Wilde's disaster could have re-convinced Englishmen that art and immorality are one. Delicacy rather than power is the typical note of the time, but at the turn of the century there were many different kinds of work being done. Kipling and Davidson specialised in the robust; Yeats in the extremely subtle; Æ in the genuinely mystical, and steadily through all modes Thomas Hardy sustained his own firm style.

Austin Dobson: 1840–1921

A Civil Servant—in the Board of Trade. From 1884 to 1901 (a lengthy enough period) he was principal clerk in the marine department.

As a poet he was a fan-painter, with a list toward the eighteenth century conceived sentimentally and without regard to Hogarth's evidence. As a metrist of light, sentimental and formal verses, he achieved a high polish not attainable by his rivals. It would not be unjust to term him a poetic French-polisher.

If his poems were not so expensive, the reader should have many more of them.

Toy-verse cannot be more deftly turned than it was by Austin Dobson; but he depended on the complacent mood of late-Victorianism, and could not have written in an age of great writing. His work, perfect though it is, would have seemed so trivial as not to be worth achieving.

155   On a Fan that Belonged to the Marquise de
Pompadour

Chicken-skin, delicate, white,
    Painted by Carlo Vanloo,
Loves in a riot of light,
    Roses and vaporous blue;
    Hark to the dainty *frou-frou*!
Picture above, if you can,
    Eyes that could melt as the dew,—
This was the Pompadour's fan!

See how they rise at the sight,
    Thronging the *Oeil de Boeuf* through;
Courtiers as butterflies bright,
    Beauties that Fragonard drew,
    Talon-rouge, falbala, queue,
Cardinal, Duke,—to a man,
    Eager to sigh or to sue,—
This was the Pompadour's fan!

Ah, but things more than polite
    Hung on this toy, *voyez-vous*!
Matters of state and of might,
    Things that great ministers do;
    Things that, maybe, overthrew
Those in whose brains they began;
    Here was the sign and the cue,—
This was the Pompadour's fan!

ENVOY

Where are the secrets it knew?
    Weavings of plot and of plan?
—But where is the Pompadour, too?
    This was the Pompadour's *Fan*!

William Ernest Henley: 1849–1903

A Gloucestershire man: but during his formative years he worked mostly in Scotland. Henley was of the Ben Jonson type, a dominant layer-down of the literary law. As Editor of various papers he confidently rewrote the work of his contributors.

A cripple from boyhood, he over-emphasised his vigour: but he certainly added a new, semi-realistic style to English poetry.

156 Before (In Hospital)

Behold me waiting—waiting for the knife.
A little while, and at a leap I storm
The thick, sweet mystery of chloroform,
The drunken dark, the little death-in-life.
The gods are good to me: I have no wife,
No innocent child, to think of as I near
The fateful minute; nothing all-too dear
Unmans me for my bout of passive strife.
Yet am I tremulous and a trifle sick,
And, face to face with chance, I shrink a little:
My hopes are strong, my will is something weak.
Here comes the basket? Thank you. I am ready,
But, gentlemen my porters, life is brittle:
You carry Cæsar and his fortunes—steady!

157 Apparition (R. L. Stevenson)

Thin-legged, thin-chested, slight unspeakably,
Neat-footed and weak-fingered: in his face—
Lean, large-boned, curved of beak, and touched with race,
Bold-lipped, rich-tinted, mutable as the sea,
The brown eyes radiant with vivacity—
There shines a brilliant and romantic grace,
A spirit intense and rare, with trace on trace
Of passion and impudence and energy.

Valiant in velvet, light in raggéd luck,
Most vain, most generous, sternly critical,
Buffoon and poet, lover and sensualist:
A deal of Ariel, just a streak of Puck,
Much Antony, of Hamlet most of all,
And something of the Shorter-Catechist.

Oscar Wilde: 1856–1900

Educated at Trinity College, Dublin, and Magdalen College, Oxford. He became an excellent Greek scholar. Considering the extreme brilliance of his talk, it is surprising that he should have written so much and so well. Just when he was at the summit of his success as a witty dramatist, he was sentenced to two years' hard labour on moral charges. When he was released, he lived in France but, whether because his spirit was broken or because he required immediate applause, he was then unable to produce any work of value.

His downfall unfortunately confirmed the millions of British Philistines in their suspicion that art is both wicked and unnecessary.

158 On the Recent Sale by Auction of Keats's Love-letters

These are the letters which Endymion wrote
To one he loved in secret and apart,
And now the brawlers of the auction-mart
Bargain and bid for each poor blotted note,
Aye! for each separate pulse of passion quote
The merchant's price! I think they love not art
Who break the crystal of a poet's heart,
That small and sickly eyes may glare or gloat.

Is it not said, that many years ago,
In a far Eastern town some soldiers ran
With torches through the midnight, and began
To wrangle for mean raiment, and to throw
Dice for the garments of a wretched man,
Not knowing the God's wonder, or his woe?

159 Theocritus

A VILLANELLE

O singer of Persephone!
  In the dim meadows desolate
Dost thou remember Sicily?

Still through the ivy flits the bee
  Where Amaryllis lies in state;
O Singer of Persephone!

Simætha calls on Hecate
  And hears the wild dogs at the gate;
Dost thou remember Sicily?

Still by the light and laughing sea
  Poor Polypheme bemoans his fate:
O Singer of Persephone!

And still in boyish rivalry
  Young Daphnis challenges his mate:
Dost thou remember Sicily?

Slim Lacon keeps a goat for thee,
  For thee the jocund shepherds wait,
O Singer of Persephone!
Dost thou remember Sicily?

John Davidson: 1859–1909

For seventeen years a schoolmaster in Scotland. He struck a note in the 'nineties more virile than those which were typical, but he did not succeed in extracting poetry from the philosophical materialism of Herbert Spencer. He once observed 'I write for Plato, Jesus Christ and Shakespeare', and yet he had some real talent behind his megalomania.

Finding that he was stricken with cancer, he deliberately walked into the sea off Penzance and drowned himself.

Even before Kipling, here is the voice of 'The Little Man' who, since he outnumbers any other kind of man, seems likely to regulate society.

The following piece is of interest as showing an early attempt to make poetry out of the commonplace and also as a kind of Phil May drawing in verse.

160　Thirty Bob a Week

I couldn't touch a stop and turn a screw,
　　And set the blooming world a-work for me,
Like such as cut their teeth—I hope, like you—
　　On the handle of a skeleton gold key.
I cut mine on leek, which I eat it every week:
　　I'm a clerk at thirty bob, as you can see.

But I don't allow it's luck and all a toss;
　　There's no such thing as being starred and crossed;
It's just the power of some to be a boss,
　　And the bally power of others to be bossed:
I face the music, sir; you bet I ain't a cur!
　　Strike me lucky if I don't believe I'm lost!

For like a mole I journey in the dark,
　　A-travelling along the underground
From my Pillar'd Halls and broad suburban Park
　　To come the daily dull official round;
And home again at night with my pipe all alight
　　A-scheming how to count ten bob a pound.

And it's often very cold and very wet;
　　And my missis stitches towels for a hunks;
And the Pillar'd Halls is half of it to let—
　　Three rooms about the size of travelling trunks.
And we cough, the wife and I, to dislocate a sigh,
　　When the noisy little kids are in their bunks.

But you'll never hear *her* do a growl, or whine,
　　For she's made of flint and roses very odd;
And I've got to cut my meaning rather fine
　　Or I'd blubber, for *I'm* made of greens and sod;
So p'rhaps we are in hell for all that I can tell,
　　And lost and damned and served up hot to God.

I ain't blaspheming, Mr. Silvertongue;
   I'm saying things a bit beyond your art;
Of all the rummy starts you ever sprung
   Thirty bob a week's the rummiest start!
With your science and your books and your the'ries about spooks,
   Did you ever hear of looking in your heart?

I didn't mean your pocket, Mr.; no!
   I mean that having children and a wife
With thirty bob on which to come and go
   Isn't dancing to the tabor and the fife;
When it doesn't make you drink, by Heaven. it makes you think,
   And notice curious items about life!

I step into my heart and there I meet
   A god-almighty devil singing small,
Who would like to shout and whistle in the street,
   And squelch the passers flat against the wall;
If the whole world was a cake he had the power to take,
   He would take it, ask for more, and eat it all.

And I meet a sort of simpleton beside—
   The kind that life is always giving beans;
With thirty bob a week to keep a bride
   He fell in love and married in his teens;
At thirty bob he stuck, but he knows it isn't luck;
   He knows the seas are deeper than tureens.

And the god-almighty devil and the fool
   That meet me in the High Street on the strike,
When I walk about my heart a-gathering wool,
   Are my good and evil angels if you like;
And both of them together in every kind of weather
   Ride me like a double-seated 'bike'.

That's rough a bit and needs its meaning curled;
   But I have a high old hot un in my mind,
A most engrugious notion of the world
   That leaves your lightning 'rithmetic behind:
I give it at a glance when I say 'There ain't no chance,
   Nor nothing of the lucky-lottery kind'.

And it's this way that I make it out to be;
 No fathers, mothers, countries, climates—none!—
Not Adam was responsible for me;
 Nor society, nor systems, nary one!
A little sleeping seed, I woke—I did indeed—
 A million years before the blooming sun.

I woke because I thought the time had come;
 Beyond my will there was no other cause;
And everywhere I found myself at home
 Because I chose to be the thing I was;
And in whatever shape, of mollusc, or of ape,
 I always went according to the laws.

I was the love that chose my mother out;
 I joined two lives and from the union burst;
My weakness and my strength without a doubt
 Are mine alone for ever from the first.
It's just the very same with a difference in the name
 As 'Thy will be done'. You say it if you durst!

They say it daily up and down the land
 As easy as you take a drink, it's true;
But the difficultest go to understand,
 And the difficultest job a man can do,
Is to come it brave and meek with thirty bob a week,
 And feel that that's the proper thing for you.

It's a naked child against a hungry wolf;
 It's playing bowls upon a splitting wreck;
It's walking on a string across a gulf
 With millstones fore-and-aft about your neck:
But the thing is daily done by many and many a one. . . .
 And we fall, face forward, fighting, on the deck.

Francis Thompson: 1859–1907

'He made helpless efforts', we are told, 'to earn a livelihood', but 'fell a prey to opium'. He was found selling matches in a London gutter, and was rescued from this abject state by Lewis Hind, an editor with insight, and by Wilfred Meynell; but, whatever his condition, Thompson never lost sight of the spiritual world. He died of consumption.

161　At Lord's

It is little I repair to the matches of the Southron folk,
　　Though my own red roses there may blow;
It is little I repair to the matches of the Southron folk,
　　Though the red roses crest the caps, I know.
For the field is full of shades as I near the shadowy coast,
And a ghostly batsman plays to the bowling of a ghost,
And I look through my tears on a soundless-clapping host
　　As the run-stealers flicker to and fro,
　　　　　　　To and fro:—
　　O my Hornby and my Barlow long ago!

162　To a Snowflake

　　What heart could have thought you?—
　　Past our devisal
　　(O filigree petal!)
　　Fashioned so purely,
　　Fragilely, surely,
　　From what Paradisal
　　Imagineless metal,
　　Too costly for cost?
　　Who hammered you, wrought you,
　　From argentine vapour?—
　　'God was my shaper.
　　Passing surmisal,
　　He hammered, He wrought me,
　　From curled silver vapour,
　　To lust of His mind:—
　　Thou could'st not have thought me!
　　So purely, so palely,
　　Tinily, surely,
　　Mightily, frailly,
　　Insculped and embossed,
　　With His hammer of wind,
　　And His graver of frost'.

John Barlas: 1860–1914

Born at Rangoon. Educated at New College, Oxford, and while there
he married a grandniece of Horatio Nelson. He himself was descended
from the heroic Kate Barlas who in 1437 saved King James (the First) of
Scotland by using her arm as a bar to the door at which his would-be
assassins were heaving.

Barlas was 'a poet of handsome presence, a Greek statue vivified',
but he had in him a streak of insanity which may have been manifested
when he fired a revolver at the Houses of Parliament in order to show
his anarchistic contempt for parliamentary institutions. He was confined
in a Scottish asylum, and was ultimately buried in Glasgow.

163   Covering Hair

> Kisses are sweetest under covering hair,
>   And whispers in its woven twilight best;
>   As flowery boughs above the chirping nest
> Make sweet and sacred all the darkened air
> Wherein abide the soft-secluded pair,
>   And know in the warm fragrance where they rest
>   The small heart beating in the downy breast
> Each of its mate:—a Paradise they share.
> This is a longing of the human heart
>   After that dream, an Eden all for two,
>   Some lonely island 'mid the ocean's blue
> Where Love may sport, and laugh, and kiss apart.
>   Therefore it was a moment past I drew
> Thine hair about mine eyes, Eve that thou art.

164   Noblesse Oblige

> 'Noblesse oblige': it was a simple creed,
>   Forgotten now, that who preferred a claim
>   To life more honoured than the general name
> Should give it for the general good at need:

And from this outworn faith arose a breed
 Of men who sickened at the thought of shame,
  Whose swords, kept bright by use, were fire to tame
On England's soil the growth of waste and weed.
He who has once loved truly is a knight,
 Knows deep down in his heart heroic worth,
  And pins upon his crest a lady's glove.
Him shall you not turn back in the grim fight:
 Uncover and own then, ye who prate of birth,
  The untitled aristocracy of Love.

Arthur Symons: 1865–

165 On the Stage

Lights, in a multi-coloured mist,
From indigo to amethyst,
A whirling mist of multi-coloured lights;
And after, wigs and tights,
Then faces, then a glimpse of profiles, then
Eyes, and a mist again;
And rouge, and always tights, and wigs, and tights.

You see the ballet so, and so,
From amethyst to indigo;
You see a dance of phantoms, but I see
A girl who smiles to me;
Her cheeks, across the rouge, and in her eyes
I know what memories,
What memories and messages for me.

166 At the Ambassadeurs

TO YVETTE GUILBERT

That was Yvette. The blithe Ambassadeurs
Glitters, this Sunday of the Fête des Fleurs;
Here are the flowers, too, living flowers that blow
A night or two before the odours go;

And all the flowers of all the city ways
Are laughing, with Yvette, this day of days.
Laugh, with Yvette? But I must first forget,
Before I laugh, that I have heard Yvette.
For the flowers fade before her: see, the light
Dies out of that poor cheek, and leaves it white;
She sings of life, and mirth, and all that moves
Man's fancy in the carnival of loves;
And a chill shiver takes me as she sings
The pity of unpitied human things.

The use of echoed words, and even of vowels, in this next lyric
could have been made only by a hypersensitive artist in language.

167   Memory

As a perfume doth remain
In the folds where it hath lain,
   So the thought of you, remaining
Deeply folded in my brain,
   Will not leave me: all things leave me:
You remain.

Other thoughts may come and go,
Other moments I may know
   That shall waft me, in their going,
As a breath blown to and fro,
   Fragrant memories: fragrant memories
Come and go.

Only thoughts of you remain
In my heart where they have lain,
   Perfumed thoughts of you, remaining,
A hid sweetness, in my brain,
   Others leave me: all things leave me:
You remain.

Ernest Dowson: 1867–1900

He increased his natural melancholy and damaged his frail health by a too frequent use of absinthe. For two or three years he suffered from an unrequited adoration of a cashier-girl in a well-known French restaurant in Soho. She was certainly a handsome wench—with 'bugle eyeballs' and coils of black hair. Dowson had a strange liking for the comforts of cabmen's shelters; he is also said to have lived for some time as a supercargo on a Thames-side wharf.

168   Seraphita

Come not before me now, O visionary face!
Me tempest-tost, and borne along life's passionate sea;
Troublous and dark and stormy though my passage be;
Not here and now may we commingle or embrace,
Lest the loud anguish of the waters should efface
The bright illumination of thy memory,
Which dominates the night; rest, far away from me,
In the serenity of thine abiding-place!

But when the storm is highest, and the thunders blare,
And sea and sky are riven, O moon of all my night!
Stoop down but once in pity of my great despair,
And let thine hand, though over late to help, alight
But once upon my pale eyes and my drowning hair,
Before the great waves conquer in the last vain fight.

169   Epigram

Because I am idolatrous and have besought,
With grievous supplication and consuming prayer,
The admirable image that my dreams have wrought
Out of her swan's neck and her dark, abundant hair:
The jealous gods, who brook no worship save their own,
Turned my live idol marble and her heart to stone.

T

'During the last two or three decades', he said, 'women have begun to write poetry of their own,—poetry made out of distinctively feminine experience: and remember the whole experience of life is conditioned by the sex into which you are born'.

(*The Old Man from Somerset*, p. 112.)

PART EIGHT

Part Eight

IN DEFIANCE OF a mere birthdate we may justly open this last section of England's poetic history with the great name of Thomas Hardy. He was always 'modern', and even in the dim eighteen-sixties he remained unaffected by either Tennyson or Browning. He achieved his own rugged style but, nevertheless, he was at heart a traditionalist. We might justly say that all the English poets who were at work during the first twenty years of this century kept touch with tradition, and that it is only since nineteen-twenty that a new bleakness and sophistication has appeared in our poetry, or, in other words, that would-be poets have again become 'clever'.

There have been so many good poets in our own time that, in a book like this one, it is only possible to choose a handful of modern poems almost at random. Kipling, as Holbrook Jackson observed, was a verse-writer whom no school or coterie seemed anxious to claim; and posterity may decide that his blend of the Bible and the Ha'penny News-paper did not achieve the distinction of poetry. A. E. Housman, whose best poems appeared in 1896, exercised for about thirty years a strong and tightening influence upon English verse which, as we have recognised, always tends to verbosity and formlessness: Yeats, a subtle artist, and 'A.E.', an amateur artist but a genuine mystic, were considerably inspired by the magnificent view of life which, set forth in Madame Blavatsky's theosophy, was a challenge to the complacent materialism of late nineteenth-century science: John Masefield, our Poet Laureate, infused fresh vigour into verse when, in 1911, he began to write his most characteristic work, the stories in colloquial language that start with *The Everlasting Mercy*; but Masefield is not at his best unless he is afforded at least ten or fifteen pages, a proportion of space not here available, for he lacks the concentration of force which alone can pack immortality into a sonnet or a lyric. Mr. T. S. Eliot, to the astonishment of his contemporaries and probably to his own surprise, has been—since the publication of *The Waste Land*—the begetter of an incalculably vast mass of amorphous free-verse for which, manifestly, he should not be held responsible. His influence in the between-war period has been so formative that, whatever posterity may think (if at all) of his multitudinous disciples, he himself has clearly obtained a *visa* to literary Elysian Fields.

Here, then, are just a few poems by a few modern authors, but they should be sufficient to indicate the innumerable cross-currents of emotion, cerebration, romantic and anti-romantic outlooks, which were thrown up by the appalling conditions of our unfortunate age.

Thomas Hardy : *1840–1928*

Born in Dorsetshire. In 1856 he was articled to an ecclesiastical architect named Hicks. He began to 'write' in 1859.

Hardy spent most of his life in the composition of novels that have a West-Country background and a sad conviction that all fine things are doomed to suffer in 'this unlucky planet'. In late life he concentrated upon the writing of poems: and the fact that the greatest of all his works, in any medium,—*The Dynasts*—was published in 1904–1906 ought to revive the creative spring in many writers who lose heart in their later 'fifties.

He was twice married.

170   In Time of 'The Breaking of Nations'

> Only a man harrowing clods
>   In a slow silent walk
> With an old horse that stumbles and nods,
>   Half asleep as they stalk.

Only thin smoke without flame
  From the heaps of couch-grass;
Yet this will go onward the same
  Though Dynasties pass.

Yonder a maid and her wight
  Come whispering by:
War's annals will fade into night
  Ere their story die.

1915.

* * *

This grave and noble poem, hewn into a novel and successful metre, was inspired by 'Mrs. Thompson' whose sailor-lover, Bywaters, murdered her husband under her 'Clytæmnestra' influence. Her letters to Bywaters had so much charm that thousands of men and women were kept awake by the knowledge that she was to be hanged.

171   On the Portrait of a Woman about to be Hanged

Comely and capable one of our race,
Posing there in your gown of grace,
  Plain, yet becoming;
    Could subtlest breast
    Ever have guessed
What was behind that innocent face,
  Drumming, drumming!

Would that your Causer, ere knoll your knell
For this riot of passion, might deign to tell
  Why, since It made you
    Sound in the germ,
    It sent a worm
To madden Its handiwork, when It might well
  Not have assayed you;

Not have implanted, to your deep rue
The Clytæmnestra spirit in you,
   And with purblind vision
     Sowed a tare
     In a field so fair,
And a thing of symmetry, seemly to view,
   Brought to derision!

January 6, 1923.

172   At Lulworth Cove a Century Back

Had I but lived a hundred years ago
I might have gone, as I have gone this year,
By Warmwell Cross on to a Cove I know,
And Time have placed his finger on me there:

'*You see that man*'?—I might have looked, and said,
'O yes: I see him. One that boat has brought
Which dropped down Channel round Saint Alban's Head.
So commonplace a youth calls not my thought'.

'*You see that man*'?—'Why yes; I told you; yes:
Of an idling town-sort; thin; hair brown in hue;
And as the evening light scants less and less
He looks up at a star, as many do'.

'*You see that man*'?—'Nay, leave me'! then I plead,
'I have fifteen miles to vamp across the lea,
And it grows dark, and I am weary-kneed:
I have said the third time; yes, that man I see'!

'Good. That man goes to Rome—to death, despair;
And no one notes him now but you and I:
A hundred years, and the world will follow him there,
And bend with reverence where his ashes lie'.

    September, 1920.

Note.—In September 1820 Keats, on his way to Rome, landed one
day on the Dorset coast, and composed the sonnet, *Bright star! would I
were stedfast as thou art*' (see p. 192). The spot of his landing is judged to
have been Lulworth Cove.

173   An Ancient to Ancients

Where once we danced, where once we sang,
            Gentlemen,
The floors are sunken, cobwebs hang,
And cracks creep; worms have fed upon
The doors. Yea, sprightlier times were then
Than now, with harps and tabrets gone,
            Gentlemen!

Where once we rowed, where once we sailed,
            Gentlemen,
And damsels took the tiller, veiled
Against too strong a stare (God wot
Their fancy, then or anywhen!)
Upon that shore we are clean forgot,
            Gentlemen!

We have lost somewhat, afar and near,
            Gentlemen,
The thinning of our ranks each year
Affords a hint we are nigh undone,
That we shall not be ever again
The marked of many, loved of one,
            Gentlemen.

In dance the polka hit our wish,
            Gentlemen,
The paced quadrille, the spry schottische,
'Sir Roger'.—And in opera spheres
The 'Girl' (the famed 'Bohemian')
And 'Trovatore', held the ears,
            Gentlemen.

This season's paintings do not please,
            Gentlemen,
Like Etty, Mulready, Maclise;
Throbbing romance has waned and wanned;
No wizard wields the witching pen
Of Bulwer, Scott, Dumas, and Sand,
            Gentlemen.

The bower we shrined to Tennyson,
          Gentlemen,
Is roof-wrecked; damps there drip upon
Sagged seats, the creeper-nails are rust,
The spider is sole denizen;
Even she who voiced those rhymes is dust,
          Gentlemen!

We who met sunrise sanguine-souled,
          Gentlemen,
Are wearing weary. We are old;
These younger press; we feel our rout
Is imminent to Aides' den,—
That evening shades are stretching out,
          Gentlemen!

And yet, though ours be failing frames,
          Gentlemen,
So were some others' History names,
Who trode their track light-limbed and fast
As these youth, and not alien
From enterprise, to their long last,
          Gentlemen.

Sophocles, Plato, Socrates,
          Gentlemen,
Pythagoras, Thucydides,
Herodotus, and Homer, yea,
Clement, Augustin, Origen,
Burnt brightlier towards their setting-day,
          Gentlemen.

And ye, red-lipped and smooth-browed; list,
          Gentlemen!
Much is there waits you we have missed;
Much lore we leave you worth the knowing,
Much, much has lain outside our ken:
Nay, rush not: time serves: we are going,
          Gentlemen.

William Butler Yeats: 1865–1939

Born in Ireland, of Irish stock. For a short time he studied in an art-school. From early years he was fascinated by occultism, and in later life built up a complex and baffling system of ideas. Perhaps the most fruitful was his contention that each person has within him an 'anti-self' which is in all ways the opposite of the apparent personality. He did much toward the creation of a new Irish drama.

There was far more of the conscious publicist in Yeats than could have existed in a man whose mysticism was really deep.

As a poet he developed several styles of which here are five specimens. *The Indian upon God*, a very early poem, is pleasantly unmannered. It comes from a time when the poet was profoundly immersed in ancient Hindu philosophy.

174   The Indian upon God

I passed along the water's edge below the humid trees,
My spirit rocked in evening light, the rushes round my knees,
My spirit rocked in sleep and sighs; and saw the moorfowl pace
All dripping on a grassy slope, and saw them cease to chase
Each other round in circles, and heard the eldest speak:
Who holds the world between His bill and made us strong or weak
Is an undying moorfowl, and He lives beyond the sky.
The rains are from His dripping wing, the moonbeams from His eye.
I passed a little further on and heard a lotus talk:
Who made the world and ruleth it, He hangeth on a stalk,
For I am in His image made, and all this tinkling tide
Is but a sliding drop of rain between His petals wide.
A little way within the gloom a roebuck raised his eyes
Brimful of starlight, and he said: *The Stamper of the Skies,*
He is a gentle roebuck; for how else, I pray, could he
Conceive a thing so sad and soft, a gentle thing like me?
I passed a little further on and heard a peacock say:
Who made the grass and made the worms and made my feathers gay,
He is a monstrous peacock, and He waveth all the night
His languid tail above us, lit with myriad spots of light.

In his second phase Yeats was obliquely influenced by the French symbolists. His work of this period is superfine, but he was in danger of reducing to a minute number the words which he could use without tearing the diaphanous texture of his poetry.

175   The Everlasting Voices

O sweet everlasting Voices be still;
Go to the guards of the heavenly fold
And bid them wander obeying your will
Flame under flame, till Time be no more;
Have you not heard that our hearts are old,
That you call in birds, in wind on the hill,
In shaken boughs, in tide on the shore?
O sweet everlasting Voices be still.

* * *

This next poem marks another clear change of style. He is now trying to introduce into his work a certain tone as of a man talking to himself. His vocabulary, in consequence, became much larger.

176   The Folly of being Comforted

One that is ever kind said yesterday:
'Your well-belovéd's hair has threads of grey,
And little shadows come about her eyes;
Time can but make it easier to be wise
Though now it seem impossible, and so
Patience is all that you have need of'.
                                        No,
I have not a crumb of comfort, not a grain,
Time can but make her beauty over again;
Because of that great nobleness of hers
The fire that stirs about her, when she stirs
Burns but more clearly. O she had not these ways,
When all the wild summer was in her gaze.
O heart! O heart! if she'd but turn her head,
You'd know the folly of being comforted.

And this handsome mosaic of gallant memory shows a yet further advance toward the use of current language—here, as so often, marvellously saved from triteness by the poet's extreme distinction of mind.

177 His Phœnix

There is a queen in China, or maybe it's in Spain,
And birthdays and holidays such praises can be heard
Of her unblemished lineaments, a whiteness with no stain,
That she might be that sprightly girl who was trodden by a bird;
And there's a score of duchesses, surpassing womankind,
Or who have found a painter to make them so for pay
And smooth out stain and blemish with the elegance of his mind:
I knew a phœnix in my youth so let them have their day.

The young men every night applaud their Gaby's laughing eye,
And Ruth St. Denis had more charm although she had poor luck,
From nineteen hundred nine or ten, Pavlova's had the cry,
And there's a player in the States who gathers up her cloak
And flings herself out of the room when Juliet would be bride
With all a woman's passion, a child's imperious way,
And there are—but no matter if there are scores beside;
I knew a phœnix in my youth so let them have their day.

There's Margaret and Marjorie and Dorothy and Nan,
A Daphne and a Mary who live in privacy;
One's had her fill of lovers, another's had but one,
Another boasts, 'I pick and choose and have but two or three'.
If head and limb have beauty and the instep's high and light
They can spread out what sail they please for all I have to say,
Be but the breakers of men's hearts or engines of delight;
I knew a phœnix in my youth so let them have their day.

There'll be that crowd, that barbarous crowd, through all the centuries,
And who can say but some young belle may walk and talk men wild
Who is my beauty's equal, though that my heart denies,
But not the exact likeness, the simplicity of a child,
And that proud look as though she had gazed into the burning sun,
And all the shapely body no tittle gone astray.
I mourn for that most lonely thing; and yet God's will be done,
I knew a phœnix in my youth so let them have their day.

Toward the end of Yeats's life, young men—and some who were not so young—made a cult of praising his latest work somewhat at the expense of the early romantic poems. This was due solely to a fashion in favour of realism and against romance.

178   Among School Children

I walk through the long schoolroom questioning,
A kind old nun in a white hood replies;
The children learn to cipher and to sing,
To study reading-books and history.
To cut and sew, be neat in everything
In the best modern way—the children's eyes
In momentary wonder stare upon
A sixty year old smiling public man.

I dream of a Ledæan body, bent
Above a sinking fire, a tale that she
Told of a harsh reproof, or trivial event
That changed some childish day to tragedy—
Told, and it seemed that our two natures blent
Into a sphere from youthful sympathy,
Or else, to alter Plato's parable,
Into the yolk and white of the one shell.

And thinking of that fit of grief or rage
I look upon one child or t'other there
And wonder if she stood so at that age—
For even daughters of the swan can share
Something of every paddler's heritage—
And had that colour upon cheek or hair
And thereupon my heart is driven wild:
She stands before me as a living child.

Her present image floats in to the mind—
Did quattrocento finger fashion it
Hollow of cheek as though it drank the wind
And took a mass of shadows for its meat?

And I though never of Ledæan kind
Had pretty plumage once—enough of that,
Better to smile on all that smile, and show
There is a comfortable kind of old scarecrow.

What youthful mother, a shape upon her lap
Honey of generation had betrayed,
And that must sleep, shriek, struggle to escape
As recollection or the drug decide,
Would think her son, did she but see that shape
With sixty or more winters on its head,
A compensation for the pang of his birth,
Or the uncertainty of his setting forth?

Plato thought nature but a spume that plays
Upon a ghostly paradigm of things;
Solider Aristotle played the taws
Upon the bottom of a king of kings;
World-famous golden-thighed Pythagoras
Fingered upon a fiddle stick or strings
What a star sang and careless Muses heard:
Old clothes upon old sticks to scare a bird.

Both nuns and mothers worship images,
But those the candles light are not as those
That animate a mother's reveries,
But keep a marble or a bronze repose.
And yet they too break hearts—O Presences
That passion, piety or affection knows,
And that all heavenly glory symbolise—
O self-born mockers of man's enterprise;

Labour is blossoming or dancing where
The body is not bruised to pleasure soul,
Nor beauty born out of its own despair,
Nor blear-eyed wisdom out of midnight oil.
O chestnut tree, great rooted blossomer,
Are you the leaf, the blossom or the bole?
O body swayed to music, O brightening glance,
How can we know the dancer from the dance?

'A.E.' (George Russell): 1867–1935

Born in Lurgan, Co. Armagh, Ireland. As a young man he served in a draper's shop, but all the time he was avidly studying theosophy and Hindu religion. He was also seeing visions. There is no doubt that 'A.E.'s' mysticism was innate, genuine and all-pervading.

He spent many years in organising a co-operative dairy scheme throughout Ireland. All through his life he painted small pictures, when he could find the time, some of them renderings of his visions, others land- or sea-scapes suffused with pantheistic feeling. He painted rapidly, and perhaps also wrote his verses rapidly: but, caring more for spiritual progress than for artistic achievement, he remained always an amateur.

'A.E.'s' poems, made from his conviction that time does not affect the immortal *atma* in man, must always bring a sense of home to those who can find little in European literature to awaken the deepest layers of the self.

179   Babylon

The blue dusk ran between the streets: my love was winged within my
   mind,
It left to-day and yesterday and thrice a thousand years behind.
To-day was past and dead for me, for from to-day my feet had run
Through thrice a thousand years to walk the ways of ancient Babylon.
On temple top and palace roof the burnished gold flung back the rays
Of a red sunset that was dead and lost beyond a million days.
The tower of heaven turns darker blue, a starry sparkle now begins;
The mystery and magnificence, the myriad beauty and the sins,
Come back to me. I walk beneath the shadowy multitude of towers;
Within the gloom the fountain jets its pallid mist in lily flowers.
The waters lull me and the scent of many gardens, and I hear
Familiar voices, and the voice I love is whispering in my ear.
Oh real as in dream all this; and then a hand on mine is laid:
The wave of phantom time withdraws; and that young Babylonian maid,
One drop of beauty left behind from all the flowing of that tide,
Is looking with the self-same eyes, and here in Ireland by my side.
Oh light our life in Babylon, but Babylon has taken wings,
While we are in the calm and proud procession of eternal things.

Here is a fine example of a poem brought down, as it were, from an uncommon height of consciousness by sheer intensity of meditation.

180   Immortality

We must pass like smoke or live within the spirit's fire;
For we can no more than smoke unto the flame return.
If our thought has changed to dream, our will unto desire,
    As smoke we vanish though the fire may burn.

Lights of infinite pity star the grey dusk of our days:
Surely here is soul: with it we have eternal breath:
In the fire of love we live, or pass by many ways,
    By unnumbered ways of dream, to death.

181   Illusion

What is the love of shadowy lips
That know not what they seek or press,
From whom the lure for ever slips
And fails their phantom tenderness?

The mystery and light of eyes
That near to mine grow dim and cold;
They move afar in ancient skies
Mid flame and mystic darkness rolled.

O beauty, as thy heart o'erflows
In tender yielding unto me,
A vast desire awakes and grows
Unto forgetfulness of thee.

* * *

Again, here is a poem in a rarefied atmosphere which has very seldom been reached by any Western poet. These poems can be effectively used as incantations to restore our sense of the spiritual world.

182 Krishna

I am Beauty itself among beautiful things
Bhagavad-Gita

The East was crowned with snow-cold bloom
And hung with veils of pearly fleece:
They died away into the gloom,
Vistas of peace—and deeper peace.

And earth and air and wave and fire
In awe and breathless silence stood;
For One who passed into their choir
Linked them in mystic brotherhood.

Twilight of amethyst, amid
Thy few strange stars that lit the heights,
Where was the secret spirit hid?
Where was Thy place, O Light of Lights?

The flame of Beauty far in space—
Where rose the fire: in Thee? in Me?
Which bowed the elemental race
To adoration silently?

* * *

An early poem, but one of the poet's best. The first verse alone has
a shimmering colour and music which are unique.

183 The Great Breath

Its edges foamed with amethyst and rose,
Withers once more the old blue flower of day:
There where the ether like a diamond glows
    Its petals fade away.

A shadowy tumult stirs the dusky air;
Sparkle the delicate dews, the distant snows;
The great deep thrills, for through it everywhere
    The breath of Beauty blows.

u

> I saw how all the trembling ages past,
>   Moulded to her by deep and deeper breath,
> Neared to the hour when Beauty breathes her last
>   And knows herself in death.

W. H. Davies: 1871–1940

Born at Newport, Wales, of Welsh stock. 'Picked up knowledge among tramps in America, on cattle boats, and in the common lodging-houses in England. Apprenticed to the picture-frame making'. He lived for six years as a tramp in the United States. The news value of this background greatly helped him to secure a reputation, but his lyric impulse and his genuine simplicity of mind would have brought him success even if he had lived a normally respectable life.

184   To Sparrows Fighting

Stop, feathered bullies!
   Peace, angry birds;
You common Sparrows that,
   For a few words,
Roll fighting in wet mud,
To shed each other's blood.

Look at those Linnets, they
   Like ladies sing;
See how those Swallows, too,
   Play on the wing;
All other birds close by
Are gentle, clean and shy.

And yet maybe your life's
   As sweet as theirs;
The common poor that fight
   Live not for years
In one long frozen state
Of anger, like the great.

185 Sheep

When I was once in Baltimore
  A man came up to me and cried,
'Come, I have eighteen hundred sheep,
  And we will sail on Tuesday's tide.

'If you will sail with me, young man,
  I'll pay you fifty shillings down;
Those eighteen hundred sheep I take
  From Baltimore to Glasgow town'.

He paid me fifty shillings down,
  I sailed with eighteen hundred sheep;
We soon had cleared the harbour's mouth,
  We soon were in the salt sea deep.

The first night we were out at sea
  Those sheep were quiet in their mind;
The second night they cried with fear—
  They smelt no pastures in the wind.

They sniffed, poor things, for their green fields,
  They cried so loud I could not sleep:
For fifty thousand shillings down
  I would not sail again with sheep.

Walter de la Mare: 1873

186 The Moth

Isled in the midnight air,
Musked with the dark's faint bloom,
Out into glooming and secret haunts
  The flame cries, 'Come'!

Lovely in dye and fan,
A-tremble in shimmering grace,
A moth from her winter swoon
  Uplifts her face:

Stares from her glamorous eyes;
Wafts her on plumes like mist;
In ecstasy swirls and sways
To her strange tryst.

E. Clerihew Bentley: 1875

The *Envoi* of this ballade will assure timid or academic personalities that it is just one of Mr. Bentley's jokes. Many of the one-line-summaries, however, set the poem, in my judgment, well above the level of a mere *jeu d'esprit*.

187   A Ballade of Souls

Aalesund, 1911

The soul of Dante was a white-hot spear;
The soul of Bonaparte, a thunder-stroke;
The soul of Bismarck was a cask of beer;
The soul of Blake was roaring flame and smoke;
The soul of Villon was a tatter'd cloak;
The soul of Washington, a perfect square;
The soul of Robespierre, a piece of coke;
But Norway has a soul of sheer despair.

The soul of Dizzy was a chandelier;
The soul of Shakespeare was a greening oak;
And Swift's, a lordly ship that wouldn't steer;
Carlyle's, a raven of stentorian croak;
And Chatterton's, a furnace none would stoke;
The soul of Nietzsche was a rotten pear;
And bluff King Hal's, a reek to make one choke;
But Norway has a soul of sheer despair.

The soul of Goethe was an opal sphere;
The soul of Chaucer was a chime that woke
The heart of England; Heine's was a tear;
And Chatham's was a mighty voice—that broke;
The soul of Calvin, that lugubrious bloke,
Was principally made of heated air;
The soul of Herbert Spencer was a joke;
But Norway has a soul of sheer despair.

ENVOI

Prince! Royal Haakon! (Did you know I spoke
Norwegian?) *Er De syg af det? Jeg er.*
You may be happy—though I doubt it, Haak;
But Norway has a soul of sheer despair.

Cecil French: *1878*

This writer, who is also a fine painter, works with such extreme care
that his poems will make no effect unless they are read slowly and with
great concentration. 'Exiles' records, of course, the mood in which a
man almost remembers one or more of his bygone lives.

188   Exiles

Exiles from we know not where,
Exiles driven now here, now there,
What do we in the world to-day—
We who hold some memory
Of the joy that was our share
In the world's lost yesterday?
Was it in resounding Rome,
By some calm Hellenic shore,
In half-fabulous lands maybe,
Rose the erewhile heart-held home
That we dream of evermore?
Now, nor south, north, east, nor west
Holds the place where we would rest
In this iron-bound, bleak to-day.
Exiles driven now here, now there,
Crazed by broken memory,
What do we in the world now, say—
We who lived when joy was—we
Exiles, exiled—O from where?

189   Before the Glass

The face that meets me in the indifferent glass
I am wearied of. Too well—or it would seem—
I know its lines and planes—all that will pass
Leaving me living as I live in dream.

In dream, forsooth, I have found it otherwise;
The self, in that more fluid world more free,
May live and love under what strange disguise
Of form, of speech—yea, even of memory.

In sleep, in death—beyond the ivory gate—
What waits the pilgrim of the ephemeral?
What form of glory or shadow—form, fate, state
Of king, priest, harlot, hunted criminal?

J. Elroy Flecker: 1884–1914

190   Brumana

Oh shall I never never be home again?
Meadows of England shining in the rain
Spread wide your daisied lawns: your ramparts green
With briar fortify, with blossom screen
Till my far morning—and O streams that slow
And pure and deep through plains and playlands go,
For me your love and all your kingcups store,
And—dark militia of the southern shore,
Old fragrant friends,—preserve me the last lines
Of that long saga which you sung me, pines,
When, lonely boy, beneath the chosen tree
I listened, with my eyes upon the sea.

O traitor pines, you sang what life has found
The falsest of fair tales.
Earth blew a far-horn prelude all around,
That native music of her forest home,

While from the sea's blue fields and syren dales
Shadows and light noon-spectres of the foam
Riding the summer gales
On aery viols plucked an idle sound.

Hearing you sing, O trees,
Hearing you murmur, 'There are older seas,
That beat on vaster sands,
Where the wise snailfish move their pearly towers
To carven rocks and sculptured promont'ries',
Hearing you whisper, 'Lands
Where blaze the unimaginable flowers'.

Beneath me in the valley waves the palm,
Beneath, beyond the valley, breaks the sea;
Beneath me sleep in mist and light and calm
Cities of Lebanon, dream-shadow-dim,
Where Kings of Tyre and Kings of Tyre did rule
In ancient days in endless dynasty,
And all around the snowy mountains swim
Like mighty swans afloat in heaven's pool.

But I will walk upon the wooded hill
Where stands a grove, O pines, of sister pines,
And when the downy twilight droops her wing
And no sea glimmers and no mountain shines
My heart shall listen still. ·
For pines are gossip pines the wide world through
And full of runic tales to sigh or sing.
'Tis ever sweet through pines to see the sky
Mantling a deeper gold or darker blue.
'Tis ever sweet to lie
On the dry carpet of the needles brown,
And though the fanciful green lizard stir
And windy odours light as thistledown
Breathe from the lavdanon and lavender,
Half to forget the wandering and pain,
Half to remember days that have gone by,
And dream and dream that I am home again!

191   No Coward's Song

I am afraid to think about my death,
When it shall be, and whether in great pain
I shall rise up and fight the air for breath
Or calmly wait the bursting of my brain.

I am no coward who could seek in fear
A folk-lore solace or sweet Indian tales:
I know dead men are deaf and cannot hear
The singing of a thousand nightingales.

I know dead men are blind and cannot see
The friend that shuts in horror their big eyes,
And they are witless—O, I'd rather be
A living mouse than dead as a man dies.

J. C. Squire: 1884

  Sir John Squire's work has always been distinguished by its sense of human littleness, by his wide sympathy and by a technique much more subtle than hasty readers will perceive. He, better than most men, can capture elusive moods, as, indeed, in this poem. . . .

192   Paradise Lost

What hues the sunlight had, how rich the shadows were,
The blue and tangled shadows dropped from the crusted branches
Of the warped apple-trees upon the orchard grass.

How heavenly pure the blue of two smooth eggs that lay
Light on the rounded mud that lined the thrush's nest:
And what a deep delight the spots that speckled them.

And that small tinkling stream that ran from hedge to hedge,
Shadowed over by the trees and glinting in the sunbeams,
How clear the water was, how flat the beds of sand
With travelling bubbles mirrored, each one a golden world
To my enchanted eyes. Then earth was new to me.

But now I walk this earth as it were a lumber room,
And sometimes live a week, seeing nothing but mere herbs,
Mere stones, mere passing birds: nor look at anything
Long enough to feel its conscious calm assault:
The strength of it, the word, the royal heart of it.

Childhood will not return; but have I not the will
To strain my turbid mind that soils all outer things,
And, open again to all the miracles of light,
To see the world with the eyes of a blind man gaining sight?

* * *

And here again is a poem simple, emotional and finely controlled.
There is not a touch wasted in this quiet portrait.

193   Winter Nightfall

The old yellow stucco
Of the time of the Regent
Is flaking and peeling:
The rows of square windows
In the straight yellow building
   Are empty and still;
And the dusty dark evergreens
Guarding the wicket
Are draped with wet cobwebs,
And above this poor wilderness
Toneless and sombre
   Is the flat of the hill.

They said that a colonel
Who long ago died here
Was the last one to live here:
An old retired colonel,
Some Fraser or Murray,
   I don't know his name;
Death came here and summoned him,

And the shells of him vanished
Beyond all speculation;
And silence resumed here,
Silence and emptiness,
 And nobody came.

Was it wet when he lived here,
Were the skies dun and hurrying,
Was the rain so irresolute?
Did he watch the night coming,
Did he shiver at nightfall
 Before he was dead?
Did the wind go so creepily,
Chilly and puffing,
With drops of cold rain to it?
Was the hill's lifted shoulder
So lowering and menacing,
 So dark and so dread?

Did he turn through his doorway
And go to his study,
And light many candles?
And fold in the shutters,
And heap up the fireplace
 To fight off the damps?
And muse on his boyhood,
And wonder if India
Ever was real?
And shut out the loneliness
With pig-sticking memoirs
 And collections of stamps?

Perhaps. But he's gone now,
He and his furniture
Dispersed now for ever;
And the last of his trophies,
Antlers and photographs,
 Heaven knows where.
And there's grass in his gateway,

Grass on his footpath,
Grass on his door-step;
The garden's grown over,
The well-chain is broken,
    The windows are bare.

And I leave him behind me,
For the straggling, discoloured
Rags of the daylight,
And hills and stone walls
And a rick long forgotten
    Of blackening hay:
The road pale and sticky,
And cart-ruts and nail marks,
And wind-ruffled puddles,
And the slop of my footsteps
In this desolate country's
    Cadaverous clay.

*   *   *

And in this lyric, a kind of pantoum, Squire has recorded miraculously and with perfect artistry another universal experience never before so memorably expressed.

194   Behind the Lines

The wind of evening cried along the darkening trees,
Along the darkening trees, heavy with ancient pain,
Heavy with ancient pain from faded centuries,
From faded centuries. . . . O foolish thought and vain!

O foolish thought and vain to think the wind could know,
To think the wind could know the griefs of men who died,
The griefs of men who died and mouldered long ago:
'And mouldered long ago', the wind of evening cried.

Andrew Young: 1885

195　Passing the Graveyard

I see you did not try to save
The bouquet of white flowers I gave;
So fast they wither on your grave.

Why does it hurt the heart to think
Of that most bitter abrupt brink
Where the low-shouldered coffins sink?

These living bodies that we wear
So change by every seventh year
That in a new dress we appear;

Limbs, spongy brain and slogging heart,
No part remains the selfsame part;
Like streams they stay and still depart.

You slipped slow bodies in the past;
Then why should we be so aghast
You flung off the whole flesh at last?

Let him who loves you think instead
That like a woman who has wed
You undressed first and went to bed.

196　A Dead Mole

Strong-shouldered mole,
That so much lived below the ground,
Dug, fought and loved, hunted and fed,
For you to raise a mound
Was as for us to make a hole;
What wonder now that being dead
Your body lies here stout and square
Buried within the blue vault of the air?

197   A Prehistoric Camp

It was the time of year
   Pale lambs leap with thick leggings on
Over small hills that are not there,
   That I climbed Eggardon.

The hedgerows still were bare,
   None ever knew so late a year;
Birds built their nests in the open air,
   Love conquering their fear.

But there on the hill-crest,
   Where only larks or stars look down,
Earthworks exposed a vaster nest,
   Its race of men long flown.

198   The Dead Crab

A rosy shield upon its back,
That not the hardest storm could crack,
From whose sharp edge projected out
Black pin-point eyes staring about;
Beneath, the well-knit cote-armure
That gave to its weak belly power;
The clustered legs with plated joints
That ended in stiletto points;
The claws like mouths it held outside:—
I cannot think this creature died
By storm or fish or sea-fowl harmed
Walking the sea so heavily armed;
Or does it make for death to be
Oneself a living armoury?

199   Man and Cows

I stood aside to let the cows
Swing past me with their wrinkled brows,
Bowing their heads as they went by
As to a woodland deity
To whom they turned mute eyes
To save them from the plaguing god of flies.

And I too cursed Beelzebub,
Watching them stop to rub
A bulging side or bony haunch
Against a trunk or pointing branch
And lift a tufted tail
To thresh the air with its soft flail.

They stumbled heavily down the slope,
As Hethor led them or the hope
Of the lush meadow-grass,
While I remained, thinking it was
Strange that we both were held divine,
In Egypt these, man once in Palestine.

200   The Round Barrow

A lark as small as a flint arrow
Rises and falls over this ancient barrow
And seems to mock with its light tones
The silent man of bones;

Some prince that earth drew back again
From his long strife with wind and mist and rain,
Baring for him this broad round breast
In token of her rest.

But as I think how Death sat once
And with sly fingers picked those princely bones,
I feel my bones are verily
The stark and final I.

I climbed the hill housed in warm flesh,
And now as one escaped from its false mesh
Through the wan mist I journey on,
A clanking skeleton.

201   The Farmer's Gun

The wood is full of rooks
That by their faded looks
No more on thievery will thrive,
As when they were alive,
Nor fill the air with the hoarse noise
That most of all is England's pleasant voice.

How ugly is this work of man,
Seen in the bald brain-pan,
Voracious bill,
Torn wing, uprooted quill
And host of tiny glistening flies
That lend false lustre to these empty eyes.

More delicate is nature's way
Whereby all creatures know their day,
And hearing Death call 'Come,
Here is a bone or crumb',
Bury themselves before they die
And leave no trace of foul mortality.

Rupert Brooke: 1887–1914

Played cricket for Rugby school. Studied at King's College, Cambridge. Was justly famed for his great physical beauty.

In 1914 he enlisted in the army and wrote some war-sonnets of high romantic enthusiasm which the world's subsequent cynicism foolishly belittled. He died, invalided, on a Greek island.

202   The Hill

Breathless, we flung us on the windy hill,
   Laughed in the sun, and kissed the lovely grass.
   You said, 'Through glory and ecstasy we pass;
Wind, sun, and earth remain, the birds sing still,
When we are old, are old. . . .' 'And when we die
   All's over that is ours; and life burns on
Through other lovers, other lips', said I,
   'Heart of my heart, our heaven is now, is won!'

'We are Earth's best, that learnt her lesson here.
   Life is our cry. We have kept the faith!' we said;
   'We shall go down with unreluctant tread
Rose-crowned into the darkness!' . . . Proud we were,
And laughed, that had such brave true things to say.
—And then you suddenly cried, and turned away.

T. S. Eliot: 1888

203   The Hollow Men

A PENNY FOR THE OLD GUY

I

We are the hollow men
We are the stuffed men
Leaning together
Headpiece filled with straw. Alas!
Our dried voices, when
We whisper together
Are quiet and meaningless
As wind in dry grass
Or rats' feet over broken glass
In our dry cellar

Shape without form, shade without colour,
Paralysed force, gesture without motion;

Those who have crossed
With direct eyes, to death's other Kingdom
Remember us—if at all—not as lost
Violent souls, but only
As the hollow men
The stuffed men.

II

Eyes I dare not meet in dreams
In death's dream kingdom
These do not appear:
There, the eyes are
Sunlight on a broken column
There, is a tree swinging
And voices are
In the wind's singing
More distant and more solemn
Than a fading star.

Let me be no nearer
In death's dream kingdom
Let me also wear
Such deliberate disguises
Rat's coat, crowskin, crossed staves
In a field
Behaving as the wind behaves
No nearer—
Not that final meeting
In the twilight kingdom.

III

This is the dead land
This is cactus land
Here the stone images
And raised, here they receive
The supplication of a dead man's hand
Under the twinkle of a fading star.

Is it like this
In death's other kingdom
Waking alone
At the hour when we are
Trembling with tenderness
Lips that would kiss
Form prayers to broken stone.

IV

The eyes are not here
There are no eyes here
In this valley of dying stars
In this hollow valley
This broken jaw of our lost kingdoms.

In this last of meeting places
We grope together
And avoid speech
Gathered on this beach of the tumid river,

Sightless, unless
The eyes reappear
As the perpetual star
Multifoliate rose
Of death's twilight kingdom
The hope only
Of empty men.

V

Here we go round the prickly pear
Prickly pear prickly pear
Here we go round the prickly pear
At five o'clock in the morning.

Between the idea
And the reality
Between the motion
And the act
Falls the Shadow
For Thine is the Kingdom

Between the conception
And the creation
Between the emotion
And the response
Falls the Shadow

Life is very long

Between the desire
And the spasm
Between the potency
And the existence
Between the essence
And the descent
Falls the Shadow

For Thine is the Kingdom

For Thine is
Life is
For Thine is the

This is the way the world ends
This is the way the world ends
This is the way the world ends
Not with a bang but a whimper.

Richard Church : 1894

204 Morning of the Twentieth Day

(From 'Twentieth Century Psalter')

Think upon her stones. Think of the city you knew,
The city you loved by instinct, as the fox its lair,
The city you loved by knowledge, as the scholar explores
The past. So I have thought upon London, the secret
City, shy in her strength, with her glory hidden;
The Roman mother defiant of kings and tyrants;
The drab, the merciless, the beautiful.

I know her streets, I conjure magic from them,
Magic drawn from reservoirs of wonder
By day, by night, walking the worn pavements.
I have felt the burden of her history
Closing about me in her courts and alleys,
Stopping me, yet forcing my quick nerves to an idleness
In which the visions came, where the past lived
And ousted the present purpose from my mind,
Held me while the centuries jostled by,
Flicked me with a scabbard, or a cloak of cloth
Hand-spun in Suffolk, lined with Paduan silk.
I have stepped aside for queens to pass
With sonnet-masters in attendance. What I saw
The other workers must have witnessed too, drifting
At lunchtime, at night, in all seasons, a myriad faces
Touched into life by the caress of London.
For I am her child, one of millions enraptured
As Chaucer, Lamb, Dickens, princes of Cockaigne,
Listeners to the eternal voice of London.

But now, to see her in the dust! To approach
The streets about St. Paul's, to tread in Temple Lane
And find the roofless hall where Shakespeare heard
His Twelfth Night revel spoken before the table
Given to the Benchers by the jewelled Gloriana:
To see where Elia, eloquent in claret,
And drunken Oliver Goldsmith stumbled home,
Stubbing a toe on the same cobble-stones
That I have trodden, until this night of horror
And holocaust, and the ruin of a world
Long learned, long loved, and never to be forgotten
Though the wind has gone over it, and it is gone!

This shall be written for those that come after,
When London, my mother, and the other loved cities of Europe
Are praising the Lord of Life with a different skyline.
This shall serve to remind them of famous townsmen,
And monuments that war withered like grass.

205   In the Backs

Too many of the dead—some I knew well—
Have smelt this unforgotten river smell
Liquid and old and dank,
And on the tree-dark, lacquered slowly-passing stream
Have seen the boats come softly as in dream
Past the green bank.
So Camus, reverend Sire, came footing slow
Three hundred years ago;
And Milton paced the avenue of trees
In miracle of sun and shade as now,
The dear, magnificent, unborn cadences
Behind his youthful brow.

Milton and Chaucer, Herbert, Herrick, Gray,
Rupert, and you forgotten others, say:
Are there slow rivers and bridges where you have gone away?
What new absorption have your spirits found,
What wider lot?
Some days in Spring do you come back at will
And tread with weightless feet the ancient ground?
O say, if not,
Why is this air so sacred and so still?

206   Youth

A young Apollo, golden-haired,
    Stands dreaming on the verge of strife,
Magnificently unprepared
    For the long littleness of life.

Phyllis Reid

207 Sonnet

If I should sing of love a thousand years
You would not know the meaning of my song,
Strange content of the human heart, made strong
By passion's ecstasy and pity's tears.
Love but a phantom of itself appears
Through other eyes, and still shall lead you wrong
Though you may read and ponder all day long
The wisdom or the folly of your peers.

Earth, ignorant of what her fruit shall be,
The myriad mysteries that she may bear,
The transient rose, or delicate olive-tree
Standing for centuries with silver hair,
Yet has more knowledge of her destiny
Than the spirit has of love, till love is there.

208 Wind

This is a giant day—
Run out and pick a tree,
Seize a great flaring beech
And wave it overhead.
Run shouting through the fields,
Leap hedges and rivers;
Mænads will spring to meet you,
Contesting the race.
Run—though you trail the clouds,
Run through the roaring world,
This is a giant day.

209　Discovery

As from the painted shining evening sky
　　Colour drains out before the day has passed,
　　Leaving a grey transparency at last,
And none may say where all those ardours die,—
So you, still young, forgetting with a sigh
　　The radiant warmth that love of her once cas
　　Over your days, remember but how fast
Flames, lit in worship, burnt out utterly.

Once when you saw the stormy sun go down,
　　Crimson streaked darkly, it had been for you
　　A furnace of the gods with iron bars
Worthy of forging Love's triumphant crown:
　　But now you shun the fire, fearing anew
To send a pale smoke wavering to the stars.

Anon.

210　Swing Low, Sweet Chariot

Swing low, sweet chariot,
Coming for to carry me home,
Swing low, sweet chariot,
Coming for to carry me home.

I looked over Jordan and what did I see
Coming for to carry me home,
A band of angels, coming after me,
Coming for to carry me home.

If you get there before I do,
Coming for to carry me home,
Tell all my friends I'm coming too,
Coming for to carry me home.

Swing low, sweet chariot,
Coming for to carry me home,
Swing low, sweet chariot,
Coming for to carry me home.

Kathleen Hewitt

2 1 1   Intrusion

To some strange room, upon some future night,
Without an invitation I shall steal,
And there will you, recalling lost delight,
Discover what one moment can reveal.

For as a woman smiles or turns her head
Or lifts a hand to smooth her tumbled hair,
Some trick of light and shade will form instead
My hand, my lips, and I'll be with you there—

A sad intruder, whom you must dismiss
Before I stir your memory with a kiss.

Anon.

2 1 2   Antagonists

It is not I who control the pulse of my heart:
   It is not I who impel the blood in my veins.
   We are bound together by strong invisible chains,
But I and the form that is with me are creatures apart.
         Whether I wake or sleep,
         Rejoice or ponder or weep,
         That other is labouring still
         With a separate will.
It bears me along through change. It is much to me
As the ship that carries the sailor across the sea,—
   A prison, a home, a cause of delight or woe,
His first and close companion, and yet not he.

   For of all the marvellous things that a man may know
As he voyages over the years, there is none that excels
The body in which he dwells.
Within the enchanted cave of the womb upcurled
It lay, shut in from the noise and glare of the world,
Remembering, under the spell of a timeless law,
The murmur of woods and waves that no man saw.

It comes of a line so vast
That none may measure its Past,
None say what kindled the fire
Transmitted by mother and sire.
Gods that were mighty in fame,
And empires now but a name,
And the splendour, the folly, the tears
And the toil of a million years—
All these it has left far back
In the dust of its love-lit track,
As the sparks that fly from the brand
In a runner's hand.

The soul weighs anchor at birth
And furrows the life of the earth;
For ships of adventure are we
And ride upon one great sea.
Not mine, not cloven apart,
Is the life that upholds my heart,
But on through the void it spins,—
It has fur and feathers and fins,
It creeps, it flutters, it flies,
It opens and blossoms and dies:
And yet though the force be one
That moves in a man or a sun,
A bird, a bloom or a tree,
It is not verily he!
The mark of man, his mingled pleasure and pain,
And all that the world has suffered, comes of the strife
Between the will of the soul and the will of life,
And the clash of these in the brain.

So, then, we come to the end of a swift journey across the English poetry of six hundred years, wondering perhaps whether the latter half of our own century will, as seems probable, witness a third springtime. The best way to appreciate poetry is to get it by heart so that we may use it as a stimulus in happy times and a consolation in hours of woe. Is it not strange to know that much unwritten poetry lies invisible on the parchment of the future, and that we shall never read those poems? For although the coming age does not seem likely to develop the subtlety of emotion and the subtlety of phrasing which are necessary ingredients of first-rate poetry, we may be confident that decade after decade young men and young women will try their hands at this difficult craft. Finally, let us remember that Dr. Johnson wisely observed that 'the purpose of literature is to help man to enjoy life, or to endure it'. That, certainly, is the value of poetry—to those who are attuned to something finer than 'a song of bawdry'.

January 19th, 1944.

APPENDIX

1 At the Cross

'Stond wel, moder, under rode,
By holt thy sone with glade mode,
　　Blythe, moder, might thou be'.
'Sone, how shudde I blithe stonde?
Ye se thin fet, I see thin honde,
　　Nayled to the harde tre'.

'Moder, do wey thy wepinge:
Y thole deth for mankynde,
　　For my gult thole y non'.
'Sone, y fele the dede stounde
The suert is at myn herte grounde,
　　Thet me byhet Symeon'.

'Moder, merci, let me deye,
For Adam out of helle beye,
　　And his kun, that is for-lore'.
'Sone, what shal me to rede?
Thy payne pyneth me to dede,
　　Lat me deze the by-fore'!

'Moder, thou rewe al of this bern,
Thou wosshe a-wai the blody tern,
　　Hit doth me worse than my ded'
'Sone, how may I teres werne?
Y se the blody stremes erne
　　From thin herte to my fet'.

'Moder, non y may the seye,
Betere is that ich one deye
　　Than al monkunde to helle go'.
'Sone, y se thi bodi byswongen,
Fet and honden thourt-out stongen,
　　No wonder that me be wo'.

'Moder, now y shal the telle
Gef y ne deze, thou gost to helle,
    Y thole ded for thine sake'.
'Sone, thou art so meke and mynde,
Ne wyt me naht, hit is my kynde,
    That y for the this sorewe make'.

'Moder, now thou miht wel leren,
What sorewe haveth that children beren,
    What sorewe hit is with childe gon'.
'Sorewe y wis, y con the telle;
Bote hit be the pyne of helle,
    More sorewe wot y non'.

'Moder, rew of moder kare,
For non thou wost of moder fare,
    Then thou be clene mayden mon'.
'Sone, help al alle nede,
Alle tho that to me grede,
    Maiden, wif, and fol wymmon'.

'Moder, may y no langore duelle,
The time is come y shall to helle,
    The thridde day y ryse upon'.
'Sone, y will with the founden.
Y deye y-wis for thine wounden,
    So soreweful ded nes never non'.

When he rose, tho fel hire sorewe,
Hire blisse sprong the thridde morewe,
    Blythe moder were thou tho.
Levedy, for that ilke blisse,
Bysech thi sone of sunnes tisse,
    Thou be our sheld ageyn oure fo.

Blessed be thou, ful of blysse,
Let us never hevene misse,
    Thourt thy suete sones myht!
Loverd, for that ilke blod,
That thou sheddest on the rod,
    Thou bring us in to hevene lyht.
                            Amen.

2   Hop along, Hubert!

Mon in the mone stond ant strit,
  On is bot forke is burthen he bereth;
Hit is muche wonder that he nadown slyt,
  For doute leste he valle he shoddreth ant shereth.
When the forst freseth, muche chele he byd,
  The thornes beth kene, is hattren to-lereth,
Nis no wytht in the world that wot wen he syt,
  Ne, bote hit ben the hegge, whet wedes he wereth.

Whider trowe this mon ha the wey take,
  He hath set his fot is other to-foren;
For none hithte that he hath ne syht me hym ner shake,
  He is the sloweste mon that ever wes y-boren;
Wher he were othe feld pycchynde stake,
  For hope of ys thornes to dutlen is doren;
He mot myd is twy-byl other trous make,
  Other al is dayes werk ther were y-loren.

This ilke mon upon heh when er he were,
  When he were ythe mone boren ant y-fed,
He leneth on is forke ase a grey frere,
  This crokede caynard sore he is a-dred;
Hit is mony day go that he was here,
  Ichot of his ernde he hath nout y-sped.
He hath hewe sum wher a burthen of brere,
  Therefore sum hayward hath taken ys wed.

Gef thy wed ys y-take, bring hom the trous,
  Sete forth thyn other fot, stryd over sty:
We shule preye the hay-wart hom to ur hous,
  Ant maken hym at heyse for the maystry;
Drynke to him deorly of fol god bous,
  Ant oure *dame douse* shal sitten hym by
When that he is dronke ase a dreynt mous,
  Thenne we shule borewe the wed ate bayly.

This mon hereth me nout, thah ich to hym crye:
  Ichot the cherl is def, the Del hym to-drawe.
That ich ye ge upon heth nulle hout hye.
  The lost-lase ladde can nout o lawe.
Hupe forth, Hubert, hosede pye,
  Ichot thart a-marstled in to the mawe.
Thah me teone with hym that myn teh mye,
  The cherld nul nout a-down er the day dawe.

3   The Clerk and the Lady

'My deth y love, my lyf ich hate, for a levedy shene,
  Heo is brith so daies liht, that is on me wel sene;
  Al y falewe so doth the lif in somer when hit is grene,
  Gef mi thoht helpeth me noht, to wham shal y me mene'.

'Sorewe ant syke ant drery mod byndeth me so faste
  That I wene to walke wod, gef me lengore laste;
  My serewe, my care, al with a word, he myhte a-way caste,
  What helpeth thee, my suete lemmon, my lyf thus forte gaste'?

'Do wey thou clerc, thou art a fol, with the bydde y noht chyde;
  Shalt thou never lyve that day mi love that thou shalt byde;
  Gef thou in my boure art take, shame the may bi-tyde,
  The is betere on fote gon, then wycked hors to ryde'.

'Wey-la-wei! whi seist thou so? thou rewe on me, thy man;
  Thou art ever in my thoht, in londe wher ich am;
  Gef y deze for thi love, hit is the mykel sham;
  Thou lete me lyve, ant be thy luef, ant thou my suete lemman'.

'Be stille, thou fol, y call the riht, cast thou never blynne;
  Thou art wayted day ant night with fader ant al my kynne;
  Be thou in mi bour y-take, lete they for no synne
  Me to holde ant the to slon, the deth so thou maht wynne'.

'Suete ledy, thou wend thi mod, sorewe thou wolt me kythe;
  Ich am al so sory mon, so ich was whylen blythe;
  In a wyndon ther we stod, we custe us fyfty sythe;
  Feir biheste maketh mony mon al is serewe's mythe'.

'Wey-la-wey! whi seist thou so? mi serewe thou makest newe;
Y lovede a clerk al par amours, of love he was ful trewe,
He nes nout blythe never a day bote he me sone seze,
Ich lovede him betere then my lyf whet bote is hit to leze'?

'Whil y wes a clerc in scole, wel muchel y couthe of lore,
Yeh have tholed for thy love woundes fele sore;
Fer from (hom) ant eke from men under the wode gore;
Suete ledy, thou rewe of me, nou may y no more'.

'Thou semest wel to ben a clerc, for thou spekest so stille;
Shalt thou never for mi love woundes thole grylle;
Fader, moder, ant al my kun ne shal me holde so stille,
That y nam thyn ant thou art myn, to don al thi wille'.

5   A Prioress

There was also a Nonne, a PRIORESSE,
That of hir smyling was ful simple and coy;
Hir gretteste ooth was but by sëynt Loy;
And she was cleped madame Eglentyne.
Eul wel she song the service divyne,
Fntuned in hir nose ful semely;
And Frensh she spak ful faire and fetisly,
After the scole of Stratford atte Bowe,
For Frensh of Paris was to hir unknowe.
At mete wel y-taught was she with-alle;
She leet no morsel from hir lippes falle,
Ne wette hir fingres in hir sauce depe.
Wel coude she carie a morsel, and wel kepe,
That no drope ne fille up-on hir brest.
In curteisye was set ful muche hir lest.
Hir over lippe wyped she so clene,
That in hir coppe was no ferthing sene
Of grece, whan she dronken hadde hir draughte.
Ful semely after hir mete she raughte,
And sikerly she was of greet disport,
And ful plesaunt, and amiable of port,

And peyned hir to countrefete chere
Of court, and been estatlich of manere,
And to ben holden digne of reverence.
But, for to speken of hir conscience,
She was so charitable and so pitous,
She wolde wepe, if that she sawe a mous
Caught in a trappe, if it were deed or bledde.
Of smale houndes had she, that she fedde
With rosted flesh, or milk and wastel-breed.
But sore weep she if oon of hem were deed,
Or if men smoot it with a yerde smerte:
And al was conscience and tendre herte.
Ful semely hir wimpel pinched was;
Hir nose tretys; hir eyen greye as glas;
Hir mouth ful smal, and ther-to softe and reed;
But sikerly she hadde a fair forheed;
It was almost a spanne brood, I trowe;
For, hardily, she was nat undergrowe.
Ful fetis was hir cloke, as I was war.
Of smal coral aboute his arm she bar
A peire of bedes, gauded al with grene;
And ther-on heng a broche of gold ful shene,
On which ther was first write a crowned A,
And after, *Amor vincit omnia.*

6   Daisies

And, as for me, though that my wit be lyte,
On bokes for to rede I me delyte,
And in myn herte have hem in reverence;
And to hem yeve swich lust and swich credence,
That ther is wel unethe game noon
That from my bokes make me to goon,
But hit be other up-on the haly-day,
Or elles in the joly tyme of May;
And that the floures ginne for to springe,
Farwel my book and my devocioun
Now have I therto this condicioun

That, of alle the floures in the mede,
Than love I most these floures whyte and rede,
Swiche as men callen daysies in our toun.
To hem have I so greet affeccioun,
As I sayde erst, whan comen is the May,
That in my bed ther daweth me no day
That I nam up, and walking in the mede
To seen these floures agein the sonne sprede,
Whan hit up-riseth by the morwe shene,
The longe day, thus walking in the grene.
And whan the sonne ginneth for to weste,
Than closeth hit, and draweth hit to reste.
So sore hit is afered of the night,
Til on the morwe, that hit is dayes light.

7 Merciles Beaute: A Triple Roundel

I. CAPTIVITY

Your yën two wol slee me sodenly,
I may the beautè of hem not sustene,
So woundeth hit through-out my herte kene.

And but your word wol helen hastily
My hertes wounde, whyl that hit is grene,
   Your yën two wol slee me sodenly,
   I may the beautè of hem not sustene.

Upon my trouthe I sey yow feithfully,
That ye ben of my lyf and deeth the quene;
For with my deeth the trouthe shal be sene.
   Your yën two wol slee me sodenly,
   I may the beautè of hem not sustene,
   So woundeth hit through-out my herte kene.

II. REJECTION

So hath your beautè fro your herte chaced
Pitee, that me ne availeth not to pleyne;
For Daunger halt your mercy in his cheyne.

Y

Giltles my deeth thus han ye me purchaced;
I sey yow sooth, me nedeth not to feyne;
  So hath your beautè fro your herte chaced
  Pitee, that me ne availeth not to pleyne.

Allas! that nature hath in yow compassed
So great beautè, that no man may atteyne
To mercy, though he sterve for the peyne.
  So hath your beautè fro your herte chaced
  Pitee, that me ne availeth not to pleyne;
  For Daunger halt your mercy in his cheyne.

III. ESCAPE

Sin I fro Love escaped am so fat,
I never thenk to ben in his prison lene;
Sin I am free, I counte him not a bene.

He may answere, and seye this or that;
I do no fors, I spoke right as I mene.
  Sin I fro Love escaped am so fat,
  I never thenk to ben in his prison lene.

Love hath my name y-strike out of his sclat,
And he is strike out of my bokes clene
For ever-mo; there is non other mene.
  Sin I fro Love escaped am so fat,
  I never thenk to ben in his prison lene;
  Sin I am free, I counte him not a bene.

8   A Slender Wench

Fair was this yonge wyf, and ther-with-al
As any wesele hir body gent and smal.
A ceynt she werede barred al of silk,
A barmclooth eek as whyt as morne milk
Up-on hir lendes, ful of many a gore.
Whyt was hir smok and brouded al bifore
And eke behinde, on hir coler aboute,
Of col-blak silk, with-inne and eek with-oute.

The tapes of hir whyte voluper
Were of the same suyte of hir coler;
Hir filet brood of silk, and set ful hye:
And sikerly she hadde a likerous yë.
Ful smale y-pulled were hir browes two,
And tho were bent, and blake as any sloo.
She was ful more blisful on to see
Than is the newe pere-jonette tree;
And softer than the wolle is of a wether.
And by hir girdel heeng a purs of lether
Tasseld with silk, and perled with latonn.
In al this world, to seken up and doun,
There nis no man so wys, that coude thenche
So gay a popelote, or swich a wenche.
Ful brighter was the shyning of hir hewe
Than in the tour the noble y-forged newe.
But of hir song, it was as loude and yerne
As any swalwe sittinge on a berne.
Ther-to she coude skippe and make game,
As any kide or calf folwinge his dame.
Hir mouth was swete as bragot or the meeth,
Or hord of apples leyd in hey or heeth.
Winsinge she was, as is a joly colt,
Long as a mast, and upright as a bolt.
A brooch she baar-up on hir lowe coler,
As brood as is the bos of a bocler.
She was a prymerole, a pigges-nye
For any lord to leggen in his bedde,
Or yet for any good yeman to wedde.

9 Lament for Chaucer

Allas! my worthi maister honorable,
This landes verray tresor and richesse!
Deth by thy deth hath harme irreparable
Unto us doon: hir vengeable duresse
Despoiled hath this land of the swetnesse
Of rethorik; for unto Tullius
Was never man so lyk amonges us,

Also who was hier in philosophie
To Aristotle in our tonge but thou?
The steppes of Virgile in poesie
Thou folwedist eeke, men wot wel ynow.
That combre-worlde that the my maister slow—
Wolde I slayn were!—Deth, was to hastyf
To renne on thee and reve the thi lyf . . .
She myghte han taried hir vengeance a while
Til that sum man had egal to the be;
Nay, lat be that! sche knew wel that this yle
May never man forth brynge lyk to the,
And hir office needes do mot she;
God bad hir so, I truste as for the beste;
O maister, maister, God thi soule reste!

10   Godspeed to his Book

Go litill tretise, nakit of eloquence,
    Causing simplèss and povertee to wit,
And pray the reder to have pacience
    Of thy defaute, and to supporten it,
Of his gudnèsse thy brukilnesse to knytt,
    And his tong for to reulë and to stere,
    That thy defautis helit may bene here.

Allace! and gif thou cumyst in ye presènce
    Quhare as of blame faynest thou wald be quite,
To here thy rude and crukit eloquens,
    Quho sal be there to pray for thy remȳt?
No wicht bot gif hir merci will admyt
    The for gud will, that is thy gyd and stere,
    To quham for me thou piteousely requere.

And thus endìth the fatall influence,
    Causit from hevyn quhare powar is comytt,
Of govirnance, by the magnificence
    Of him that hiest in the hevin sitt.
    To quham we think that all ourë hath writt,
    Quho coutht it red agone syne mony a zere,
    Hich in the hevynis figure circulere.

Unto impnis of my maistèris dere,
  Gowere and *Chaucere*, that on the steppis satt
Of rethorike, quhill thai were lyvand here,
  Superlative as poetis laureate,
In moralitee and eloquence ornate,
    I recommend my buk in lynis seven,
    And eke thair saulis unto the blisse of hevin.

13 To a Lady

Sweit Rois of vertew and of gentilness,
Delytsum Lyllie of everie luftyness,
  Richest in bontie, and in bewtie cleir,
  And everie vertew that is (held most) deir,
Except onlie that ye ar mercyless.

In to your garthe this day I did persew,
Thair saw I flowris that fresche wer of hew:
  Baithe quhyte and reid moist lufty wer to seyne,
  And halsum herbis upone stalkis grene;
Yit leif nor flour fynd could I nane of Rew.

I dout that Merche, with his cauld blastis keyne,
Hes slane this gentill herbe, that I of mene;
  Quhois petewous deithe dois to my heart sic pane
  That I wald mak to plant his rute againe,
So confortand his levis unto me bene.

INDEX OF AUTHORS

INDEX OF FIRST LINES

ate Due

COLONIAL BOOK SERVICE
45 FOURTH AVE.
New York City 3, GRamercy 5-8354
We Hunt Out-of-Print Books